Quality
in
Postgraduate
Education

EDITED BY
ORTRUN ZUBER-SKERRITT
AND YONI RYAN

KOGAN
PAGE

First published in 1994

Kogan Page Limited
120 Pentonville Road
London N1 9JN

British Library Cataloguing in Publication Data

A CIP record for this book is available from the British Library.

ISBN 0 7494 1413 8

Printed and bound in Great Britain by
Biddles Ltd, Guildford and King's Lynn

Quality
in

Contents

Notes on Contributors

Tania Aspland is a lecturer in curriculum and professional studies in the Faculty of Education at the Queensland University of Technology. Her interests are in teacher education and gender issues in the supervision of overseas students in Australia.

Dr Robert Brown is the Principal Scientific Publications Officer with the Queensland Department of Primary Industries, where he runs action learning programmes on how to publish research papers that are both easier to write and easier to read.

Christine Bruce has been a librarian at the Queensland University of Technology since 1987 where she has designed and implemented information literacy programmes for undergraduate and postgraduate students across all disciplines. Her most recent publication is the HERDSA Green Guide No. 13, *Developing Students' Library Research Skills*.

Dr Linda Conrad is a lecturer in the Griffith Institute for Higher Education at Griffith University. She has research interests in postgraduate supervision (especially supervisory support groups) and gender issues in higher education. During her recent study leave, she was a Visiting Research Associate at the Institute for Research on Women at Rutgers University, New Brunswick, New Jersey.

Dr Pam Denicolo is Assistant Head of the Department of Educational Studies at the University of Surrey, Director of Professional Courses Unit, and Director of the Centre for the Advancement of Teaching in Higher Education (CATHE). She is also director of the postgraduate research degrees programme.

Lewis Elton is Professor Emeritus of Higher Education, University of Surrey. He is an independent consultant in higher education. In this capacity he acts as Further and Higher Education Adviser to the Employment Department. He is a Fellow of the American Institute of Physics and of the Society for Research into Higher Education and an Honorary Life Member of the Staff and Educational Development Association.

Dr Nanette Gottlieb is a senior lecturer in the Department of Japanese and Chinese Studies at the University of Queensland, and is also Postgraduate Coordinator for the Japanese section.

Adele Graham is a member of the Higher Education Research Office at the University of Auckland. Working primarily in the area of academic staff development, she is interested in challenging and changing teaching practices in higher education, postgraduate supervision practices in particular.

Barbara Grant teaches in the Student Learning Centre and the Higher Education Research Office at the University of Auckland. As a teacher, she is particularly interested in postgraduate supervision and the practices of thesis management and writing. In her academic work, she is interested in the intersection of poststructuralist theories and radical (including feminist) education theories in relation to higher education.

Professor Roger Holmes has served as Deputy Vice-Chancellor (Research) at Griffith University since 1992. He is an active researcher in the area of biochemistry and molecular biology, with particular interests in alcohol metabolism, corneal biochemistry and gene families. He currently serves on the AVCC Standing Committee on Research.

John Jones is Head of the Higher Education Research Office at the University of Auckland. He taught and researched at the Universities of Wales, Malawi and Papua New Guinea in Physics and Education. His current interests encompass a wide range of aspects of teaching and learning in higher education, especially in relation to staff development and the implementation of quality systems.

Professor Ingrid Moses is Deputy Vice-Chancellor (Academic) at the University of Canberra and author of the HERDSA Green Guide on *Supervising Postgraduates* and the DEET Report on *Barriers to Women's Participation as Postgraduate Students* and was a member of the Research Training and Careers Committee of the Australian Research Council.

Thomas A. O'Donoghue is a lecturer in curriculum theory in the Department of Education at the University of Western Australia in Perth. His interests are in curriculum history, teacher education and curriculum development in the developing world.

Dr Estelle M. Phillips is a research fellow at the Open University (UK) and independent educational consultant specializing in giving advice to universities on the institutional adequacy of their provision for doctoral students. She designs and conducts training seminars for PhD supervisors on the skills necessary for effectiveness in their role. She is co-author of the book *How to Get a PhD*.

Professor Maureen Pope is Head of the Department of Community Studies at the University of Reading; the Department is responsible for the education of counselling and vocational guidance specialists, community nurses, youth and social workers. She is an experienced supervisor, and is widely recognized for her work in personal construct psychology.

Dr Yoni Ryan is a lecturer in the Academic Staff Development Unit at Queensland University of Technology. She has particular interests in postgraduate supervision and open learning practices.

Professor Peter Sheehan is Pro-Vice-Chancellor (Research and Postgraduate Studies) at the University of Queensland. He is past Chair of the Australian Research Grants Committee of the Australian Research Council (ARC). He is also Deputy Chair of the ARC and President of the Academy of Social Sciences in Australia.

Jan Whittle is a lecturer in the Staff Development Unit at the University of Hong Kong. At the time of writing she was a lecturer in the Centre for University Teaching and Learning at the University of South Australia and had responsibility for the provision of academic staff development.

Dr Ortrun Zuber-Skerritt is Associate Professor in the Griffith Institute for Higher Education at Griffith University, and a part-time faculty member of the International Management Centre, Pacific Region. Her research and development interests are in Higher Education and Management Education, including Action Learning, Action Research and Process Management.

List of Acronyms

AGPS	Australian Government Publishing Service
AIDAB	Australian International Development Assistance Bureau
AVCC	Australian Vice-Chancellors' Committee (Australia)
CAE	College of Advanced Education (Australia)
CEDAM	Centre for Educational Development and Academic Methods (Australia)
CSHE	Centre for the Study of Higher Education (Australia)
CVCP	Committee of Vice Chancellors and Principals (Britain)
DEET	Department of Employment, Education and Training
DORCISS	Association of Directors of Research Centres in the Social Sciences (Britain)
ESRC	Economic and Social Research Council (Britain)
HEC	Higher Education Council (Australia)
HERDSA	Higher Education Research and Development Society of Australia
HERO	Higher Education Research Office (New Zealand)
NBEET	National Board of Employment, Education and Training (Australia)
NFER	National Foundation for Educational Research (Britain)
SERC	Science and Engineering Council (Britain)
SRHE	Society for Research into Higher Education (Britain)
SSRC	Social Science Research Council (Britain)
USDU	Universities' Staff Development Unit (Britain)

Foreword

Roger Holmes

Higher education institutions around the world have become aware of the importance of quality assurance in the operation and delivery of their academic programmes. This applies especially to those universities in countries such as the United Kingdom and Australia, for which the distribution of substantial government support funding is directly linked to an independent assessment of the quality of teaching and learning, and of research and community service activities. This linkage of quality assurance outcomes with substantial differential funding provision has been catalytic in moving quality assurance into the mainstream of university work for academic staff and many general staff.

The major beneficiaries of a well-run quality assurance system in higher education are the students and graduates, who will have experienced many opportunities to provide comment and feedback on their experiences. Employers and other stakeholders will also have been consulted and included in this process. Academic staff should have gained adequate feedback to positively influence their teaching and learning activities and supervisory skills, as well as the course structure and content of academic programmes. Overall, the quality and performance of the university will have been improved by these quality assurance measures.

Research postgraduate training is unique among academic responsibilities in providing a direct linkage between teaching and learning activities and research. Typically, quality assurance programmes separate these functions and concentrate on teaching and learning in association with undergraduate or postgraduate courses, or on research issues, focusing on input and output measures of research performance and productivity.

Research postgraduate training, however, provides for an integration of these separate roles of higher education institutions, and can be legitimately dealt with under both headings.

This publication is therefore very timely and appropriate, in the light of increased awareness and implementation of quality assurance principles and practices, and the central position of research postgraduate training programmes within universities. The book will assist universities, faculties, departments and schools, as well as individual supervisors, in improving the quality and effectiveness of research postgraduate training and supervision responsibilities. It draws on the experiences of a wide range of experts within the university system and establishes a framework for setting benchmarks of quality performance and excellent outcomes.

The editors, Ortrun Zuber-Skerritt and Yoni Ryan, have arranged an excellent series of papers, selected to cover relevant areas and the skills required to support a quality research postgraduate programme. These range from strategic planning issues, through to thesis writing, staff development — particularly in enhancing supervisory skills, effective supervision of overseas students, maintaining good communication and supervising literature reviews.

The publication is suitable for new and experienced researchers in the design, implementation and evaluation of the programmes of academic organizational units for research postgraduate students and/or supervisors. The book will also assist in designing staff development programmes for new supervisors of research postgraduate students, and in the identification of areas relevant to quality assurance in research postgraduate training.

May I warmly commend the authors on the wide and comprehensive coverage of issues related to quality assurance and the research postgraduate training programmes of higher education institutions.

Roger S. Holmes
August, 1994

Introduction

Ortrun Zuber-Skerritt and Yoni Ryan

Issues of quality, institutional research culture and processes which encourage, achieve, sustain and assure high quality teaching and research in our universities have been matters of intense debate in Britain and Australia in recent years.

Quality has a generally understood meaning, but it is very difficult to define. It is often used as a synonym for excellence, and its specific connotations are explored further in the context of postgraduate education in Peter Sheehan's chapter here. **Postgraduate** (or graduate) study in this book refers to higher degrees which have a substantial amount of research as a major component, by contrast with coursework Masters degrees, or even coursework doctoral programmes.

The book will be of interest to all higher education institutions, and to supervisors of postgraduate students, as well as to students themselves, because it canvasses not only systemic responses to the increase in postgraduate numbers but also particular matters of concern, such as research training, thesis writing and supervisory practices. Hence it is structured in two parts.

Part One (Chapters 1–6) discusses issues of quality and institutional research culture. This includes the importance of institutional and departmental infrastructure, criteria for evaluating theses and research applications, research in the new universities, women and overseas students. Part Two (Chapters 7-14) suggests educational processes and strategies by which high quality research and supervision may be achieved, including residential staff development programmes, managing the writing process, strategies for improved communication, supervising literature searches, and using contracts, checklists and guidelines.

Ingrid Moses' opening chapter sets the framework of the book by emphasising the importance of departmental and institutional infrastructure for the quality of postgraduate study. Yet she concludes that in the end the 'quality of staff and students is still the key variable'. Chapter 2 is a revised version of **Peter Sheehan**'s keynote address at the Residential Staff Development programme in 1993 described in Chapter 7. Sheehan argues that key factors affecting the quality of the thesis are similar to those affecting the quality of a research application to external grant agencies. **Lewis Elton** and Task Force Three in Britain report in Chapter 3 on their investigations of staff training needed to promote more efficacious teaching, examination of theses, and research in our universities. They provide detailed recommendations for institutional and departmental training programmes.

In Chapter 4, **Jan Whittle** describes the development of a policy framework in a 'new' university to establish university-wide procedures, such as an agreed Code of Good Practice for Research Degree Supervision, and a Register of Research Degree Supervisors. Drawing on universal social and institutional gender inequities, **Linda Conrad** identifies the particular contextual problems facing female students, and suggests a number of practical ways in which institutions can engender 'women-friendly' practices in Chapter 5. In the following chapter **Tania Aspland** and **Thomas**

O'Donoghue consider the influx of overseas students to Australian universities, and on the basis of a case study, explore the difficulties faced by students of differing cultural backgrounds, particularly in relation to attitudes to authority, and the amount of direction students expect.

Part Two turns to more specific processes which might be adopted by institutions and individual supervisors. In Chapter 7, **Ortrun Zuber-Skerritt** proposes residential staff development programmes which focus on the many issues involved in supervision, and which operate as a catalyst for further programmes at the institutional and departmental level — a train-the-trainers programme. The actual writing of the thesis is often the cause of greatest anxiety for students. In Chapter 8 **Robert Brown** argues that success can be assured through reconceiving writing as a marketing exercise, while **Nanette Gottlieb**, in Chapter 9, argues for the use of concept maps, processes of time management, and clarification of examiners' criteria.

Pam Denicolo and **Maureen Pope**, in Chapter 10, explore the use of personal construct psychology as a mode of clarifying the pressures on individual students through grid, 'snake' and narrative techniques and concept maps. Chapter 11, by **Estelle Phillips**, explores the nature of communication breakdowns by comparing student and supervisor narratives about their relationship during study.

In Chapter 12, **Christine Bruce** defines the nature, process and product of a literature review and considers the vital training necessary for advanced information retrieval skills. Arguing that the demographics of postgraduate students have changed from full-time young adults to part-time mature adults, **Yoni Ryan** suggests in Chapter 13 that contracts and checklists could prove effective measures to deal with the difficulties faced by institutions, staff and students as a result of these changes in the student population.

Finally, in Chapter 14, **Barbara Grant** and **Adele Graham** report on the guidelines for communication they have developed at the University of Auckland, New Zealand, and the variable success they have had in introducing use of such guidelines, despite student enthusiasm. John Jones adds an afterword setting the philosophical context of the project.

Acknowledgement

The editors pay full tribute to the desk-top publishing skills of Erica Maddock, who reformatted or rekeyed and remained cheerful throughout 'the production process'.

Part One

Issues of Quality and Institutional Research Culture

Chapter 1

Planning for Quality in Graduate Studies

Ingrid Moses

Introduction

Over the past few years graduate studies have attracted attention from governments, institutional researchers, student bodies and those concerned with equity and access as well as supranational bodies.

Economic and social well being are seen as closely related to how well prepared our future scientists, future academics or the professoriate are, and whether the continuing education of our leaders in the public and private sector and the professions is comparable and produces equivalent or better outcomes than in other countries.

Graduate education is a growth area in higher education. In Australia, we include in graduate studies (or postgraduate studies as it is generally called) postgraduate certificates and diplomas, Masters degrees and PhDs, and professional doctorates (e.g. DBA, DPhil, DEd, DLitt). The growth of these areas is illustrated in Table 1.

Table 1: Postgraduate enrolment in Australia in 1982 and 1992

	1982	% of total enrolment 1992	1992	% of total enrolment 1992
Higher degree				
Research	12,990	3.8	24,286	4.3
Coursework	11,857	3.5	29,275	5.2
Postgraduate				
Cert/diploma	30,965	9.1	49,894	8.9
Total	55,812	16.3	103,455	18.5

Higher degree students are only a minority of students; however they are an increasing minority and as a body are as large as the total enrolment in Australian universities in 1960, when there were just over 53,000 students.

At Masters level we tend to differentiate between coursework and research degrees, although the boundaries are fluid and artificial. Masters courses have an important function but in the following I want to concentrate on research degrees, notably PhDs. It is mainly through our researchers, at postdoctoral level, and as academic staff members and scientists that we stay in touch with the international community of scholars and contribute to an extension of knowledge.

The quality debate

The 1980s were the decade of efficiency and effectiveness in higher education and accountability for both. Thus **planning** for quality in graduate education in contrast to trusting the academic staff and academic departments to ensure and deliver quality is not new.

In July 1992 the Higher Education Council published its draft advice to the Minister on *The Quality of Higher Education*. Relatively little was said about research education (HEC, 1992), but the Council noted:

> ... the enrolment of students in research training programmes should be dependent on the existence of a strong and active research presence in that area. The Council is concerned that there is evidence of expansion into research training occurring 'the other way around' — that is, driven by demand from prospective students, with little regard for the capacity to provide them with a quality education at that level. (33)

The Council acknowledged links between teaching, research and professional practice and commented:

> An institution which does not have as part of its ethos the search for and transmission of new knowledge will not be one capable of instilling in its staff, students and graduates the willingness and ability to assess critically the bases of current thinking, and strive continually for new solutions.

> ... while all institutions should develop a research culture, and the values inherent in quality research activity, this does not mean that all academics, at all times, must be actively engaged in research, nor that every university will comprehensively cover the full spectrum of research activities in all of the disciplines and fields of study that they offer. It is better that institutions be selective and do a few things well, rather than many things badly. (34)

The question, then, of selectivity, of concentration, of fostering quality, not quantity, has remained on the agenda.

Quality in PhD education — supervisors, students and the education process[1]

The quality of PhD education is to a very large extent determined by the postgraduate students themselves. Their formal qualifications in the discipline and research training, their prior experiences as students, as professionals, and as persons shape their expectations and their approaches to study, and these and their motivations have great impact on how students experience graduate study.

Figure 1: Quality in PhD education

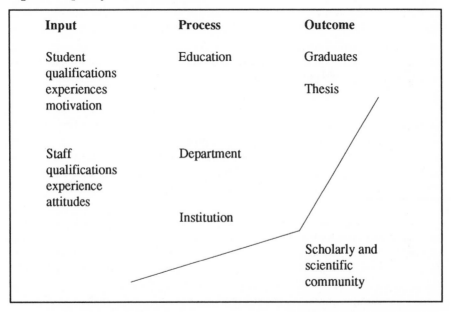

Academic staff as supervisors of these postgraduate students also contribute to the quality of PhD education. Their formal qualifications which signify subject competence and research training, their active involvement in research and publication, as well as their knowledge of the research process, constitute competence as supervisors which is important to the success of graduate students. Their attitudes, their own philosophy of higher education and of PhD education in particular, contribute to the quality; their attitudes, often based on their own past experience, shape the interaction with students — the amount of direction and control, of guidance and structure, and of freedom and autonomy their students experience.

The postgraduate student population has changed dramatically over the past few years, and staff need to take account of that, change some of their practices, some of their attitudes, and acquire and hone some new skills.

The process is the education students experience over three, four, five, six years. It is a teaching-learning process, supervised research training, a process which takes students from a directed, structured programme to a substantial piece of research which demonstrates their research performance and certifies them as independent researchers henceforth.

What happens in these years, in the educative process, is very much determined by the department. [I use this term to connote the basic academic unit.] As we all know, the department:

- provides the resources, ethos, and environment in which staff–postgraduate student and student–student interaction can flourish — or not
- in which postgraduate students feel welcome and respected as fellow researchers — or not
- in which postgraduates are integrated and nurtured — or not.

And as all of us well know, the institution has an impact on the quality of PhD education by signalling the importance of graduate studies to its staff, students and departments. Resources provided to the department, rewards for supervision, guidelines for supervision, training for supervisors, adequate administrative procedures — all the 'quality assurance' mechanisms so much debated in the public forums now, have an impact on that quality.

When we talk about 'output' we do not mean merely a product. Above all we are talking about individual people, graduates, who as individuals have experienced a highly personal supervised research training programme over several years and have gained during that time — which is often longer than their undergraduate studies! — advanced knowledge, skills and understanding. What our graduates learn during the education process is what equips them later to work as academics, researchers, or professionals in leading positions.

But entry to these positions is by the 'Thesis of Merit', a product indeed. The criteria for the thesis are similar around Australia: a demonstration of originality (however defined), of the ability to work independently, and of understanding of the broader context, a contribution to knowledge, and sometimes even the suitability of the thesis for publication (e.g. at the University of Queensland).

The thesis examination process takes the 'quality' issue outside the university and puts it into the broader disciplinary community in Australia or overseas. The convention in Australia is that several of the examiners are external to the university, and often they are from overseas. Assessment is never internal as can happen in graduate schools in the US. This ensures that the PhD graduate is accepted as a full member of the wider disciplinary community, it underlines the international scope of scholarship, and it also highlights the importance of the supervisor as teacher and mentor and of his or her knowledge of the scientific conventions, the schools of thought in the field, and the suitability of examiners. Thus there is a direct link back to staff qualifications and experience.

Quality assurance in graduate study

We are being judged already by the quality of our graduate students and the educative process, and from 1994 onwards, $70 plus million will be distributed on 'quality' criteria. Hence institutions need to look afresh at graduate study and the educational experience of graduate students.

Table 2: Quality assurance in graduate study

Institutional admission criteria
  • student qualifications and experience

Institutional policies
  • supervisor qualifications/accreditation
  • departmental/school resources
  • supervision guidelines
  • half-yearly reports
  • interim assessments

Departmental/school policies
  • assistance to supervisors
  • assistance to students
  • monitoring of supervision process

Institutional research
  • monitoring of completion times and rates
  • monitoring of half-yearly reports
  • regular reviews of examiner reports
  • regular feedback from students

Institutions largely control whom they admit as postgraduate students — even though there are conventions. A good Honours degree, certainly a first class Honours degree, admits students to any PhD programme. If students do not have this qualification they may be admitted with an 'equivalent' qualification; institutions can determine how this equivalence is demonstrated. This is particularly important in the new universities — or the new faculties in older universities, which often draw on a student population which has a less traditional educational career path. Most students from the former College of Advanced Education (CAE) sector would need to demonstrate 'equivalence'. Hence institutions which admit these students — and it is laudable that the rigidity has gone — need to make available courses and opportunities for students to gain or enhance skills in areas which were covered in the traditional Honours degree.

Student experiences, and particularly motivation, also have an impact on the educative process, and it helps supervisors to know about these. Recent studies in various universities show that many of the factors which influenced students in their decision to enrol in a PhD were job-related. But nearly three-quarters of students at the University of Melbourne in a survey some years ago (Powles, 1988) were intrinsically interested in research. In a newer university, the University of Technology Sydney, a study conducted in 1992 produced similar results.

Table 3: Greatest influence on decision to enrol in research degree (%)

	PhD	M
Aspiring to academic career	22	20
To improve job prospects	31	43
To develop high-level research skills for current profession	30	35
Extension of knowledge for current prof.	36	42
Personal satisfaction from being engaged in research and discovery	50	48

Clearly, student motivation to enrol in a research degree has an impact on what students expect from supervisors and from graduate study itself.

Institutions also determine the qualifications a supervisor needs to have; this is normally a qualification at least at the same level as the degree to be supervised. Staff who do not have this degree may usually supervise if they have a substantial and current research involvement and publication record, and/or if they act as co-supervisor or associate supervisor with a principal supervisor.

In some institutions, notably newer ones, research areas or nodes need to be accredited or individual researchers or teams are accredited to supervise research students. This ensures that there is a critical mass of researchers, both staff and students, to provide the intellectual stimulation and opportunities for feedback and interaction students need.

Resources made available to departments, the infrastructure, are essential for quality assurance, as are supervision guidelines, regular reports on student progress, some assessment early in the candidature, and the monitoring of completion times and rates.

Supervision guidelines, half-yearly progress reports, and other forms of interim assessment, including public seminars, all provide a structure for both staff and student in which they can progress.

At departmental level, assistance to supervisors must be given. With the large numbers of research students we have very large numbers of supervisors, and many of these are first-time supervisors. Departments need to think about 'training' such supervisors, helping them to become effective; they need to consider resources at departmental basis, acknowledging supervision in workloads, meetings where supervision issues are discussed, seminars in which supervisors and students give and get feedback on student work, and a research culture in which supervisors and students are embedded and to which they contribute.

Students want assistance, too. The following points in Table 4 are taken from a study of women postgraduates and reflect both student and supervisor views (Moses, 1990: 41ff).

Table 4: Good departmental and institutional practices

Financial assistance
Access to child care
Information about graduate study and employment
Encouragement for enrolment in Honours and research degrees
Supervisors and other staff as role models and mentors
A vibrant research environment

The first four points make it easier for students to move from undergraduate to graduate study. The last two points are about the relationship between student and staff and the integration into a research culture, the initiation into scholarly communities.

This table, again, makes clear that supervision is one of the key elements in graduate study. But it also illustrates how supervision has to be seen in context. We are no longer talking about a small number of scholars working with a small number of research students. We are now talking about many thousands of students engaged in various research degrees, and about several thousand supervisors who are influenced in their work by the context in which they teach and research.

Much of what is depicted in Table 4 is internationally assured through graduate schools. In Australia, graduate schools have been discussed for a number of years; and several have come into existence. However, in themselves the graduate schools do not provide the answers to the ills which can befall graduate students. Data from North American studies show that graduate students there experience the same problems as students here — financial and motivational difficulties, and inadequate supervision. There are long completion times and high drop-out rates. Indeed, a recent historical analysis by Bowen and Rudenstine (1992), *In Pursuit of the PhD*, makes the Australian data look positively healthy. Compulsory coursework and organization in graduate schools do not seem to have led to less attrition or timely completion. Similarly, students in a Canadian study of graduate education (Holdaway, 1992) had very similar complaints to Australian students and the problems identified in the study and the solutions sound nearly identical to the issues and conclusions we draw in Australia. A recent British study by Becher, Henkel and Kogan (1994) finds similar systemic and discipline-specific problems.

I need to stress the importance of institutional research. Unless we know whether our students progress, how long they take, and what the difficulties are that they experience, we cannot plan for quality.

A study of the 1983 cohort of higher degree students conducted for the Australian Vice-Chancellors' Committee looked at the progression over a six-year period. Most students of that cohort did not complete in standard time — this is not only the students' but also the supervisors' problem. Many part-time students do not complete at all. This is much more than a departmental or institutional problem; part-timers need to be accommodated more positively by institutions.

Some students are more vulnerable than others and it helps to realize where we as supervisors need to be aware of potential problems. The data from the AVCC study indicated that the successful students were the 'traditional' PhD students — young, male and in the natural sciences. They are advantaged by a more structured research degree, often working as members of a team. These students have less financial worry than those without scholarships and they have had substantial research training.

The students who dropped out were mainly enrolled in disciplines with traditionally high autonomy for individual researchers and research students; these students were also older, part-time, were not on scholarships, had changed university and had not had research training in an Honours degree.

However we do not see a higher proportion of women in this drop-out group, although women predominate in such disciplines. Being a woman does not predispose one to greater likelihood of dropping-out — all factors being equal, women are as likely to complete, though they take longer.

We need to follow up these national studies in our own institutions.

The following are some questions asked in a recent study of research students in a new university (Moses, unpublished) with categories adapted from those that emerged from an ARC/AVCC–sponsored symposium on supervision (Moses, 1992a). The categories have been grouped into those relating to access to funds, access to infrastructure, support facilities and awareness of opportunities.

Table 5: Funding access

'The level of funding is sufficient for my research work.' Funding for library searches Funding for photocopying Funding for incidentals Funding for conferences Funding for other travel connected with study Funding for fieldwork Funding for experimental work Funding for visits to other research teams or laboratories Opportunities for casual tutoring

More than a quarter of students in this university believed they had insufficient access to conference and other travel funds which they considered necessary for their work, and more than a fifth noted that funding for experimental work, fieldwork, visits to other research teams or laboratories was insufficient.

Table 6: Infrastructure access

> *'The availability of the following infrastructure items is sufficient for my research work.'*
>
> Computing facilities ✓
> Library facilities ✓
> Laboratory space ·
> Technical equipment ✓
> Room or office space
> Desk
> Phone
> Audio-visual facilities
> Common room

Library facilities, notoriously inadequate in the newer universities, caused greatest inconvenience to students, followed by a lack of room or office space. Space problems are experienced in old and new universities. If we believe that research students contribute to the intellectual discourse in a department and benefit themselves from the formal and informal interchanges with staff and peers, then provision of space becomes a vital infrastructure item.

Table 7: Support facilities

> *'The level of support items is sufficient for my research work.'*
>
> Representation on departmental committees
> Technical support
> Editorial support for writing
> Typing
> Mentor system
> Seminars to present work
> Research group meetings
> Research methods seminars/advice
> Access to visiting speakers and other experts
> English language assistance programmes
> Orientation programme of the department and/or the university

More than a quarter of students found editorial support for writing and access to typing wanting, and also found research group meetings and access to visiting speakers and other experts inadequate. More than a fifth wished for a mentor system, and research methods seminars and advice, as well as an orientation programme for the department and/or the university.

Table 8: Awareness of opportunities

> *'I have been made aware of the following opportunities.'*
>
> Made aware of opportunities to publish
> Made aware of opportunities to present at conferences
> Made aware of opportunities for project funding
> Made aware of visiting scholars in school

The four items indicate the extent to which students are mentored and integrated into the research programme and research culture of a department. Large proportions of students were not made aware of the above opportunities, yet supervisors themselves had seen these as important components of effective supervision and mentoring.

An important rule is always to differentiate between the essential and the desirable. And while we want to ensure both quality of outcome and quality of educational experience as a process, we need to ask what actually impedes progress. We concentrated above on infrastructure and other support. The last table focuses on supervision.

Table 9: Supervision

> *'Do you consider that any aspects of your supervision are seriously impeding your progress?'*
>
> Supervisor availability
> Lack of supervisor comment/guidance
> Lack of qualified supervisors/supervisor lacks
>   knowledge/supervisor gives incorrect information
> Supervisor not interested or motivated
> Supervisor workload too great
> University/school/department devalues postgraduate learning

Few students commented that their progress was seriously impeded because of supervisors' failures. The above reasons are in order of frequency mentioned. However, when asked about the level of satisfaction with particular aspects of supervision, significantly more students expressed concern about the (lack of) guidance they received on research design, fieldwork/experiment, on topic selection and definition, followed by feedback on reports/presentations and written work.

The results for all of these items indicate huge differences across the university's departments. As university averages would indicate, the most severe problems occurred in the traditionally least structured areas which were also new to PhD studies.

Conclusion

Clearly the amount of guidance and feedback students need varies between disciplines, and within disciplines depend on each student's ability, preparedness and motivation. Supervisors need to negotiate this with each student, keeping in mind that the student needs to demonstrate in the end independence and mastery.

All of the results from this study as from those previously and currently conducted at La Trobe and the ANU, indicate that we need to rethink what we do with our students in their graduate studies and to rethink the role of supervisors. Departments and institutions, as much as supervisors, influence the quality of supervision which academics in a mass higher education system can give. We need to move away from putting all of the responsibility onto one supervisor to a collaborative system in which input and responsibility are shared, but without detracting from the mentoring opportunities which benefit our research students.

Our experience and research show we can plan for improved quality of graduate study, and institutional research helps planning. In the end, however, the quality of staff and the quality of students are still the key variables.

Note

1.   This section is taken from a symposium paper 'Quality in PhD education — issues in women's participation', delivered at the ANU, 1 July 1992 (Moses, 1992b).

References

Becher, T., Henkel, M. and Kogan, M. (1994). *Graduate Education in Britain.* London: Jessica Kingsley.

Bowen, W.G. and Rudenstine, N.L. (1992). *In Pursuit of the PhD.* New Jersey: Princeton University Press.

Higher Education Council (1992). *The Quality of Higher Education.* Canberra: AGPS.

Holdaway, E. (1992). 'The organisation of graduate studies', in D.J. Cullen (ed.), *Quality in PhD Education.* Canberra: CEDAM and the Graduate School, ANU.

Moses, I. (1990). *Barriers to Women's Participation as Postgraduate Students.* Canberra: AGPS.

Moses, I. (ed.) (1992a). *Research Training and Supervision,* Proceedings from the ARC and AVCC sponsored conference. Canberra: AVCC, NBEET.

Moses, I. (1992b). 'Quality in PhD education — issues in women's participation', in D.J. Cullen (ed), *Quality in PhD Education.* Canberra: CEDAM and the Graduate School, ANU.

Powles, M. (1988). *Know Your PhD Students and How to Help Them.* Melbourne: CSHE, University of Melbourne.

Chapter 2

From Thesis Writing to Research Application: Learning the Research Culture

Peter Sheehan

Introduction

Postgraduate education is the key to strengthening academic and professional expertise in our universities. Through research education and training, advanced and updated professional education, and in-depth specialization within particular fields, tertiary institutions are better equipped to provide high quality research for the general advancement of knowledge, to develop closer international and professional links, and to provide teaching staff to cope with the growth in all areas of higher education, including higher education itself. Universities have a special place in that endeavour. The system is poised, as it were, at a turning point. If the system is to take full advantage of the growth in undergraduate education, we must prepare for considerable expansion in the provision of postgraduate education.

Let us consider the concept of 'research culture'. It is an important one. Postgraduate scholarship activity reflects it, as does the activity of the academic community in submitting applications for funding. Writing a research application reflects the concept of a research culture in similar ways. This chapter first addresses briefly the concept of 'research culture' and then the relevance of quality.

The concept of research culture

There is remarkably little consensus about the definition of 'culture' (Hofstede et al., 1990). Weiner and Vardi (1990) choose to define culture in terms of shared values that place normative pressures on members of organizations. One of the clearest descriptions of 'culture' is by Edgar Schein: 'Culture is what a group learns over a period of time as that group solves its problems of survival in an external environment, and its problems of internal integration' (1990: 111). Dill (1982) points out that the culture of an academic group is much more complex than that in other institutions, drawing as it does on cultural inputs from the subscribing academic professions, the different academic disciplines, and the nature of the specific enterprise. Thus one cross–disciplinary research team might start with a fundamentally different cultural mix from another research team, even in the same institutional setting. Overall, the concept of 'research culture' can be taken to refer to the salient features of a research group on a variety of dimensions, and in particular, it can be taken to refer to the salient features of an **effective** research group.

Historical development of the concept of culture

Concepts representing the surface manifestations of culture, such as 'group norms' and 'climates' have been used by psychologists for a long time (e.g. Lewin et al., 1939), perhaps reflecting the focus on observable behaviour in psychology in earlier decades. The application of the concept of culture to organizations within a given society occurred only recently (in the 1950s and 60s), as organizational psychology began to differentiate itself from industrial psychology, with the increasing interest that emerged in organizational phenomena and their effectiveness.

In 1979, Pettigrew extended the anthropological concept of 'culture' to the particular context of everyday working groups. He proposed that the need for people to function effectively together within a given social setting gave rise to a particular group culture and he described this concept of organizational culture as the 'system of publicly and collectively accepted meanings operating for a given group at a given time' (1979: 574). This system of terms, forms, categories and images was seen as interpreting a group's own situation to themselves.

An especially important paper relevant to research cultures was Wodarski's (1991) article, 'Promoting research productivity among university faculty: An evaluation'. This paper discussed a successful multifactor experiment at the University of Akron in the USA where the intervention aimed to create and maintain a positive culture for research. It did this by improving the development of a more adequate information exchange system, focusing on a systematic approach to securing funds, seminars on grants, indirect cost returns, unplanned research expenditure, and other support activities.

It is only recently that the concept of 'culture' as such has been applied in mainstream literature to organizations, and only very recently to research settings.

Factors affecting research cultures

Bland and Ruffin (1992) argue that the factors affecting research cultures do not operate in research groups as isolated characteristics. They liken these factors to 'fine threads of a whole fabric, individual, yet while interwoven, providing a strong, supportive and stimulating backdrop for the researcher'. They further make the point that 'while at a distance the productive enterprise looks like a highly robust entity, upon closer inspection, it is revealed to be a delicate structure highly dependent on the existence and effective working of numerous individual, organizational and leadership characteristics' (1992: 385).

After an extensive review of the literature on research productivity, Bland and Ruffin (1992) identified a set of 12 characteristics which can be found in research-conducive environments. Whereas these are not written from a cultural perspective, they clearly contain a mix of contextual features including many which impact on the culture of the group. These characteristics are as follows:

1. clear goals that serve a coordinating function
2. research emphasis
3. distinctive culture

4.   positive group climate
5.   assertive participative governance
6.   decentralized organization
7.   frequent communication
8.   accessible resources, particularly human
9.   sufficient size, age and diversity of the research group
10.   appropriate rewards
11.   concentration on recruitment and selection
12.   leadership with research expertise and skill in both initiating appropriate organizational structure and using participatory management practices.

Bland and Ruffin state that the differential impact of each of these 12 factors is unclear. What is clear, however, is that the leader has a disproportionate influence. They further emphasize the 'overarching interdependency' of all 12 factors.

Overarching rationale — quality

The overarching rationale that sustains a research culture must appeal to the concept of 'quality'.

Quality is a concept with a generally understood meaning but there is no one among us who would not find it very difficult to define. The *Random House Dictionary* bravely attempts to define it as 'a characteristic, property or attribute that denotes a high grade, great excellence, accomplishment, or attainment'.

The concept of quality has several specific meanings and they all relate significantly, I believe, to the process of peer review. That process is relevant both to thesis submission and to making a research application.

First, the term 'quality' denotes research that stands out as meritorious in a larger pool of work. This meaning is important, because it refers to the normative framework within which similar work is assessed. This frame of reference partly defines the statistical probability that an application will be supported, or a degree awarded.

Second, a quality product is of such a kind that peers will judge that it has merit. The ultimate yardstick of excellence is the successful application of the process of peer review. This mode of evaluation is flawed, ultimately impressionistic and affected by many factors (not all of which are understood), but there is nothing more valid to replace it.

Third, the judgement of the excellence of research must be such that there will be reasonable consensus concerning its quality. Peers may disagree, but a meritorious proposal for funds, or thesis being evaluated for a degree, ought to obtain agreement across judges and judged merit should (ideally) be reliably evident.

Fourth, the merit of good work should be evident both with respect to the quality of the research itself, and the quality of how the proposal to conduct the work is communicated to others. Failure to be 'supported' will result from a deficiency in either — the degree will not be awarded, or the grant given.

In the context of these remarks, let me define now what I mean by meritorious research. I think the definition fits a variety of research products — both a thesis and a research application.

> A meritorious research project is a well-defined research programme investigating a significant problem or major issue in the theory or practice of a discipline, or a research programme aiming toward the development of new knowledge in the area, fundamental or applied. Its worth should be evident to others and earn the respect of peers.

In both a thesis and a research application then, the nature of the research must be obvious and communicated clearly. The research should be well-defined both in terms of the adequacy of experimental design that underlies the work, and the ease with which the arguments made can be understood by others (one's peers).

In writing an application for funding or a thesis, one must be aware first and foremost that the responsibility rests with the person writing to communicate the quality and significance of a research programme clearly and well. The situation is analogous to the process of editorial review of a work submitted for publication. There is a peron (or persons) sitting in judgement who must be convinced of the merit or quality of the work. Peer assessment is used as an instrument to collect evidence of quality. This process of evaluation may at times be flawed, but for the most part peer review is expected to be consistent with the final judgement. One always hopes that such consistency will be present.

Let us turn now to evaluation of the quality of a thesis in particular. In doing so, I will hazard a definition of what I regard as a 'good thesis' and draw out what I think are the major principles at stake, summarized in Table 1. All flow from the presence of a vigorously operating research culture. Along the way, major guidelines for assessment will be formulated. It should be noted that what follows is more consistent for theses relevant to the application of experimental design than to non-experimental work such as occurs in many fields of study within the humanities. Many of the principles, however, are relevant and broadly applicable.

Table 1: Principles affecting the quality of a thesis

1.	Quality (*vs* quantity)
2.	Succinctness
3.	Perfect format
4.	Critical tone
5.	Sound methodology
6.	Freedom from errors in statistics
7.	Meeting objectives
8.	Impartiality

Evaluation of the quality of a thesis

The Examiner's Report form used by the University of Queensland in the examination of its higher degree theses asks examiners in making their report to assess the quality of the thesis. It is of interest to note that comments are requested particularly on the following:

(a)   the extent to which the candidate has demonstrated
            originality,
            critical insight, and
            capacity to carry out independent research;
(b)   the extent of the contribution to knowledge made by the thesis, and in particular its contribution to the understanding of the subject with which it deals; and
(c)   the suitability of the thesis for publication.

Students should understand that a thesis is **not** a publication. Rather, I would define a thesis as a testimonial in scientific report writing form of the progression of a candidate's thinking toward the solution of a particular problem. Comment on different types of theses (coursework, and PhD) may help to illustrate the point. A Masters coursework thesis has to solve a problem or make a substantial contribution in the same way as a PhD thesis does. A coursework thesis typically investigates an issue of some practical or professional relevance and shows the careful application of scientific reasoning. A doctoral thesis, on the other hand, should make a substantial contribution to the area of the discipline in which the thesis is written, and be publishable (in principle) as a series of studies.

Issues in assessment

With reference to Table 1, the following factors affect the quality of a thesis.

(a)   **Quality (*vs* Quantity).** Students should avoid thinking that amount of work will impress examiners. Quality of scholarship is what is primary, given that the above criteria are met.
(b)   **Succinctness.** A thesis must demonstrate a logical development of an argument threading through a serial list of studies. A useful strategy to adopt to emphasize this progression is to separate essential material from less essential material by including the latter in appendices to the thesis. One should think especially carefully about the introduction to a thesis. An introductory section to a thesis needs to put the problem into context and show a relevant grasp of the literature, but should not be written to establish how much the student knows about the discipline as a whole. It is wise also to think carefully about how theory should be used. Few theses can reasonably be expected to decide conclusively between one theory and another. Theory helps organize the data and when writing a thesis it may be most useful to view

the theory being tested not as something to be 'proved', but as a way of thinking that organizes the data around a coherent viewpoint.

(c) **Format.** Format should be perfect. If the research work can be criticized methodologically, no examiner should be led to assume there is an untidy mind illustrated by blemishes in presentation. A model of clarity and exposition sets the stage for an uncritical examiner. If the research cannot be perfect, at least the format can.

(d) **Critical tone.** A thesis should primarily demonstrate evidence of analytical ability. Whatever the area of the thesis or its approach to the discipline, there should be evidence that the student appreciates the limitations of what he or she has done. The two most important facets of this ability are: (1) constructive criticism of others and criticism of self as well as others using the same standards of evaluation; (2) application of sound principles of logic that is demonstrated by the flow and consistency of the work. This guideline is independent of the level of the thesis (Honours, Masters, or PhD).

(e) **Methodology.** There should be no major methodological pitfalls or errors of logic in the argument. Assumptions behind a methodology should always be discussed and recognition given to when they are not sustained (e.g. a study is not really a replication, or the control of some variable breaks down).

(f) **Errors in statistics.** There are different types of errors to consider. Take a thesis citing quantitative statistics, for example. Gross errors such as conducting an analysis of variance on frequency data are different, for example, from errors of assuming interval scaling (*vs* ordinal scaling), or allowing heterogeneity of variance in the data being analysed. Any limitations in statistical method should be recognized. The student should be especially careful not to indulge in excessive displays of statistical sophistication — where, for example, the logic of the hypotheses is lost in statistical overkill.

(g) **Objectives.** Content should always be considered in relation to the major objectives of a thesis. The main objectives should be listed at the outset of the research, and the thesis written so that the text is perfectly consistent with them.

(h) **Impartiality.** Personal preferences should be avoided, and the student should always be careful to present alternative viewpoints to the theory that is being preferred so that the assessor can know that other 'options' were considered. Finally, in relation to style, the best theses are those that are written in such a way as to enthuse the reader about the phenomena being investigated and the candidate's commitment to research. Rewriting is necessary to achieve this goal, and requires intensive liaison with the supervisor.

A good thesis

At this stage a definition of a 'good thesis' can be attempted. A sound thesis should provide a critical analysis of a topic, be critical of the author as much as of others and always point to further work that needs to be done. It should bear on a particular problem (that does not yield too excessive a number of hypotheses) in a focused fashion and should be written succinctly and in flawless format. It should use theory cautiously, not recklessly, and its design should always tally with the objectives of the work as stated in the text of the thesis at the outset. The programme of research should flow logically and relentlessly in the text of the thesis, with the main text being reserved for the major steps of the developing argument. The thesis must have a position and it must be stated clearly, and this position must always be argued in a way that is fair to what others in the literature might think about the phenomena with which the thesis is concerned.

Evaluating a research application

The process of writing an application bears important similarities to writing a thesis. I will not go into comparable detail about research applications, but choose to make this point by listing 16 'common concerns' drawn from my experience of evaluating hundreds of research applications. Some of the concerns are necessarily peculiar to funding applications (e.g. defence of budget, and commencing the work) but for the most part there is a remarkable commonality between the issues pertinent to the evaluation of a thesis and those related to the assessment of a grant proposal. All but one of the first 13, for example, are directly common to both. These concerns are:

1.   lack of commitment to the topic
2.   failure to communicate liveliness and enthusiasm for the work
3.   poor precision or definition of the project
4.   lack of evidence of academic content and communication of scholarship
5.   impressionistic observations and subjective comment
6.   use of prescription in place of argument
7.   lack of discussion of relevant data with similar content
8.   insufficient details given about the work
9.   failure to demonstrate thorough familiarity and experience with relevant processes and techniques associated with the work
10. inadequate justification of the budget — e.g. scope of request, and listing of priorities
11. overall lack of awareness of a normative frame of reference
12. unprofessional presentation
13. poor organization with no road signs reinforced by direct and concise language for skimming
14. poor knowledge of the granting scheme's procedures and rules (e.g. eligibility, length of application, size of grant, and number of applications)
15. poor awareness of new procedures and rules
16. failure to capitalize on ongoing work.

Standards and assessment criteria for dissertations and theses have been proposed by Madsen (1983) and are listed in Table 2. They reinforce the same point and again demonstrate commonality.

Table 2: Standards and assessment criteria for dissertations and theses (after Madsen, 1983)

Masters by Research

1. Evidence of an orginal investigation or the testing of ideas
2. Competence in independent work or experimentation
3. An understanding of appropriate techniques
4. Ability to make critical use of published work and source materials
5. Appreciation of the relationship of the special theme to the wider field of knowledge
6. Worthy, in part, of publication

PhD

In addition to 1 – 6 above:
7. Originality as shown by the topic researched or the methodology employed
8. Distinct contribution to knowledge

Conclusion

This chapter began by listing the characteristics of a research culture. Such a culture requires a real commitment; it is distinctive, positive and participative; it benefits most from decentralization; and there should be frequent communication. Further, the culture also requires accessible resources and should recognize and sustain diversity. Above all, the concept of quality permeates it and there is an overarching interdependence of all its factors.

I leave to last the question of what structures are needed to foster a research culture in universities. Others in this book take up this issue in more detail, but let me conclude by offering (consistent with the characteristics of a research culture listed above) one kind of structure—operating at a decentralized level, and in a participative fashion — which actively fosters a research culture. The guidelines, illustrated in Table 3, focus on how to attract external funding but they are easily generalized to incorporate postgraduate education.

Table 3: Action to encourage research in departments

- Every department should have a research committee
- Groups should encourage the formation of departmental research committees and monitor support programmes initiated at departmental level
- Efforts should be made in departments by their research committees to identify particular research projects and encourage staff responsible to apply for support for them
- Committees at department level should review completed draft applications and conduct practice interviews
- Strong and active researchers in departments should not be too heavily loaded with teaching and administrative responsibilities
- Group and departmental research committees need to monitor and react to what happens in external funding rounds
- The level of research involvement of women needs particular attention, as well as the specific needs of different disciplines

In conclusion, it might be said that perhaps the overall aim of all the contributors to this book is to encourage the research culture of our institutions and to point to the need to implement guidelines to foster research activities at the grassroots (departmental) level. For reasons stated, this incorporates applying for research grants, facilitating research in departments, and encouraging and facilitating postgraduate research.

Author's note

The author would like to thank Rosemary Robertson for help in the preparation of this paper.

References

Bland, C.J. and Ruffin, M.T. (1992). 'Characteristics of a productive research environment: Literature review'. *Academic Medicine* **67**: 385-397.
Dill, D.D. (1982). 'The management of academic culture: Notes on the management of meaning and social integration'. *Higher Education* **11**: 303-320.
Hofstede, G., Neuijen, B., Ohayv, D.D. and Sanders, G. (1990). 'Measuring organizational cultures: A qualitative and quantitative study across twenty cases'. *Administrative Science Quarterly* **35**: 286-316.
Lewin, D., Lippitt, R. and White, R.K. (1939). 'Patterns of aggressive behavior in experimentally created "social climates"'. *Journal of Social Psychology* **10**: 271-299.

Madsen, D. (1983). *Successful Dissertations and Theses.* San Francisco: Jossey-Bass.

Pettigrew, A.M. (1979). 'On studying organizational cultures'. *Administrative Science Quarterly* **24**: 570-581.

Schein, E. (1990). 'Organizational culture'. *American Psychologist* **45**: 109-119.

Weiner, Y. and Vardi, Y. (1990). 'Relationships between organizational culture and individual motivation: A conceptual integration'. *Psychological Reports* **67**: 295-306.

Wodarski, J.S. (1991). 'Promoting research productivity among university faculty: An evaluation'. *Research on Social Work Practice* **1**: 278-288.

Chapter 3

Staff Development in Relation to Research

*Lewis Elton and members of the Task Force on
Staff Development in Relation to Research*

Introduction

Over the past 30 years, the concept of staff development has been successively extended. Originally the area with which it was largely concerned was that of furthering the discipline background and knowledge of academic staff, through attendance at conferences and meetings, secondments to research centres or to industry, and obtaining advanced qualifications. At that stage, its base was largely departmental. During the 1970s, the concept came to be additionally associated with the improvement of teaching, until in the universities it came to be almost wholly identified with this new area, while in the polytechnics (recently upgraded and now referred to as 'the new universities'), both the new and old areas came to be subsumed under staff development. The base for the new area was normally outside departments, in special staff or educational development units. Such units naturally did not consider themselves competent to handle the earlier task of improving disciplinary knowledge.

Most recently, it has been realized that the research area, with which the improvement of disciplinary knowledge had been primarily concerned, had within it an area that was not primarily discipline-related and which consequently might well be within the remit of a staff development unit. This is the concern of the present chapter, an edited version of the Report of Task Force Three[1], established by the Universities' Staff Development Unit (USDU, 1994), to investigate 'Staff Development in Relation to Research'. It omits the appendices of the original Report. While the Report refers to the situation in Great Britain, its conclusions are likely to have general applicability.

The remit of the Task Force

When we first came to discuss our role, we immediately realized that we were dealing not just with one area, but with three that were essentially distinct from each other and all of which were in need of support through staff development. They were:

- support of staff in their work with research students
- support of staff in their own discipline-oriented research
- support of staff in their work directed towards pedagogic research in their discipline.

The first of these had to be extended, through the addition of two very different activities:

* support of examiners of research students
* training of research students in support of teaching.

The second of these is the only area where we make proposals for working directly with students.

As our work progressed, we came to identify gaps in our initial perception of our task. Although it was possible to incorporate some of these within the areas laid down, there remain certain gaps of which we are very conscious. They are:

* support for the development of research careers and in particular, adequately meeting the needs of staff on short-term contracts
* support of ancillary research staff
* support of the special needs of the new universities.

For the first two, time ran out on us, but there is little doubt that they should be included. The third is different, in that it depends on the assumption that the needs of the new universities are identifiably different from those of the old universities. To the extent that until recently the new universities have not received special research funding, this seemed a reasonable assumption. The reality which we found is that the needs of the new universities are as varied as those of the old and, while to some extent they may differ in degree, they do not differ in kind.

Staff development is about change, and successful change normally requires a combined 'bottom up' and 'top down' approach, in which change is engendered from the bottom and facilitated from the top. Hence this chapter is likely to have two audiences. The first consists of individuals with a staff development role, whether they are full- or part-time, and whether they are in special units or in discipline departments. Such a role may not even be formally recognized, particularly for some of those in departments, but that does not make this chapter less relevant to them. Indeed to the extent that all staff development is an activity that is mutual and one which all staff have to recognize as important, this is addressed to all academic staff. The second audience consists of individuals in decision-making positions, at departmental, institutional and national levels. Unless they clearly recognize the need for the kind of staff development which we propose, provide adequate resources for it and recognize its relevance to institutional rewards and promotions, little if anything will happen.

Support of staff in their work with research students

Supervision and the nature of the PhD

The supervision of research students and all that is included in this concept raises questions at every level. At the most fundamental level are questions concerning the nature of the PhD programme. To what extent is it a general education for the formation of researchers, a specific training in research, or a means of generating research outcomes? It clearly has aspects of all three and, although all three purposes are legitimate and pursued in all disciplines, they have different weights in different disciplines. Although it is not within the remit of a staff development programme to discuss the nature of the PhD, to the extent that the purposes of PhD programmes are complex and subject to disagreement, staff development programmes lack the security of agreed objectives. However, in part this complexity arises from a feature of academia, to which we shall have to make reference more than once, namely the lack of self-reflection on fundamental issues and their inadequate discussion among colleagues. Many, although not of course all, of the differences between academic practices turn out to be resolvable, once self-reflection and discussion are applied to them, and it is an important part of staff development to encourage and facilitate both.

The training of supervisors

We next turn to supervisory practice. Supervision is a teaching activity and academics traditionally learn how to teach, not through training, but from their experience as students and as teachers. Even at undergraduate level, where both these experiences have great variety, and the normal cycle of teaching is repeated sufficiently frequently for improvement through self-reflected experience to be a possible reality, it is now beginning to be accepted that training is important. At the level of research supervision, where there is usually a unique student experience and where the majority of staff supervise only a small number of research students, learning from experience can hardly ever be an adequate preparation. This is so even if, as is common now, staff act at least once (and rarely more frequently) in an apprentice role to more experienced supervisors, who may have had no mentoring training. Such training is important, but if it is not immediately available to particular supervisors, then they ought to be aware of advice generally available, such as that given in Appendix 1e of the full Report of this Task Force.

It is not possible to lay down yet the content, methods or duration of any formal course through which supervision in all its aspects can be taught. What can be done and is beginning to be done very successfully is to bring supervisors together, and enable them to analyse their own practices and those of their colleagues in mutual discussion. Such an approach is particularly appropriate for those aspects of supervision — and they are the most important ones — that have a strong interpersonal element, while those primarily concerned with the development of a knowledge and skills base may respond better to more formal staff training. It is necessary to emphasize that the possession of such knowledge and skills on the part of staff is a necessary but not a sufficient condition for being able to impart them to others. Another point to be noted is that while staff with little or no experience are more likely to profit from staff development activities that involve others in the same discipline, more experienced staff tend to profit from sharing experiences with those from other disciplines. Finally there is an organizational aspect to supervision, ranging from the institutional provisions relating to monitoring a student's progress to such general questions as those concerning intellectual property rights, all of which have to be addressed in the training of supervisors.

A managed partnership between supervisor, student and institution

Our approach to the training of supervisors has thus far been quite conventional, respecting the traditional resistances of academic staff to any form of managerialism. However, we must now acknowledge the culture of the 1990s, with its stress on quality and accountability, which requires universities to establish formal structures where previously there often were none or only barely adequate ones. Supervisor, student and institution should engage in a managed partnership and an agreed code of practice. There is little doubt that many students would prefer the certainties that such a framework and code of practice can provide for them. Although we make suggestions in the full Report as to the nature of the framework and what it should contain, including not uncontroversially the recognition that students should be prepared for varied forms of employment, we leave the details of both nature and content to negotiation between universities, CVCP and the Research Councils.

Is PhD supervision research or teaching?

We want to draw attention to an unfortunate consequence of the fact that research supervision is often not given a formal time allowance, perhaps because it is considered an aspect of research rather than of teaching. It then becomes something that academics are expected to carry out in their own time, as is the case for their own research, rather than in properly allocated time as is the case for their teaching. Not surprisingly, this can result in research students being given inadequate supervision time and any staff development associated with research supervision coming very low in staff time priorities.

Recommendations

The following are then our recommendations in respect to the training of research supervisors:

1.   Supervisors of research students should receive a proper time allowance for both the tasks of supervision and any training and development for them.
2.   All research supervisors should receive an adequate training in relevant general skills of research supervision and its management, including the development of appropriate attitudes.
3.   This should be done in part through formal programmes and in part through discussions with colleagues of varying experience in their discipline, facilitated by staff developers, through which they can share and profit from each other's experiences and develop appropriate attitudes.
4.   All research supervisors should act as assistant supervisors to experienced supervisors before they act on their own. This involves the experienced

supervisor acting in a mentoring role, a task which in turn requires some staff
development.
5.   More experienced supervisors should consider meeting regularly to exchange
      experiences and discuss practices with colleagues in other disciplines.
6.   Universities should consider establishing an agreed code of practice for
      research supervision and training for it.
7.   Universities should give serious consideration to the managerial implications
      of research supervision and training for it.

Support of examiners of research students

Examiners of research students, like most research supervisors, rely largely on their
own experience in order to learn their job and improve on it. One advantage that they
have over supervisors is that they always work in pairs, as an internal and an external
examiner, so that over the course of some years they can learn a variety of approaches.
The extent to which this is effective is difficult to assess, but it must be rare for
examiners to discuss matters which relate to their performance with each other. They
also have a disadvantage in comparison with supervisors — the experience of being
examined as a student is often so stressful that it is exceedingly unlikely for it to
become a model for the student who in due course becomes an examiner. It may be
safely concluded that examiners ought to receive some training.

Standards

It is difficult, in the absence of relevant research, to establish whether examiners work
to common standards or whether these standards, if they exist, are efficiently
transmitted to new examiners. A more formal means of establishing and then
transmitting such standards is clearly desirable.

External and internal examiners

An important point to note is that the tasks of external and internal examiners are not
entirely the same. External examiners are usually chosen for their knowledge and
expertise in the narrow field of a student's work, while internal examiners should be
more concerned with the general knowledge of the student in the wider area in which
the student's specialism is set. This would make sense, for it is usually difficult to find
staff in a department, other than the student's supervisor, who are expert in the
student's specialism. Yet we have insufficient data to decide if this procedure is
indeed typical. What is certain is that external examiners carry more weight, which
implies that the specialized knowledge is likely to carry more weight than general
knowledge.

     Until recently, supervisors in many British universities acted as internal
examiners, but as a result of the Reynolds Report on Examiners this is no longer the
case. The reason for the recommendation was of course that a supervisor could hardly

suddenly become an independent examiner. What has received far too little attention is the fact that the relationship between student, supervisor and the examination process is quite radically different in these two examination regimes, which affects not only the examination itself, but the whole teaching and learning process that precedes it.

Recommendations

We make the following recommendations regarding the training and development of examiners:

1. Examiners should have an introduction to the theory of examining, so that they can link it to their practice.
2. They should attend events in which they share their experiences and concerns with colleagues, with the aim of developing appropriate attitudes towards their tasks and establishing common standards.
3. They should be familiar with relevant parts of the USDU 'Handbook for External Examiners in Higher Education' (Partington et al., 1993).
4. They should not normally be allowed to practise as examiners unless they have had training of this kind.

Training of research students in support of teaching

The use of research students to assist in undergraduate teaching is of long standing. Their role has usually been as tutors or as laboratory demonstrators; it has generally been accepted that they should work no longer than six hours per week in term time. This has in the past often referred to contact hours, with no extra time provided for out-of-contact time, whether for preparation, marking or — least of all — training. The result of this has been that research students have at times not been paid for any of their work in support of teaching in time other than contact time. Thus there is a history to the current situation of using research students in support of undergraduate teaching which may affect it unfavourably.

Now that it has come to be recognized, at least in principle, that research students do need some formal training in their teaching support role, it is not surprising that this training parallels that given to new teaching staff. It is important therefore to stress from the outset that in our view, students should not in the main be expected to act independently as teachers; they should normally act in support of teaching staff.

What form should the training take?

Although the majority of research students treat their teaching role with interest and conscientiously, they cannot be expected to treat it as their prime commitment, which is, and rightly so, to be research students. At the same time, it can and must be expected that they and all staff involved treat research students' teaching tasks very seriously.

All concerned should receive appropriate training. Current evidence would appear to indicate that it may be more difficult in practice to convince the staff of this than the students, and this would be wholly in line with the situation that new staff face in similar circumstances.

As for what training is appropriate, all experience with new staff indicates that such first training must be very practical, if it is to be useful and acceptable. The next question is whether such training should precede first practice or run in parallel with it. Here the argument that it should precede practice so as to save undergraduates from acting as guinea pigs is not as strong as the argument that if the training is integrated with practice it will be perceived as more relevant, and hence more effective. Thus we suggest that the initial training should take the form of about half a day per week of very practical training for, say, ten weeks, closely associated with the ongoing teaching, which itself should be supervised.

Such training, about half of which should be private study, can only be effective in small groups, which should in general be discipline-specific. Other areas of training, e.g. more theoretical work or work that is institution- but not discipline-specific, could follow, and for this larger groups would be appropriate. Perhaps ten half-days would be needed, but this could include any private study time. The supervisor of the teaching, who should normally be the teacher the student supports, acts in a mentoring role.

An important consideration is the time students give to the training, which will of course form part of their total commitment of six hours, i.e. one day per week for about 30 weeks in a year. The suggested training programme would occupy about twelve days, which is cost-effective if it prepares students for teaching over two to three years, i.e. for research students on a normal three-year programme, but grossly inefficient if they are on a one-year programme. For such students, something much shorter would be needed to be efficient, but it is extremely doubtful whether anything so short could also be effective.

Even for research students on a three-year programme it is clear that initial training will have to be very specific to the task in hand, which should rarely be one in which they act independently. However, if they act in support of staff, then such staff need training in three roles: in their own teaching, in the supervision of the associated teaching of their students and in the training of their students. Of these, only the last can be delegated to a colleague with specific training for it. It may perhaps be assumed that in future all university teachers will either have received adequate training for their own tasks or have profited from their experience to an extent that may make such training unnecessary. It may be further assumed that whatever teaching they delegate is such that they themselves have experience of it and that they treat their supervisory role conscientiously. This then leaves the actual training task, which we suggest should be concentrated in a small number of disciplinary colleagues, who themselves may require some training, to be provided by professional staff developers. Such people would also be involved in the more general training which is to follow the first training.

A critique of current training provision

The proposals which we make can only be tentative, since there is at present a serious shortage of development and evaluated practice in this field. We are concerned that under increasing financial pressures, there will be a reluctance to undertake such training and that this will lead to a deterioration in the quality of the undergraduate learning experience. Another danger is that courses for research students will be modelled too closely on existing initial courses for university teachers. Their respective needs are not the same.

Whatever form a course takes, we believe that it is essential for it to be seriously evaluated, in a way that goes much beyond the immediate satisfaction of the participants. In particular, any evaluation should include answers to the following questions:

1. How well do the actual teaching tasks of the students match the course objectives and to what extent may the different needs of students require different course provisions?
2. To what extent are these tasks in support of teaching done by staff and to what extent are they carried out independently?
3. Are there parts of the course that specifically address the problems of working in support?
4. Was the course evaluated after the participants had had some experience of using what they had learnt?
5. Was the course evaluated by staff whom the participants supported?
6. What sort of training did those staff have, either in their teaching function or in the function of mentors to the participants?
7. To what extent can training at a distance be an effective component in a training programme for research students?

More comprehensive training and certification

Finally we turn to the question of whether research students should be prepared specifically for a future as university staff. There is little doubt that if they receive a good training for their ongoing tasks, this will stand them in good stead also for future tasks, but there is no way that such limited training can or should replace the training that new university staff should receive. On the other hand, there may be some students who would like to prepare themselves for future and much more substantial roles as university teachers. Clearly such students should not be discouraged, and to provide something for them on a voluntary basis, that may conceivably reduce a little the need for their initial training as university teachers, could be helpful and might even lead to a qualification. The short courses discussed earlier might at least be rewarded by an attendance certificate and a testimonial from the teacher(s) whom the students were supporting. However, to see either the shorter or the longer type of course as a way of reducing the need for the initial training of university teachers would in our opinion be a wholly retrograde step.

Recommendations

The training of research students in the support of teaching is still in its infancy and there may well be substantial changes in it over the coming years. In the meantime, we propose the following recommendations:

1.   Students in their teaching role should normally act only in support of teaching staff; only in exceptional circumstances should they act independently.
2.   The times for which students are paid in connection with teaching must allow for all the work done in connection with the teaching as well as for all associated training. It should not normally exceed six hours per week during term time.
3.   The training of students should be aimed directly at the tasks which they have to undertake. Such training should be compulsory and it should be fully evaluated some time after students have started teaching.
4.   More general training can be provided on a voluntary basis.
5.   The staff whom the students support should themselves have received training, both as teachers and as mentors to the students.
6.   The compulsory part of the training should lead to an attendance certificate, while the voluntary part may well lead to a certificate, which could provide partial exemption from the initial training given to academic staff.

Support of staff in the management of their own research

The increasing complexity of much research, the demands for quality assurance and accountability, the impact of legislative change, for example in the areas of intellectual property and health and safety, and the need for researchers to raise their own funds, have made the researcher's life very much more complicated in recent years.

To some extent this has clearly led to a more professional approach, through the establishment of full-time research support and industrial liaison officers, the appointment of full-time administrators to manage major research centres and the designation of senior academic staff as centre directors. But even for the individual academic, holding a single or a small portfolio of grants, some managerial functions are now unavoidable.

Hence training in research management has become an essential element of staff development at several levels. This is as important in the old universities as in the new ones, although staff in the latter may be even more conscious of the need for it. In contrast to much staff development, this is an area where the demand is real and substantial, but its provision is at present somewhat limited. [USDU's Task Force One (forthcoming) is currently formulating a framework and guidelines for management and leadership development for higher education staff.] Since quite a high proportion of the training required is in the knowledge area, the use of self-study materials and distance modes of training may be particularly appropriate. Much of the training will also be needed by research support staff.

Any such training should be seen in the context of a proper career development strategy. This has been particularly lacking in recent years, most notably for contract researchers with little or no job security, but also for permanent staff for whom circumstances dictate a transition from an academic to a managerial role. Such issues cannot adequately be addressed here. However, such training would at least provide research staff with the basis of a transferable skill which could be an asset in non-academic occupations should the need arise.

Recommendations

In relation to training in research management, we propose the following:

1.   Existing expertise in research management should be coordinated through national networks such as the Association of Directors of Research Centres in the Social Sciences (DORCISS).
2.   This should lead to the national provision of training for staff at several levels, i.e. the individual academic, the research centre/company director, the research centre manager, and university-based research support staff.
3   Training for academics and for research managers within research centres, as well as for research support staff, should in the main be provided regionally and locally.
4.   Training provision should move towards modularization and could ultimately lead to certification.
5.   Much of the training is particularly suited to be delivered at a distance through self-study materials.
6.   USDU's Green Paper (forthcoming) on the work of Task Force One will provide a useful guide to management development in higher education.

Support for staff in their work directed towards pedagogic research

The pedagogy of higher education is a discipline, overlapping but significantly different from the pedagogy of education at other levels. Hence all the normal canons of academia apply to it, i.e. research must be carried out in it, it must have a body of literature and a communication system to acquaint its members with results of that research, and it must provide education and training at undergraduate and postgraduate levels. At the same time, the discipline is still struggling to establish itself in academia.

The nature of pedagogic disciplinary research and the need for training

Although there is more than one way to conduct the kind of research appropriate to innovative teaching practice, the form most commonly employed is action research, an essential feature of which is that research and action are carried out in tandem, usually by the same person. For most academic staff, their own disciplines require quite different forms of research and, while undoubtedly research experience in one discipline is to some extent transferable to another, it would be unwise to assume that such experience would be an adequate preparation for research in this other field. It seems to us that there is therefore a need for such academic staff to undertake research training in action research, which must include both the ability to carry out research oneself and appreciation of the significance of the research done by others. A form of training programme likely to be acceptable and effective is one that is problem-oriented and resource-based.

While for some staff, research is a by-product of their teaching, other staff may develop a more general interest in pedagogic research in higher education for its own sake, generally related to teaching and learning in their discipline. This additional and more general training is best obtained in education departments which specialize in the pedagogy of higher education and will not therefore be considered here.

Training the trainers

The proposed problem-oriented training programme would need to be supported by a programme for the training of the trainers involved in it. This should be based on well-tried methods which turn experience into expertise, i.e. self-reflection; feedback from those whom they train; cooperative work, e.g. in learning sets, with other trainers and professional advisers; and evaluation. There should be no specific training courses for the trainers, since the logic of this would lead to the problem of an infinite regression of the trainers of the trainers of the .... . At the same time it must be acknowledged that in the present stage of development many such trainers are in a position where they would themselves greatly profit from the training programme suggested above for academic staff.

Recognition of the need for training

In stressing the need for the provision of staff development and training in pedagogic research, we may have given an impression that at present there is no competent pedagogic research in higher education. Such an impression would be false. Nevertheless, the results are more uneven than would be expected, if pedagogic research in higher education were a well-established research field. There is also not nearly enough of it. Furthermore those who engage in such research are themselves aware of their need for training, a matter that became very apparent at, for instance, a recent symposium on 'Improving student learning: research and practice', organized by the Oxford Brookes Centre for Staff Development.

Recommendations

We therefore propose the following recommendations regarding pedagogic research in higher education:

1.   There is a need for adequately resourced training of staff who wish to engage in pedagogic research of their subject.

2.   The training should be problem-based and should contain a local as well as a national element. The latter should almost certainly use a distance mode.
3.   The training of trainers on such a programme should be based on self-reflection, cooperation with other trainers and evaluation. There should be no formal courses for the training of trainers.
4.   There should be appropriate training for decision makers, so that they appreciate and support the needs of pedagogic researchers.
5.   Funding Councils should provide a financial climate conducive to the pursuit of pedagogic subject research.

Practical aspects of training in support of research

Finally, we must consider the implementation of the training. While this could be in the form of face-to-face lectures, seminars or workshops, there are many alternatives. These include informal methods such as mentoring and discussion meetings, and methods based on self-study, individualized learning or resource-based learning. The following issues should be considered:

*   setting up a group to plan and oversee the training programme
*   resources
*   staffing the programme
*   the purpose, content and form of the programme
*   evaluating effectiveness.

These issues and the following questions should guide development of training in support of research:

1.   Who should the programme be for?
2.   What should be the precise purpose of the programme?
3.   What should be in the programme (its content)?
4.   What form should the programme take? (i.e. what training methods should be used?)
5.   What should be the pattern of attendance?
6.   What, if any, assessment procedures should there be and should there be any certification?
7.   How should the programme be monitored (evaluated) for judgement and improvement?
8.   What support provision is required — e.g. special materials, library, computer lab, seminar room?
9.   What should be the background and experience of the staff running the programme?
10.   Who should be the contact person or organizer?
11.   How much, if anything, will participants be charged?
12.   What should be the structure of any committees in connection with the programme?

13.   What are the initial costs of setting up the programme and what are the ongoing
       costs of running it?

These questions also serve as a basis for documenting the programme for the purpose
of quality audit and quality assessment and they can provide the substance of a
publicity flyer.

Conclusion

We believe that the areas which we have covered here are all important and are all in
need of a greatly expanded effort in staff development involving as they do the
training of staff and future staff in that *sine qua non* of university culture, research.
Furthermore, the proposals which we have made do not call for large resource inputs,
and the return in terms of quality enhancement could be very substantial.

[1] The members of the Task Force were:

Professor Howard Barnes, Unilever Research.
Professor Robert Burgess, CEDAR, University of Warwick.
Dr Pat Cryer, Higher Education Consultant.
Mr Colin Cumming, Head of Postgraduate Training Support and Fellowship Groups,
        ESRC.
Professor Lewis Elton, Professor Emeritus, University of Surrey.
Dr Kate Exley, Staff Development Officer, University of Nottingham.
Miss Joan Hughes, DORCISS Research Administrators Group.
Mr James Irvine, Chair, National Postgraduate Committee.
Dr Michael Jubb, Deputy Secretary, The British Academy.
Dr John Kirkland, Head of Research Services Bureau, Brunel University.
Professor John Laver, Chairman, Centre for Speech Technology Research, University
        of Edinburgh.
Ms Anne McIntyre, Senior Scientific Officer, Postgraduate Training Division, ESRC.
Professor Patrick O'Brien, Director, Institute of Historical Research, University of
        London.
Dr Estelle Phillips, Open Business School, School of Management, The Open
        University.
Professor Murray Stewart, School of Advanced Urban Studies, University of Bristol.

References and further reading

Advisory Board for the Research Councils (1993). *Nature of the PhD*. London:
        Office of Science and Technology.
American Association for Higher Education (1993). *Preparing Graduate Students
        to Teach*. Washington DC: AAHE.

Committee of Vice-Chancellors and Principals (1986, 1988, 1989). *Academic Standards in Universities*. London: CVCP ('The Reynolds Report').

Cryer, P. (ed.) (1992). *Effective Learning and Teaching in Higher Education*. Sheffield: USDU.

Elliott, J. (1991). *Action Research for Educational Change*. Buckhingham: Open University Press.

Elton, L. (1993). 'University teaching: a professional model for quality', in R. Ellis (ed.), *Quality Assurance for University Teaching*. Buckingham: SRHE/Open University Press.

ESRC (1991). *Postgraduate Training Guidelines*. Swindon: ESRC.

McMichael, P. and Garry, A. (1991). *Strategies for Supervision: A Handbook*. Edinburgh: Moray House.

National Postgraduate Committee (1992). *Guidelines on Codes of Practice for Postgraduate Research*. Troon, Ayrshire.

National Postgraduate Committee. (1993). *Guidelines for the Employment of Postgraduate Students as Teachers*. Troon, Ayrshire.

Partington, J., Brown, G. and Gordon, G. (1993). *Handbook for External Examiners in Higher Education*. Sheffield: USDU.

Phillips, E.M. and Pugh, D.S. (1987). *How to Get a PhD*. Buckingham: Open University Press.

Piper, D.W. (1992). 'Are professors professional?' *Higher Education Quarterly* **46**: 145-156.

Schön, D.A. (1983). *The Reflective Practitioner*. London: Temple Smith.

SERC (1991). *Research Student and Supervisor: An Approach to Good Supervisory Practice*, 2nd ed. Swindon: SERC.

SERC (1993). *Review of Engineering Board Education and Training Programmeme*. Swindon: SERC.

Shaw, A. and Gaskin, K. with Brittain, K. *Research Centre Management Training Initiative: A Survey of DORCISS Members*. Centre for Research in Social Policy, University of Loughboriough.

USDU's Task Force One (forthcoming). 'A Framework for Leadership and Management Development in Higher Education'. Sheffield: USDU.

USDU's Task Force Three (1994). 'Staff Development in Relation to Research'. Occasional Green Paper No. 6. Sheffield: USDU.

Chapter 4

A Model for the Management of Research Degree Supervision in a Post-1987 University

Jan Whittle

Introduction

In late 1987 the Australian federal government announced its intention to reorganize the structure of tertiary education by establishing a 'unified national system' of large, amalgamated institutions (Dawkins, 1987). The amalgamation process combined the former 19 universities and 57 colleges of advanced education into 37 institutions, all with university status. The removal of the 'binary divide' in tertiary education has caused unprecedented upheaval in the administrative, management and academic sectors of universities. This chapter is concerned with the impact of the Dawkins reforms on the provision of research degree programmes in the 'new' universities in the unified system.

The task of developing competitive research degree programmes and providing quality supervision presents special challenges for those post-1987 Australian universities which do not have a strong history of research and postgraduate education. The challenges arise from limited institutional infrastructure to support research, lack of staff with experience in conducting research and providing research degree supervision, and a high proportion of research degree candidates who have not been exposed to research activities in their undergraduate degree programmes. Many faculties representing disciplines from the former colleges of advanced education are offering research degree programmes for the first time; and faculties representing professional disciplines are expanding their research Masters programmes and offering new doctoral programmes.

This rapid expansion of research degree programmes in the 'new' universities has changed the nature of academic work for many staff. There is an expectation that all academic staff should participate in research activities, and pressure has been placed on staff without research degrees to upgrade their qualifications and develop new teaching skills. In emerging research disciplines, such as nursing, where there is no research tradition or infrastructure to draw upon, staff face the task of developing a research culture from scratch. Furthermore, in an effort to meet student demand, those staff who do have the necessary research experience and academic qualifications to supervise research degree candidates are under pressure to take on excessive numbers of students. Further, students without research training tend to place heavy demands on supervisors' time in order to adjust to the expectations of research degree study. These factors have created a situation of work overload for staff and inadequate supervision for students.

The following discussion focuses on the approach taken by one post-1987 university to managing its research degrees programme, and developing and maintaining high quality supervision practices. The approach is characterized by centralized administration and management of research degrees, with academic decision making devolved to the faculty level. Key elements include a comprehensive code of practice for supervision which provides the framework for the interaction of academic staff and students; a mechanism for the accreditation of supervisors; organizational support; needs-based staff development initiatives; and structured research skills training for research students.

The University of South Australia

In 1991, the South Australian Institute of Technology and three campuses of the South Australian College of Advanced Education amalgamated to form the University of South Australia. At this time, there were three doctoral and 18 research Masters degree programmes available in the former Institute, and no research degrees at all in the former College. Over the next three years, the research degree profile expanded significantly, and, by 1993, there were 398 postgraduates enrolled in 26 doctoral and 32 research Masters degrees across the University. In comparison with the other two universities in South Australia, the proportion of students undertaking research degrees is relatively low: research students at the University of South Australia make up less than 2.0 per cent of the total student population, compared with 10.5 per cent at Flinders University, and 12.0 per cent at the University of Adelaide (1992 data). Nevertheless, the task of supervising research students is a new responsibility for many academic staff, and presents difficulties for those staff who have limited research experience.

As a strategy to improve its research profile, the university has, over the past two years, assisted staff in developing their research skills through a system of mentorship by experienced researchers. In this scheme, both the mentors and the novice researchers receive funding to release them from teaching activities. In addition to receiving advice and support for their research projects, staff participate in a range of workshops on research skills.

Review of existing policies and practices

Each of the former tertiary institutions brought to the new university different educational traditions, practices and attitudes to research and research training. For example, entry requirements, examination policies and expectations regarding thesis content and standards for research Masters degrees were not consistent across the university. Although formally united as a single university, the level of experience with and the approaches taken to research degree education clearly reflected former institutional allegiances. Not surprisingly, a great deal of confusion existed about 'correct' research degree policies and practices.

With a view to streamlining the provision of postgraduate education, the Pro-Vice-Chancellor (Research) commissioned the author early in 1993 to review the existing policies and practices, and to develop a proposal for the management of research degrees in the University of South Australia. The proposal was submitted in June, and contained 60 recommendations for research degree programmes and processes for monitoring and evaluating academic quality and standards in teaching and learning at this level. The author based her recommendations on a review of the relevant literature and the University of South Australia's policies on research degrees and supervision, extensive discussions with key University of South Australia staff, and consultations with personnel involved in the management, support and teaching of research degrees programmes in eight other Australian universities. The recommendations related to a range of issues including the management model and administrative structure, definitions of research degrees, allocation of research degree places, supervision policy, developing the *Code of Good Practice: Research Degree Supervision*, monitoring student progress, examination policy, support for research students, equity considerations, and library resources (Whittle, 1993). The proposal was accepted by the Research Degrees Committee and working parties were established to implement the recommendations. By December 1993, the Academic Board of the university had endorsed several new policies relating to the management of research degrees and supervisory practices.

Management and decision-making structure

A brief overview of the decision-making structure relating to research degrees will provide the context for the discussion of the university's approach to the management of supervision. Traditionally, Australian universities have adopted a decentralized approach to the management of research degrees in which faculties have responsibility for both academic decision making and most administrative matters. This approach has made it difficult for institutions to establish uniform administrative procedures, and has led to a highly variable quality of research degree supervision across disciplines. To avoid these problems, the university has established a centralized administrative and management structure, and retained academic decision making at the faculty level. This system provides an effective and efficient means of delivery of services, support and advice to staff and students, and has the educational benefits of drawing on specific expertise within disciplines for academic issues related to research degrees. Quality control of academic standards and coherence of research degree provision across faculties has been provided for through a central academic committee comprising representatives from each faculty.

The university is organized into nine faculties and 40 schools. The faculties represent the following broad discipline areas: Aboriginal and Islander Studies; Applied Science and Technology; Art, Architecture and Design; Business and Management; Education; Engineering; Health and Biomedical Sciences; Humanities and Social Sciences; and Nursing. Each faculty comprises a number of schools, each representing a specific field of endeavour. For example, the Faculty of Health and Biomedical Sciences is made up of the Schools of Occupational Therapy, Pharmacy and Medical Sciences, Physiotherapy, and Medical Radiations.

Figure 1:   Research degrees decision-making structure University of South Australia, 1993

```
┌─────────────────────────────────────────────────────────────────┐
│                        Academic Board                             │
│         (Code of Good Practice: Research Degree Supervision)      │
└─────────────────────────────────────────────────────────────────┘

┌─────────────────────────────────────────────────────────────────┐
│                   Research Degrees Committee                      │
│   (Scholarships Panel)   (Examination Panel)   (Candidature Panel)│
└─────────────────────────────────────────────────────────────────┘

┌─────────────────────────────────────────────────────────────────┐
│              Faculty Research Management Committee                │
│          (Faculty Research Degrees Management Plans)              │
└─────────────────────────────────────────────────────────────────┘

┌─────────────────────────────────────────────────────────────────┐
│                  Research Degree Coordinators                     │
│                        (School based)                             │
└─────────────────────────────────────────────────────────────────┘

┌─────────────────────────────────────────────────────────────────┐
│                    Principal Supervisors                          │
│         (Register of Research Degree Supervisors)                 │
└─────────────────────────────────────────────────────────────────┘

┌─────────────────────────────────────────────────────────────────┐
│                    Associate Supervisors                          │
└─────────────────────────────────────────────────────────────────┘
```

Against this academic organizational framework, the research degrees decision-making structure can be plotted as in Figure 1. Oversight of the university's research degrees programme is vested in the Research Degrees Committee (RDC) which has authority in all matters relating to research degrees. Membership of the RDC is drawn from senior academic staff in each faculty, the student body, and the Research Office, and also includes a person to monitor equity issues. Its central role is to develop policy and monitor academic quality and standards in research degrees and to make recommendations to the Academic Board. The Examination, Candidature and Scholarships Panels are sub-committees of RDC.

Each faculty has a Research Management Committee (RMC) which has responsibility for developing five-year Research Degrees Management Plans (RDMPs) which are submitted to the RDC for approval. RDMPs must include a list of staff who are on the *Register of Research Degree Supervisors*, the number of research candidates that faculties can support, and a guarantee of adequate resources to support research students (including physical space, equipment, ongoing and appropriate supervision). They must also indicate how candidates' research proposals dovetail with the research objectives of the faculty, describe how research seminar programmes will be conducted, and outline the mechanisms for processing students' annual review of progress and the procedures for selection of examiners. Faculty RDMPs are the key documents for monitoring quality in research degrees in the university. Faculty

RMCs make recommendations to RDC on academic matters relating to research degrees including the appointment of examiners, scholarship allocations, acceptance of research proposals and continuation of candidature. Each faculty is also responsible for appointing research degree coordinators whose role is to oversee the supervision of research students within schools.

Management of research degree supervision

There are three main elements to the university's approach to the management of research degree supervision: a policy framework, organizational support, and staff development.

Policy framework

The university has adopted a policy of **co-supervision** which ensures that each research candidate has a principal supervisor who has prime responsibility for the candidature, and an associate supervisor who provides support to the principal supervisor. The requirement for principal supervisors to undertake supervision training is an important means of quality assurance and, to the author's knowledge, the first move by a university in Australia to formally restrict access to supervisory responsibility. The university's policy of co-supervision provides for the mentoring and informal training of associate supervisors through their collaboration with experienced supervisors. Two policy documents which have recently been endorsed by the Academic Board provide a framework for establishing, supporting and maintaining good supervisory practices. These are the *Code of Good Practice: Research Degree Supervision*, and the *Register of Research Degree Supervisors*.

Code of Good Practice: Research Degree Supervision
Guidelines for the interaction of academic staff and students are contained in an 11-page *Code of Good Practice: Research Degree Supervision*. The *Code*, which was developed by the author in conjunction with a 15-member Reference Group, articulates the consensus that exists currently within the university about the characteristics of good supervision, and delineates the locus of responsibility for maintaining and monitoring academic quality and standards in research degrees.

The university's *Code* is similar to other codes of supervision practice in that it describes the roles and responsibilities that the institution, faculties, research degree coordinators, supervisors and students have in regard to their mutual obligation to ensure that research education is conducted in the most effective manner. Importantly, however, the *Code* also embodies two features which distinguish it from other Australian codes of supervision practice. First, the *Code* is intended to be an evolving, 'living' set of guidelines, which will change over time as new knowledge about teaching and learning at research degree level emerges. The *Code* stresses that the university recognizes that the concept of good supervisory practice is a contested one which is not only concerned with approaches to supervision but which is invariably context-specific, and involves moral, ethical, ideological and political considerations.

Thus, the *Code* acknowledges that research and supervision practices will vary in relation to research cultures, fields of inquiry and individual projects (University of South Australia, 1993a). An important purpose of the *Code* is to invite ongoing critical review and debate within the university about what constitutes good practice and, accordingly, the *Code* will be reviewed on an annual basis through a process of consultation and evaluation.

The second distinguishing feature of the *Code* is its emphasis on the responsibility of supervisors to adopt teaching practices which enable **all** students, regardless of their background or characteristics, to have an equal opportunity to learn and to demonstrate that learning, in accordance with the aims of the degree programme. The *Code* states that 'a fundamental characteristic of good supervision is that academic staff constantly reflect on their approaches to supervision' and that supervisors have a responsibility, grounded in the principles of social justice, to 'maximize the opportunities each graduate will have to contribute to society' (University of South Australia, 1993a). This means that supervisors are expected to vary their teaching in relation to the needs, values, experiences and abilities of individual students. The university's history and its access and equity policies have created a diverse postgraduate population of students drawn from a wide range of ethnic, socio-economic and educational backgrounds. For example, in 1993, overseas students represented 15 per cent of research degree candidates, and students from non-English speaking backgrounds, 30 per cent (University of South Australia, 1993b). In this environment, it is important for supervisors to be sensitive to individual student needs and flexible about their approaches to supervision so that effective working relationships can be established.

Register of Research Degree Supervisors
There has been no formal process in Australian universities for the training or accreditation of research degree supervisors. Traditionally, academic staff have assumed responsibility for supervision on an *ad hoc* basis, and have relied on their personal experience of being supervized as a model for their own practice. This has resulted in the quality of supervision ranging from excellent to very inadequate (Whittle, 1991). The quality of supervision is one of the main factors which influence the quality of research theses and the ability of candidates to complete their degrees on time. Several studies have indicated that the majority of candidates depend on their supervisors as the main source of support and encouragement during their candidature, and that unsatisfactory supervision has a strong negative effect on the participation and performance of research students (Higher Education Council, 1990; Moses, 1989; Powles, 1989; Whittle, 1992).

As a strategy to establish, maintain and monitor excellence in the quality of the supervision, the University of South Australia has established a mechanism for the accreditation of academic staff who have responsibility for supervising doctoral and research Masters students. It is university policy that staff who wish to act as principal supervisors must first be admitted to the *Register of Research Degree Supervisors*. To be admitted to the *Register*, academic staff must have 'a higher degree by research or have an equivalent record of scholarly achievement', and be 'currently engaged in research methodologically appropriate to the discipline', and have undertaken 'appropriate training in research degree supervision' (University of South Australia, 1993c). The policy also provides for a regular review of membership of the *Register* and the removal of staff who no longer meet the requirements of admission.

Implementation strategies for policy framework
In addition to the development of a policy framework for research degree supervision, the university has established implementation strategies to disseminate information about the new initiatives and to ensure that staff and students adhere to policies. Strategies include formalized lines of communication through decision-making structures, regular distribution of hard copies of new policy documents, and discussion of new initiatives in staff development workshops.

For example, the implementation strategies for the *Code of Good Practice: Research Degree Supervision* included the following processes. Members of the Research Degrees Committee (RDC) had responsibility to inform their faculty Heads of School, research degree coordinators, and relevant committees about the development of the *Code* and its endorsement by the Academic Board. In addition, through their membership of faculty Research Management Committees, RDC members provide advice to their faculty on matters arising from the *Code*. A copy of the *Code* was distributed to all supervisors and research degree students at the start of the academic year, together with other university policies and regulations concerning research degrees and supervision, which had been updated to include cross references to the *Code*. Academic staff and postgraduates have opportunities to discuss the *Code* and provide evaluative feedback on it through participation in staff development programmes on supervision and student induction programmes respectively.

Organizational support

Two strategies for supporting academic staff and maintaining excellence in supervision have been embedded in the academic organizational and management structure of the university. First, faculties have a responsibility through their Research Degree Management Plans to ensure that the **workload of supervisors** in research, teaching, supervision and other duties permits them to have sufficient time to provide students with proper supervision. This strategy aims to protect supervisors from work overload and to discourage unsatisfactory supervision practices which can result from staff taking on too many research candidates.

Second, faculties must appoint senior academic staff members as **research degree coordinators** whose central role is to coordinate research degree matters, oversee the quality of research degree supervision, and monitor the progress and welfare of research students. Faculties also must provide **adequate resources** and make workload adjustments to support coordinators in the performance of their duties. Coordinators are chosen on the basis of their excellent interpersonal skills and extensive experience in research and research degree supervision. They play an important role in providing a link between the faculty research management committee and staff at the school level by disseminating information from management and representing the interests of staff in their schools. Research degree coordinators are the first point of contact for research students and act as a resource on research degree matters for both students and staff. They also have responsibility for conducting annual reviews of student progress which include separate interviews with supervisors and students and the production of a written report. The annual review process provides coordinators with a mechanism for monitoring the quality of supervision and staff adherence to the *Code of Good Practice: Research Degree Supervision*. Coordinators also act as mediators and facilitate the resolution of conflicts between students and supervisors.

Staff development: training and support for supervisors

The value of providing training and support for supervisors has been recognized in both the well-established and the 'new' universities, and most institutions now provide some form of staff development in this area. Staff development programmes range from short, 'one-off' workshops on supervision to systematic, ongoing support programmes. The former type of staff training can be conceptualized as a 'top-down' approach as the process and content of workshops are developed in isolation from the participants, and generally are generic in nature.

In contrast to this, a 'bottom-up' approach in which the participants identify their areas of developmental need involves educational developers and academic staff collaborating on the design of the training programme which can be tailored to the disciplinary context in which the staff are working. Research on educational change indicates that the short, 'one-off' workshop approach to staff development has a limited effect on changing teaching practices for at least two reasons. First, staff find it extremely difficult to implement new approaches to teaching in the absence of continuing support and encouragement; and second, 'one-off' programmes lack the relevant context as they are not designed to meet the specific needs of individuals or disciplinary groups (Fullan, 1991).

The university's academic staff development unit has responsibility for providing training programmes, support and advice for staff in their teaching role, including those involved in supervising research students. The philosophy underpinning the unit's approach to academic staff development emphasizes the provision of long-term, on-going support for staff, and the provision of a range of training and support strategies which are tailored to the needs and interests of individual staff, faculties and schools (Reid and Whittle, 1993). Thus the majority of the unit's activities emerge from liaison with faculties and schools. The unit provides university-wide 'one-off' workshops on aspects of teaching and learning, including an induction programme for supervisors. The academic staff development unit also convenes special interest discussion groups, and provides support and advice to staff on an individual basis. In addition, there are opportunities for staff development through inter-institutional programmes on supervision which enable staff to form networks with colleagues in other South Australian universities.

University-wide induction programmes

Each semester, university-wide supervision induction programmes are conducted to introduce staff to university policies on research and supervision, the role and responsibilities of supervisors, and key issues and concerns relating to research degree study. Various methods are used to stimulate discussion about the role and responsibilities of supervisors and to encourage staff to reflect on what teaching and learning theories underpin their own approaches to supervision. The author has found role perception rating scales, case studies, and expert panels of supervisors and students have been effective in this context. The induction programme enables staff from a range of disciplines to share their experiences and perceptions of supervision, and provides opportunities for reflection on practice.

It is important to note that the induction programme is intended to be the first step in a continuing programme of support for supervisors. During the induction programme, staff are encouraged to establish networks for peer support, and further staff development activities are organized to meet the needs and interests of the participants. For example, often issues will be raised in the induction workshops which staff wish to explore further and special interest groups are formed to fulfil this purpose. In the past, interest groups have been established for staff to discuss supervising overseas students, distance supervision, supervising women in non-traditional fields of research, supervising the writing process, and distinguishing between the requirements for research Masters and doctoral theses.

Feedback the author has obtained from academic staff via questionnaire evaluations of staff development workshops indicates that considerable benefits accrue from inter-disciplinary discussion of supervision. Staff benefit from being exposed to issues, concerns and solutions experienced in disciplines other than their own, as this broadens their perspective and encourages the development of flexible approaches to supervision. However, it is also important for staff to have opportunities to discuss supervision issues with colleagues within their own fields of research, so that discipline-specific strategies for effective supervision can be shared. It is therefore helpful when organizing induction programmes, to provide staff with a balance of same-discipline and cross-discipline discussion groups.

Faculty/school-based support for supervisors

The university also provides faculty-based and school-based staff development programmes in response to staff requests. The opportunity to work with a single faculty or school means that discipline-specific tasks can be used to explore good supervisory practices. There are several reasons why training programmes of this kind are likely to have a high success rate in changing attitudes and supervision practices. First, because the need for staff development has been identified by the academic unit, staff 'own the problem' and have a vested interest in working towards finding solutions. Second, as these programmes are faculty or school initiatives, they have the support of deans, heads of schools and other senior academic staff. This level of support is vital for the successful implementation of new pedagogical approaches which may require redistribution of resources or changes to traditional ways of operating within the academic unit. Third, the 'local' focus of the staff development tends to encourage an ethos of open communication and discussion among staff which provides a basis for educational change.

A research skills/supervision training programme which was conducted at the university in the first semester of 1993 illustrates this needs-based, discipline-specific approach to staff development. The university's academic staff development unit was approached by representatives of the Faculty of Social Sciences for advice and support regarding supervision in their research Masters programmes. The Faculty, which had very few staff qualified to act as principal supervisors, was faced with the problem of providing supervision for 28 new research Masters students. The author, in collaboration with senior faculty members, developed a semester-long programme of seminars and workshops to provide both supervision training for staff and research skills induction for the novice students. This innovative programme used a team-teaching approach to supervision, and provided the opportunity for the entire cohort of supervisors and students to work together. The seminars were designed to have an applied focus so that students were able to work on their own research proposals throughout the programme. Topics covered by the programme included roles and responsibilities of supervisors and students, time and data management, writing a thesis proposal, how to structure a thesis, and methodological approaches in social science. Workshop presenters included the programme development team, several faculty supervisors and staff from the university library. Formal presentations were kept brief as the central objective was to encourage a high level of discussion among the participants through small group activities and whole group open forums. A full discussion of the workshop programme and its evaluation can be found in Whittle (forthcoming).

The rationale for providing a collaboratively taught workshop programme was grounded in the assumption that the quality of teaching would be enhanced by providing opportunities for staff to discuss different approaches to research and supervision. That is, it was anticipated that staff would gain developmental benefits from shared knowledge about teaching research students, and that students would benefit from exposure to a range of academic approaches. A further reason for adopting a team-teaching approach was to reduce the burden of responsibility for supervision on individual staff and to encourage all faculty members to contribute to the induction of students into research processes.

The traditional approach to postgraduate teaching at research degree level in the social sciences and humanities generally involves one-to-one supervisor-student teaching. An associate or co-supervisor may also be available to the student, but usually plays a minor role. Thus, responsibility for providing advice and support falls largely on the shoulders of a single academic. This teaching model can present problems if personality clashes occur, in inter-disciplinary projects requiring a range of academic expertise, or where the research interests of the staff member and the student are not well matched. The team-teaching approach to research skills development does not attempt to replace the one-to-one supervision model, but rather acts as a complementary support strategy for both students and staff.

In addition to benefits to student learning which go hand-in-hand with improvements in teaching, the workshop programme also aimed to enhance the learning environment for research students by reducing the social and intellectual isolation often experienced by candidates in the social sciences and humanities, which part-time candidature can exacerbate. The workshop programme aimed to provide opportunities for the development of open communication between staff and students, peer interaction between students, and to integrate students into the research culture of the discipline. Furthermore, the workshop programme provided a focus for the development and strengthening of the research ethos of the faculty.

The current demand for institutional accountability and the emphasis on quality in university teaching has placed pressure on academic staff to evaluate their teaching. Evaluation of research supervision is an important reflective tool which staff can use to improve their teaching practices. Feedback from evalution can also be used for promotional purposes. However, the evaluation of teaching at research supervision level is fraught with difficulties due to the long-term and special nature of the one-to-one student-teacher relationship. Moreover, biased evaluation of supervision after graduation is inevitable since research students continue to rely on supervisors as referees for applications for employment, post-doctoral positions, scholarships and research grants. Team-teaching of groups of research students, such as that used for the Faculty of Social Sciences workshop programme, provides opportunities for the peer evaluation of supervision practices, as academic staff in this teaching context are actively involved in each other's work. This collaborative approach to supervision also presents the possibility of reliable student evaluation of supervision as students can comment on the team's approach to supervision without the fear of personal disadvantage which may be associated with evaluating individual supervisors.

The approach to research induction which has been described above could also be used at the department or school level, or by inter-disciplinary research groups which support postgraduates. Research skills training will be of particular value to candidates who are at risk of having poor completion times or who have not had the advantage of completing an Honours degree prior to embarking on a research degree. By providing students with structured research skills training at the commencement of their degree programmes, staff can work as a team to improve the teaching and learning environment at the postgraduate level and help students to get off to a good start in their candidature. Furthermore, staff in disciplines which do not have a strong research background will benefit from the collaborative teaching approach, and the workshop programme will stimulate the development of a research culture.

Evaluation of the management model

Systematic evaluation of the policy framework, organizational support, and staff development programmes discussed above form an essential aspect of the University of South Australia's quality control of its management of research degree supervision. At the time of writing this chapter, it was too early to comment on the effectiveness of these new initiatives; however, there are several strategies in place for evaluation.

Staff who participate in the induction programme and other training and developmental activities designed for supervisors are asked to critically evaluate those programmes by means of an open-ended questionnaire survey conducted at the close of each programme. These data will be used to improve on staff development programmes and inform policy development. The *Code of Good Practice: Research*

Degree Supervision will be reviewed annually on the basis of feedback from academic staff who attend workshops, and data obtained from a comprehensive questionnaire survey of all supervisors and postgraduate students. The five-year Faculty Research Degrees Management Plans will provide a benchmark against which the ability of individual faculties to meet their objectives for research degree management can be judged and evaluated. The annual review of the progress of research students in which supervisors and students are interviewed separately will provide research degree coordinators with a rich source of information about the effectiveness of supervision and adherence to university policies.

Conclusion

In this chapter it has been argued that many academic staff in the post-1987 universities face special challenges in fulfilling their roles as research degree supervisors. It is evident that the morale of academic communities in the 'new' universities has diminished in the environment of rapid change and job uncertainty that the amalgamation process has created. It is important, therefore, that institutions provide adequate support to assist their staff to cope with the demands which the removal of the binary divide in tertiary education has brought about.

The approach taken by the University of South Australia in managing research degree supervision is offered as a model for the provision of a high quality teaching and learning environment. The university has established a policy framework for good supervision practices and has provided a system of training and support for academic staff. While each university has its own unique characteristics and must develop strategies to meet its specific needs, the model presented here can be used as a framework for management of supervision in those universities which, by virtue of the recent amalgamation processes, have limited research infrastructure, limited staff expertise in supervision, and a rapidly expanding research degree programme.

References

Dawkins, J.S. (1987). *Higher Education: A policy discussion paper*. Canberra: AGPS.

Fullan, M.G. (1991). *The New Meaning of Educational Change*. London: Cassell.

Higher Education Council (1990). *Higher Education: Courses and Graduate Studies*. Canberra: AGPS.

Moses, I. (1989). *Barriers to Women's Participation as Postgraduate Students*. Canberra: AGPS.

Powles, M. (1989). *How's the Thesis Going?* Melbourne: Centre for Studies in Higher Education, University of Melbourne.

Reid, A. and Whittle, J.I. (1993). 'A Model of Staff Development for Pedagogical Change'. Paper presented at the 1993 HERDSA Conference, Sydney.

University of South Australia (1993a). *Code of Good Practice: Research Degree Supervision*. Adelaide: University of South Australia.

University of South Australia (1993b). *Statistics.*   Adelaide: Planning Unit,
    University of South Australia.
University of South Australia (1993c). *Register of Research Degree Supervisors.*
    Adelaide: University of South Australia.
Whittle, J.I. (1991). 'Postgraduate Participation and Performance: Research Students
    at the University of Adelaide'. Unpublished Masters Thesis, University of
    Adelaide.
Whittle, J.I. (1992). 'Research Culture, Supervision Practices and Postgraduate
    Performance', in O. Zuber-Skerritt (ed.), *Starting Research — Supervision
    and Training.* Brisbane: Tertiary Education Institute, The University of
    Queensland.
Whittle, J.I. (1993). *Proposal for Research Degrees Programme.* Internal report,
    University of South Australia.
Whittle, J.I. (forthcoming). 'Collaborative Supervision and Research Skills Training',
    in I. Dunn (ed.), *Research and Development in Higher Education*, Vol. 16.

Chapter 5

Gender and Postgraduate Supervision

Linda Conrad

Introduction

The purpose of this chapter is to discuss some of the problems facing women postgraduate students and ways in which supervisors can respond in order to address long-entrenched discriminatory patterns in a constructive way. It is widely recognized that institutions must urgently address their need to increase the proportions of women postgraduate students and to make the university environment a supportive one for women. The problems of female postgraduate students are directly related to ancient and global social and institutional inequities. Yet those problems are experienced by individual women working with individual supervisors — usually men. The question central to this chapter is: what are the difficulties faced by female postgraduate students and what can supervisors (usually men) do to make a difference?

Background

Women number about half of undergraduate students in Australia overall including Honours students (although there are disciplinary imbalances). But female postgraduate students, especially in some fields and at the PhD level, are much fewer. Women who enrol as postgraduates are at greater risk than are men of late completion or withdrawal (Powles,1989).

Women postgraduate students must cope with economic inequities, differentiated social and family responsibilities, and a 'chilly' institutional environment. That chilly environment has been documented by Hall and Sandler (1991), who also make a number of suggestions for introducing change.

The economic inequities begin, of course, with women's lower incomes in society at large. At the university level, this economic inequity is repeated. Women are less likely to have the financial support of scholarships. First-class Honours degrees translate into postgraduate scholarships, and more first-class Honours degrees are given in the disciplinary area of the natural sciences in which women are less well represented. Furthermore, women's entry is often by alternative routes, which may not be seen as equivalent to first-class Honours degrees to which postgraduate scholarships are closely tied. Women's ability to earn an income while doing a postgraduate degree is limited, and the possibility of their earning a higher income may be delayed because women generally have much greater responsibility for the care of children, partners and parents. Such barriers to women's participation as postgraduate students have been clearly documented (Moses, 1990; Powles, 1986, 1987a, 1989).

Governments, institutions, departments and individual supervisors have a role to play in eliminating these barriers. The focus of this chapter, however, is what individual supervisors can do. Supervisory action includes efforts to modify the institution to make it a more supportive context for women's postgraduate work. The goal is to increase the retention rates for women postgraduates, encourage their completion in good time, and bring about greater satisfaction and success for both women postgraduates and their supervisors.

Difficulties faced by women postgraduate students

Research into women postgraduate students and their supervision suggests that women on the whole tend to have less time with their supervisors than do men. One study showed that male students spent more than twice as much time with teaching staff as did female students, with a correlation of .9 being found between gender of student and time spent in certain social science fields, although a later study suggested that other factors are important (Jenkins, 1985). Powles (1989) found that women consulted their supervisors less frequently than did men and that younger PhD students consulted more often than older students (most women, of course, are older than men when they start higher degrees).

Women express greater dissatisfaction with their supervision than do men. There are many possible reasons for this dissatisfaction. We might speculate that women's lack of confidence makes them feel that they need more than they are getting from their supervisors, or that different conventions of communication governing the patterns of conversation among men and women (Deakins, 1992) may make it more difficult for female students to interact with their usually male supervisors. As Phillips has shown in her chapter here, even communication between male students and male supervisors is fraught with misunderstanding. Still another possibility is that the chilly environment facing women generally affects their views of supervision. Women have been shown to be less likely than men to rate their academic environments as friendly and helpful (Powles, 1987b).

Women are more likely to let their perfectionism stand in the way of their completion of the thesis (Germeroth, 1990). However, 'perfectionism' can be viewed either as a laudable rigour or as an eccentric obsessiveness — and the latter may often be the interpretation of a woman's exhaustive efforts to prove that she is worthy in a place where, according to the cliché, a woman has to be twice as good as a man to be considered half as good. Women express a lack of confidence, even when their high performance would not warrant it. In a study by Moses (1990: 29), some women reported that they worked constantly 'to be taken seriously'.

Women are more likely to have periods of suspension and more transfers between full-time and part-time than do men — and people who suspend are more likely to withdraw than those who maintain an uninterrupted period of study. Part of the explanation for women's interruptions is that they are older than men when they begin postgraduate study. At this time they have partners and families to whom they have responsibilities that may interfere with study (Powles, 1989). It is useful to note that the 'normal' time for postgraduate study is during a woman's childbearing years.

Women are much more often than men supervized by someone of the opposite sex. Senior women academics are exceedingly rare. According to Juddery (1993), not quite 32 per cent of Australian academics are women. Of that 32 per cent, 80 per cent are at lecturer level or below (compared to 48 per cent of men at those levels). Only 5 per cent of women are above Senior Lecturer level, although 23 per cent of men are at that level. This means that it is fairly unlikely that women who are postgraduate students will be supervized — or even have contact with — women at higher academic levels. It is well known that a 'critical mass' of women is necessary to provide role models for women. As Moses (1990: 18) has pointed out, citing Reilly (1985: 7-9), 'In order for modelling behaviour to occur . . . there needs to be an adequate number of women particularly in senior level positions of the career structure (one is not enough)'. Berg and Ferber (1983: 639) in a US study suggest that:

> students and faculty of the same sex interact most comfortably. Since the ratio of male faculty to female students exceeds the ratio of female faculty to female students in every field and each type of discipline within fields in our study, women students are at an inescapable disadvantage in finding mentors.

Berg and Ferber also note that women students tend to be more successful in completing postgraduate degrees where the proportion of female academics on the staff is relatively higher.

Bargar and Duncan (1982) have deplored the fact that the vicissitudes of genuine research are often obscured by the conventions of reporting research so that research is 'mystified' for all postgraduate students. That mystification may be a particular problem for women. Women report feeling alienated from male supervisors who use intimidation and shaming, or who 'leave advisees feeling objectified' or depersonalized or who use 'overly intellectualized approaches' (Heinrich, 1990: 4) that can be interpreted as adding to the mystification of the PhD process. For example, presenting the thesis as an esoteric engagement of great ideas or a *magnum opus* is excessively daunting when the thesis can alternatively be seen as a job to be done at a research training stage.

Issues of power and sexuality often permeate women's descriptions of their relationships with male supervisors. Women have reported feeling distanced from male supervisors when those supervisors treated them as sex objects (Heinrich, 1990). Treatment as 'sex objects' can cover a number of kinds of behaviour of varying levels of seriousness, ranging from uncomfortably received flattery to sexual harassment and rape. Certainly the relationship of supervisor and student, because of the power differential, has the potential to be inappropriately sexualized. Some universities provide a clear statement that any sexual relationship between student and staff member is considered to be unprofessional. Although there may be no attempt to police staff and student behaviour, such a university policy can ensure that staff members accept full responsibility should later action be brought against them for sexual harassment.

Especially in fields in which men predominate (and these are in the majority), women may feel isolated from other students as well as from staff. Male students 'interact less' with female than with male students (Berg and Ferber, 1983: 631). Hence the kind of informal supervision that peers may provide is less accessible to women than to men. Female postgraduate students may be less involved in the social life of the faculty and may find that informal routes of entry into the faculty's research culture are not available to them (Bulbeck, 1994: 2).

Although no research is available on gender effects in communication between supervisor and student, studies in a variety of contexts have suggested that communication conventions differ between men and women (Deakins, 1992; Graddol and Swann, 1989; Kramarae and Treichler, 1990; Smythe and Huddleston, 1992). As Deakins (1992: 156) has observed, 'the stage is set for misunderstanding and conflict when the two sexes interact and must struggle to communicate using systems which operate largely unconsciously and which do not always match'. Hence, if men are seen as more intellectually solid than women, the judgement may be reflecting differences in communication styles rather than differences in a student's grasp of the field.

Supervisors' attention to the difficulties faced by female postgraduate students

Given the findings of studies into gender and postgraduate study, what can be done by supervisors to improve the supervision of female students? Not all findings imply specific action to be taken, but it is possible to make some suggestions that supervisors can keep in mind when dealing with female students. It cannot be overemphasized here that differences that have been identified as distinguishing men and women are the result of social and cultural constructions of gender and do not necessarily characterize all or even most individuals. Hence any suggestions must be considered as part of an overall strategy that calls for sensitivity to the situation of particular students in particular circumstances.

The supervisor's influence on the context

Supervisors can actively intervene to change the context in which supervision takes place.

A major way to assist women as postgraduate students is to improve the university climate for women by working to eliminate their isolation. It is useful to enhance opportunities for female postgraduate students to meet women from other institutions, whether senior academics or other female students. Supervisors can encourage the development of small, informal groups of students to provide one another with peer support. Where possible, gender balance within any group of which women are a part would be helpful. The supervisor may wish to arrange regular meetings with all or some of his or her postgraduate students, thus encouraging group solidarity that will maximize interaction among students. Some research into postgraduate supervisory groups or peer support groups suggests that such groups may eliminate one of the most significant factors leading to withdrawal from postgraduate study — intellectual and social isolation (Conrad, 1991; Phillips, 1989;

Zuber-Skerritt, 1992). Supervisors should encourage departments or faculties to provide support to part-time students (who are more often women than men), providing them work space on campus and/or common rooms, for example, and arranging for peer support through opportunities for social and intellectual interaction, preferably in a non-competitive, non-hierarchical setting.

When participating in making staffing decisions, supervisors should call attention to the importance of ensuring that increasing numbers of women join the academic staff and become available as role models and potential supervisors for women. Furthermore, anything that the supervisor can do to encourage the institution, faculty or department to enhance the status of female academic staff will have a useful indirect effect on postgraduate students whether they are supervized by women or are looking to women as mentors.

The supervisor's interaction with postgraduate students who are women

Given the evidence that female postgraduate students receive less time from supervisors than do male students, it is important for supervisors to make every effort to spend ample time with female postgraduates. Frequent meetings should be arranged, and the supervisor should as often as possible converse with female students informally to build a relationship in which women can feel confident approaching the supervisor. Being aware of the student's extra-university responsibilities in setting meeting times is also important.

Supervisors need to ensure that they take women seriously. They need to respect women's work, showing trust, appreciation and flexibility to increase women's confidence to do their best. Even women who have proved their excellence still lack confidence and need a supportive environment. It goes without saying that every attempt should be made to avoid intimidating or humiliating any female (or male) student and that every effort should be made to demystify the process of postgraduate research, that is, to present it as a do-able piece of work. Confiding one's own initial disappointments, followed by eventual success, may be one way to achieve this and to create a sense of shared experience.

Supervisors should try to achieve a balance of professional and personal concern for the student, scrupulously excluding sexual overtures or sexist language. It is always difficult to achieve what feels like a 'natural' and relaxed relationship while being on one's guard against 'mistakes'. Rather than focusing on the avoidance of mistakes, it is best to keep always in mind respect for the student and a concern for helping that student do her best work.

Possible differences between women and men in communication styles need to be kept in mind as well. The following suggestions for cross-sex communication between supervisor and student are inferentially developed (but not tested experimentally) from research reported in a number of studies of communication (e.g. Deakins, 1992; Graddol and Swann, 1989; Kramarae and Treichler, 1990; Mapstone, 1990; Smythe and Huddleston, 1992). However, a useful caution is necessary: not all women by any means have modes of communication that are 'typical' as shown by research, and differences also depend on context. The emphasis should be on the supervisor's increasing sensitivity to student interaction characteristics (as well as the supervisor's own interaction features) in order to maximize the chances of clear communication.

- A supervisor may need to help a student in a supportive way to think through what she wants to do rather than to 'tell' the student what to do. Women tend to share experiences and mention problems in order to elicit emotional support to help them come to their own solutions rather than to seek detailed advice on what to do. Direct advice can be given, of course, but enabling the student to work out the best strategy may be more effective.

- Being aware that a female student may share personal information in order to strengthen the supervisor-student relationship rather than to avoid discussion of the thesis is important. Women tend to use self-disclosure to build solidarity whereas men avoid self-disclosure and want to stick to business. This can be inferred as leading to situations in which women feel that men are maintaining their powerful status rather than 'being themselves'; men, on the other hand, may feel women are injecting irrelevant personal information into discussions.

- Women tend to wait for a space to be given to them before they speak rather than interrupting to discuss their own concerns. This suggests that supervisors need to avoid long perorations and allow for pauses in which women can feel comfortable to speak without competing for time.

- Supervisors need to pay close attention not only to what they say to students but to what they do. Generally speaking, women tend to pay more attention than do men to the non-verbal or paraverbal language of the person with whom they are speaking. So if a supervisor doodles while the student explains a problem — however intently the supervisor might be listening — the likelihood is that the student may interpret this as a sign that the supervisor considers her work to be trivial or boring. Women often nod or say 'umm' to indicate that they are listening; but men often use these signals to indicate agreement. It is important to know this difference to avoid misinterpreting a female student's paraverbal signals and to ensure that one's own signals are not misinterpreted.

- Women's language tends to imply doubt, uncertainty, or tentativeness. There is some evidence that this is because women lack confidence, but it is also possible that this is a strategy for maintaining harmony and showing respect for another's possibly very different views.

- Harmony in relationships is a high priority for women. Special effort should be made to a) couch disagreement in a way that shows respect for and some commonality with the student and b) provide a climate in which disagreement is welcomed and appreciated and defensiveness avoided. In her study in a higher education setting of male and female experiences of, and attitudes to, argument, Mapstone (1990) found that all of the women were concerned about the possible harm that disagreement might lead to, and half felt that there had to be some mutual agreement on values if an argument was to be 'safe'. Except in situations where they had equal status with colleagues or were with close friends, women expected that their disagreement would be interpreted as criticism whereas men expected that their disagreement would be recognized as a rational response.

Conclusion

The supervisor can make a significant difference in a woman's experience of postgraduate study — and in her success. The supervisor can attempt to influence the institution to improve the climate of the department or faculty for women students in two major ways: a) by implementing a variety of strategies to help eliminate the isolation of female postgraduate students; b) by participating in selection decisions that bring more women to academic positions and in activities that work to enhance the status of women academics. The supervisor can also go beyond the institution to help put the postgraduate student in touch with the larger academic community, for example, helping female students to make extra-departmental contact with female academics and postgraduate students.

The supervisor can also look to one-to-one interaction with the student. He or she can ensure that women postgraduate students are taken seriously, that they are encouraged and supported without any intimidation or sexualising of the relationship and that they are given ample time and attention. That attention needs to include sensitivity to communication styles so that the most essential requirement of supervision is met — that the supervisor and student understand each other.

References

Bargar, R.R. and Duncan, J.K. (1982). 'Cultivating creative endeavor in doctoral research'. *Journal of Higher Education* 53(1): 1-32.

Berg, H.M. and Ferber, M. (1983). 'Men and women graduate students: Who succeeds and why?'. *Journal of Higher Education* 54(6): 629-648.

Bulbeck, C. (1994). 'The unintended gender effects of policy and practice on postgraduate research at Griffith University: Summary'. Nathan, Qld: Australian Institute for Women's Research and Policy.

Conrad, L. (1991). 'Peer participation in supervising postgraduate research', in A.R. Viskovic (ed.) *Research and Development in Higher Education*, Vol. 14, papers presented at the 17th annual conference of the Higher Education Research and Development Society of Australasia, at Victoria University of Wellington, New Zealand, 29 August - 1 September. Campbelltown, NSW: HERDSA, 42-49.

Deakins, A. (1992). 'The tu/vous dilemma: Gender, power, and solidarity', in L.A.M. Perry, L.H. Turner and H.M. Sterk (eds), *Constructing and Reconstructing Gender: The Links Among Communication, Language and Gender*. Albany: SUNY Press, 151-161.

Germeroth, D. (1990). 'Lonely days and lonely nights: Completing the doctoral dissertation'. Paper presented at the Annual Meeting of the Speech Communication Association, November.

Graddol, D. and Swann, J. (1989). *Gender Voices*. Oxford: Basil Blackwell.

Hall, R.M. and Sandler, B.R. (1991) *The Classroom Climate: A chilly one for women?*. Washington, D.C. Project on the Status and Education of Women, Association of American Colleges.

Heinrich, K. (1990). 'Toward gender sensitive advisement of women doctoral students'. ERIC (unpublished paper).

Jenkins, S. (1985). 'Gender differences in graduate student relationships with their major faculty advisors'. Dissertation, University of Oregon.

Juddery, B. (1993). 'Postgrad handicap in equality chase – report'. *Campus Review* 3(23): 1 September 9-15.

Kramarae, C. and Treichler, P.A. (1990). 'Power relationships in the classroom', in S. Gabriel and I. Smithson (eds), *Gender in the Classroom: Power and Pedagogy*. Urbana: University of Illinois Press, 41-59.

Mapstone, E.R. (1990). 'Rational men and disagreeable women: The social construction of argument'. Presented at the London Conference of the British Psychological Society, City University, London, 17-18 December.

Moses, I. (1990). *Barriers to Women's Participation as Postgraduate Students.* Canberra: Department of Employment, Education and Training.

Phillips, E. (1989). 'Institutional responsibilities to postgraduate students: The college approach'. *HERDSA News* 11(1): 5-8.

Powles, M. (1986). 'Chips in the academic wall: Women and postgraduate study'. *The Australian Universities Review.* 29(2): 33-37.

Powles, M. (1987a). *Women's participation in tertiary education: A review of recent Australian research.* Melbourne: University of Melbourne, CSHE.

Powles, M. (1987b). *PhD Candidates at the University of Melbourne.* Report to the PhD Committee of the University of Melbourne.

Powles, M. (1989). 'Higher degree completion and completion times'. *Higher Education Research and Development* 8(1): 91-101.

Smythe, M-J. and Huddleston, B. (1992). 'Competition and collaboration: Male and female communication patterns during dyadic interactions', in L. Perry, L. Turner and H. Sterk (eds), *Constructing and Reconstructing Gender: The links among communication, language, and gender.* Albany: SUNY Press, 251-260.

Zuber-Skerritt, O. (1992). 'Helping postgraduate students learn', in O. Zuber-Skerritt (ed.), *Action Research in Higher Education.* London: Kogan Page, 36-55.

Chapter 6

Quality in Supervising Overseas Students?

Tania Aspland and Thomas O'Donoghue

The background

Crossley (1992: 25) and Crossley and Broadfoot (1992) have drawn attention to the number of educationalists engaged in consultancies in the developing world but without training in international education or relevant experience of the cultural contexts in which they go to work. Nevertheless, they have been encouraged to undertake such work by their universities which are seeking funds in an increasingly competitive higher education environment. There is an accompanying concern about the nature of the academic experiences of overseas students at a time when there has been an enormous increase in students from the developing world attending universities in the developed world. In particular, there is mounting disquiet about the tendency to slot overseas students into courses designed for 'first world' situations, without much consideration being given to the appropriateness of such courses for educational practice in their countries of origin. The appropriateness of the teaching styles adopted for the promotion of learning amongst overseas students is also beginning to receive attention. Bilbow (1989: 85), for example, has drawn attention to the fact that, particularly at undergraduate level, lectures may pose severe problems for those from non-English speaking backgrounds because of linguistic, discoursal and cultural factors.

In the case of postgraduate students, the difficulties being experienced by overseas students and their supervisors in the thesis supervision process are also giving cause for concern and need to be investigated from a number of perspectives. This chapter attempts to highlight the need for research related to overseas students from one such perspective, namely, the thesis supervision experience as interpreted by students, with a focus on the situation in one developed country, Australia.

The nature of the Australian education experience for overseas students

Over the past five years, the Australian federal government has encouraged higher education institutions to market educational services overseas. Much of the resulting effort has centred around attracting full-fee paying students from South-East Asia. The success of the effort is attested to by the fact that Australia has an overseas student market valued at around $350,000,000 (DEET, 1991: 54-55).

The total number of overseas students in Australian universities increased from 22,018 in 1986 to 60,629 in 1991, with full-fee paying overseas student numbers increasing in the same period from 1,468 to 29,339 (DEET, 1991: 54-55). Most of these students are from Malaysia, Hong Kong and Singapore, but there is growing interest from other countries such as South Korea and Indonesia (Jones, 1992: 15). A much smaller group of students includes those on Australian International Development Assistance Bureau (AIDAB) funded scholarships as part of Australia's aid to the developing world (AIDAB, 1992: 70). Under the direction of the Minister for Trade and Overseas Development, AIDAB has primary responsibility for providing policy advice to the Australian government on international issues, as well as planning and implementing Australia's programme of international development cooperation.

Many Australian educational institutions assume that the impressive national increase in overseas students will continue. However, as Smart and Ang (1992: i) put it:

> ... there is some evidence to suggest that to project this point of view into the 1990s may be overly optimistic in relation to some countries. Certainly, if the assumption is wrong, the costs to institutions are high and this argues for, at least, careful monitoring of trends in our major source countries.

The institutions themselves also need to monitor carefully at least two interrelated aspects of their own on-site operations which will determine whether or not students will continue to come to Australia, namely, the appropriateness of their welfare support and of the education they offer.

With regard to the welfare component, Australia's record to date would appear to be a good one. With respect to the experiences of Singaporean students, for example, it has been reported (Smart and Ang, 1992: 22) that:

> Australia is seen as a safe place to study in a mild climate. It also has the great advantage of geographic proximity to Singapore and a similar time zone... Australia is one of the most liberal countries in terms of work rights, allowing overseas students to work 20 hours a week. There is also a general impression that Australia is a more affordable destination in terms of fees and living expenses than the United States and the United Kingdom.

However, overseas students also expect the **quality** of the education which they receive to be high. Of particular concern is the perception that some universities are now prepared to lower their standards and take in any students who can pay, regardless of their academic record (Australian Industry Commission, 1991: 171-2; Burns, 1991; Smart and Ang, 1992: 24). This applies not only at the undergraduate level but also at the postgraduate level.

The writing of a thesis constitutes a major component of the requirements for a postgraduate degree. The quality of this work must be high in order to maintain a university's reputation for academic excellence and to ensure that overseas students get value for their money. This, in turn, demands a high level of quality supervision responsive to students' needs within the institutional requirements for the course of study (Ballard and Clanchy, 1984: 89-97). Accordingly, there is a need in universities for vigilance in performing the difficult role of supervising higher degree students.

However, as the next section demonstrates, all is not well in this domain not just in the case of the supervision of overseas students but in the area of supervision of higher degrees in general.

Supervision of higher degree students

Contemporary research in Britain highlights a variety of concerns about higher degree studies. As *The Times Higher Education Supplement* of 6 December 1991 reported:

> Administrators are worried about the poor completion rates, institutions are concerned about the dearth of good doctoral students in many fields; supervisors believe that they receive inadequate resources to do their job properly.

Some concerns have also been expressed that inadequacies exist in the supervision of higher degree students. The Winfield (1976) Report examined a range of studies (Makrotest, 1987; Marsh, 1972; Rudd, 1975; Whalley, 1982) and demonstrated significant dissatisfaction on the part of students with the nature of the supervision they received. A variety of other studies highlighted a number of aspects of this dissatisfaction. The lack of regular meetings between student and supervisor has been identified (Halleck, 1976; Rudd, 1985; Wason, 1974; Welsh, 1979; Wright and Lodwick, 1989) as a major factor leading to a lack of enthusiasm for research, disorientation with respect to the central research questions, lack of clarity in writing and a poor rate of completion. The failure of supervisors to adequately guide students in the design of their study programme (Brown and Atkins, 1988), to ensure they have adequate preparation for data collection and analysis (Delamont and Eggleston, 1983) and to facilitate the development of report writing skills (Brown and Atkins, 1988; Lowenthal and Wason, 1977; Wason, 1974) has also been highlighted. The fact that different students require different relationships with their supervisors, ranging from a high level of dependency to a high level of autonomy, is another matter which is often overlooked by supervisors (Cox, 1988; Krebs, 1967; Schön, 1987; Welsh, 1979).

A number of these concerns have also been raised on the Australian scene (Moses, 1985; Zuber-Skerritt, 1992). This has led to a certain amount of research (Connell, 1985; Moses 1985; Powles, 1989a, 1989b; University of Queensland Union, 1983), some of which has highlighted such difficulties as unsatisfactory completion times (DEET, 1991) and an unsatisfactory drop-out rate (Powles, 1989a). As elsewhere (Brown and Atkins, 1988), much of the research is still only at the exploratory stage. At the same time, however, what does seem clear is that the problems which exist have been amplified since the amalgamation of the former colleges of advanced education to form universities within the new Unified National System of higher education.

According to Powles (1989a: 21), changes associated with restructuring in higher education in Australia have occurred at a time when 'postgraduate study is currently under fierce scrutiny'. An associated development which gives cause for concern is that many 'new' university staff members, who as employees in the former colleges of advanced education were primarily concerned with teaching rather than research, have become supervisors for the first time of candidates writing theses (Hansford and Maxwell, 1993: 171). Accordingly, it would not be surprising to find that overseas postgraduate students in these institutions in particular are experiencing difficulties in their thesis preparation.

In May 1992 the National Liaison Committee for Overseas Students in Australia conducted a general survey of overseas students in the country and the results were published under the title *Australian Education: Excellent or Dismal* (1992). Of significance is the conclusion that unless standards improve nationally, students will take their business elsewhere (Jones, 1992). The 1,100 international student respondents rated campus support services and teaching quality as average. However, with respect to the postgraduate respondents, almost a third believed that their institution had provided them with inadequate facilities and workspace; nearly half felt they received inadequate information about supervision requirements prior to enrolment; and almost a third were not convinced that their regularly submitted written work was returned to them as quickly as it should have been.

There have been some attempts to demonstrate what can be done in order to better prepare the incoming students for what is expected of them by their potential supervisors. Manuals such as Ballard and Clanchy's *Study Abroad: A Manual for Asian Students* (1984) are useful, as is the advice of writers like Ginsburg (1992: 6):

> Studies commissioned by the Australian government in an attempt to improve higher education for students from Asian countries indicate a need to ensure better preparation in terms of both 'study skills' and knowledge of Australian cultural norms, together with practice at participating in discussion... students need to modify the world-view of their native culture and the academic culture in which they were educated if they are to gain acceptance in this new academic context.

However, research on styles of supervision (Wilson, 1980; Zuber-Skerritt, 1988) also brings to the fore the need for supervisors to be responsive to the unique constructs brought to the situation by the student, placing high on the educational agenda a notion of supervision that is student responsive and open to modification. The danger in the current university context in Australia, which is characterized by instrumental forms of rational thinking and policy, is that supervision of this type could be undermined and depoliticized in ways that portray the overseas students as an abstraction, removing them from practices 'which might give meaning to individual wants, needs and visions of justice' (Apple, 1990: 9).

In Australia, as elsewhere, the information base pertaining to the nature of supervision of overseas students from this perspective (Smawfield, 1989: 51-61) is sparse. A need exists to research the area thoroughly with a view to acquiring a better understanding and illumination of the nature of teaching and learning most appropriate for this little-understood student cohort. The following reports the findings of a case study which attempted to begin to explore the matter by focusing on a small group of overseas Master of Education (MEd) students at one university and to use these students' 'voices' to add a qualitative dimension to the existing small body of quantitative findings on the national scene. The tone, quality, language and feelings of the students are outlined in the belief that they constitute vicarious experience and can problematize for potential researchers the academic life of overseas students in Australia. This, it is to be hoped, will in turn encourage in-depth research into the area and thus contribute to the improvement of that academic life.

The supervision of overseas Master of Education students at one Australian university

Background

The MEd programme was first offered at the university in question in 1991. It was marketed as a degree which could be completed in one year full-time or two years part-time, unlike the situation in some of the traditional universities which generally stress that these are minimum completion times and that students should normally expect to be enrolled for a longer period. In September 1992 the MEd coordinator indicated that major difficulties were being experienced by the five enrolled overseas students and their supervisors in the thesis supervision process. None of these students spoke English as a first language. Three of them — a Melanesian female (S1), an Asian female (S2) and an Asian male (S3) — were full- fee paying students. The other two, an African female (S4) and a Melanesian male (S5), were on AIDAB scholarships.

Methodology

A qualitative methodology was selected since the aim of the research was to gather feedback from the overseas students about the experience of supervision by getting 'inside the perspectives of the respondents' (Vulliamy, 1990: 100). A skilled interviewer with 22 years experience as an educationalist in developing countries was chosen because of his ability to foster a 'conversation piece, not an inquisition' (Simons, 1982: 37) and because of a belief that his experience would assist in facilitating the elicitation of true reponses and in reducing 'noise' (Field, 1987: 61) in the communication process. It was also felt that his experience was such that he could handle any problems in language interpretation by changing the wording of questions to suit each particular respondent.

The fact that the interviewer was also enrolled in the MEd course and, while not a full- fee paying student, had established a friendly non-threatening relationship with the interviewees, was also seen as having advantages. In particular, it was considered a safeguard against the common response in some non-European cultures of interviewees feeding researchers what they think they want to hear. It is also contended that this choice predisposed the interviewer to being able to give students the maximum opportunity to voice their concerns and express the complexities of their expectations of supervision and their evolving relationships with supervisors.

The interviews were conducted over a period of two months. Each interviewee was interviewed in total for about five hours. As part of the effort to promote a non-threatening and 'open' atmosphere, the interviews were conducted in the informal environment of the interviewees' homes. Cognisance was taken of Vulliamy's (1990: 100) advice that the interviewees should do most of the talking and that questions should be designed to elicit open responses. At the same time, the interviewer made use of probes to elicit the most complete descriptions of participants' perceptions of their relationships with their supervisors. The interviews with four of the interviewees were tape-recorded. The interviews with the fifth interviewee were, at that person's request, recorded as hand-written notes. Each interview was transcribed as soon as possible after it was conducted so that the interviewer's still fresh recollections could be written up. In every case the record was taken back to the students to ascertain the level of acceptability of what was said and meant, and it was then refined where necessary.

The analysis of the students' transcripts followed the procedures outlined by Marton (1988: 155). Utterances in the transcripts found to be of interest for the questions being investigated were selected and marked. These selected quotes then made up the data pool which formed the basis for the next step of the analysis where utterances were brought together into categories on the basis of their similarities, and categories were differentiated from one another in terms of their differences. Each of the four categories which emerged — alienation from the university, the human qualities of the supervisor, the teaching strategies of the supervisor, and the supervisor's cultural understandings — will now be considered in turn.

Alienation from the university

A useful conceptual framework to apply to the task of interpreting the educational experiences of overseas students as related by themselves is to view education as cultural transmission, a social process occurring within social institutions (Singleton, 1974: 23) and entailing the construction and negotiation of shared meanings. A significant aspect of the process is the acquisiton of cultural knowledge or enculturation. Viewed from such a perspective, people who are learning to operate as members of a culturally defined setting can be seen as having acute information needs. Schutz (1964: 93-94) identifies the knowledge correlated to the social pattern of a new cultural context which newcomers must acquire as a collection of trustworthy recipes which are both precepts for action and interpretive schemes. That is, newcomers need both practical 'know how' and understandings of underlying attitudes and value systems. In adopting such a perspective it is also helpful to view university post-graduate students as falling into one of a number of groups, each of which is at a different stage of removal from possessing the necessary behavioural skills and from having adopted the cultural standards necessary for success. It is suggested that within the Australian education system, the greatest gap is likely to be evidenced in the experiences of people who have recently arrived from another country for the purpose of undertaking a higher degree. In the conduct of their academic work, including thesis preparation, such people are likely to encounter not only the more obvious language difficulties, but also more subtle differences in beliefs and value systems about the nature of knowledge and learning.

It would appear that, from the very outset, any chance that the five students interviewed might have had of quickly coming to a shared understanding with their supervisors of what was involved in preparing a thesis had been hampered seriously by the university's marketing policy. All of the five students interviewed were unhappy with the fact that while they were given the impression prior to coming to Australia that it would be normal to complete the required course work and thesis in one year, the attitude of their supervisors from the time of first meeting was that this would be an almost impossible task. This added greatly to the stress which they were experiencing in coming to terms with living in a new culture. A sense of the associated feeling of resentment can be gauged from the following extract:

> S2: I have paid over $8,000 in fees and I have living expenses, all paid from funds provided by my family. Now I find that I cannot complete my research in one year. I am definitely not getting value for money in terms of helpful guidance and supervision.

Only one of the students, in fact, had completed all of the requirements by the end of the year and attributed her success to dedication by her supervisor over and above what she would consider normal.

This is not to deny that it is possible to research and write up a thesis within a year. However, it is arguable that for most students it would necessitate commencing one's course with a very well-defined area of interest to be pursued if not a clearly formulated, narrowly focused set of questions to be investigated. This, in turn, pre-supposes students well-read in the field on commencement, something which was certainly not the case with the interviewees in this study, as reflected in the following extracts:

> S1: I needed a lot of guidance. I feel that I needed a supervisor that would not leave me to my own devices as I had very little idea what I was about. I would like a supervisor to be able to give me guidance, tell me perhaps what I suggest to do for a thesis won't work, ask me to read things to give me a clearer idea on what I could research.
> S3: I needed strong and helpful supervision because of my own language problem and difficulties with adjustment. Books and articles are so hard to find on a topic that I might research. What can I do?
> S5: Every two weeks I meet with my supervisor. He has assisted me in choosing my research topic.

To some extent there appears to have been an expectation on the part of the students that there would be a fairly clear prescription of the general area they would have to select for their research and that within that area a clear set of topics would be identified for them from which they could choose one to pursue. That this was so is not, of course, surprising. Australian academics are reminded regularly of the different learning styles and expectations of overseas students. Ginsburg, for example, (1992: 6) states that for many overseas students:

> ... knowledge is not open to challenge and extension...and academic education may have little to do with the getting of wisdom. The teacher decides what

knowledge is to be taught, and the students accept and learn that knowledge. The lecturer is the authority, the repository of knowledge, leading the student forward into this knowledge, a respected elder transmitting to a subordinate junior.

However, it would appear that no great effort was taken by the university during recruitment to impress upon the students the importance which would be attached by their supervisors to the self-generation of research questions and to the capacity for independent management of the research project. Here one is reminded of Burns' (1991) contention that there is no evidence that Australian universities are confronting the issues related to the significance of fundamental differences in the learning styles of overseas students and Western academic traditions. In this respect, they would do well to be mindful of Grace's (1992) work where, building on Schutz's (1964) analysis, she identified two broad strategies for bridging cultural distance: to provide explication and interpretation of the institutional culture; and to acknowledge, communicate with and utilize the world of the student.

The 'human' qualities of the supervisor

Harris and Holmes (1975) have drawn attention to the fact that 'newcomers to the academic game', because they are unfamiliar with the culture of higher education, find it difficult to acquire strategic knowledge such as how to identify the essential parts of a course. The situation, as Cohen (1982) points out, is compounded by the fact that people who are members of cultures are not always conscious of their membership and may take for granted information which needs to be made explicit to newcomers. Furthermore, as Louis (1980) notes, newcomers and those who are marginal members of a culture are typically unaware of their need to understand context-specific interpretive schemes and the fact that they are in ignorance of them. This kind of situation is evident in the interviews, where students described themselves as vaguely feeling that they were in 'the dark' or else said they knew they lacked information, but did not know what questions to ask. They also spoke about the university's lack of a 'human' touch and of 'the crucial importance' of students, prior to commencing their studies, having 'some formal orientation to the content of the course, what is expected and how to go about it'.

Reflecting back on her experience with respect to her thesis preparation, one of the students articulated clearly how she saw the problem and what the institution could do to address it:

S1: I did have a lot of problems when I first began to think about my thesis. I went to a particular lecturer whom I thought I knew quite well. I sought that person's advice. I was really put down very badly and told to go back to the lecturers I was dealing with in research methods, that it was their place to help me. I felt disappointed because I did not want a particular help, just a general help and some things to think about before settling on a subject. I just generally needed a chat; some sort of dialogue that would set me straight, that would show me the way.

This student felt very strongly that there should be a central person one could go to initially and just throw around ideas — 'someone who is in the know' — arguing that if such a person had been available to her it would have saved her a lot of time and frustration. She went on to argue that the 'central person' should be able to talk to incoming students, work out their area of interest and match them up with lecturers with similar areas of interest. The students should then, 'without any obligation', be able to go and see the different lecturers because 'you really have to get to know a supervisor before you take him or her on'.

Another common sub-theme highlighting the interviewees' sensitivities with regard to the need for 'human' qualities in a supervisor was reflected in their notions that supervisors should display a personal interest in students' research topics. Four of the interviewees perceived lack of such an interest on the part of their supervisors and they expressed sentiments bordering on anger:

> S1: It is important to have someone who is interested in the work. He was not really interested in what I am doing.
>
> S2: I felt it was a business arrangement. She was not really interested in me or my work. I feel that little interesting debate took place. All I was asked to do was go through and explain what work I had done over the previous fortnight.
>
> S3: Two or three weeks ago I asked my supervisor for models and theories on TESL teaching and learning and she replied 'it's not my area'. Why did she not tell me before?
>
> S5: They do not care for us overseas students. Why didn't they ask me what kind of supervisor I wanted? The authorities need to make sure we have the right supervisor.... I cannot compete with native students. I need someone who is really interested in what I am doing.

These perceptions reflect Burns' (1991: 67) findings that generally, overseas students feel that academic staff in Australia are uncaring and uninterested in their students.
    The fifth interviewee also stressed the importance of the supervisor taking a personal interest in the students' research. In this case, however, the matter was highlighted in her relating of a positive experience in this regard:

> S4: Sometimes it happens that you would be given some ideas by your supervisor and you incorporate them in your work. The next time when you read out those same ideas they will be crushed by him. I said to myself that this person is a human being like me and what he is trying to do is incorporate an idea which he thought was good at first and now finds that it is not good. We could argue over the point and I am happy about that.

She went on to place great importance on the fact that her supervisor took her 'as a colleague and not as a student', introduced her to other lecturers and explained her area of research to them. She concluded: 'I was not working on my own. Other lecturers were interested in what I was doing. Some of them brought some material as a help. They accepted me. I felt happy'.

An associated sub-theme which emerged was that the interviewees felt it was vital that a supervisor should be an authority in the topic of research; somebody who, as it was put, would be able to say: 'Why don't you look at this author' or 'there is a good article in there'. Of the five interviewees four felt that they suffered serious demotivation because of the fact that their supervisors had not conveyed the impression to them that they were experts in their fields. This reflects Samuelowicz's (1987) contention that overseas students commonly share an excessive regard for authority and intellectual expertise and display a readiness to accept authority without question. The challenge for supervisors is to develop strategies for the promotion of independent learners (Brookfield, 1985; Mezirow, 1985) which take into consideration the fact that this is the background out of which overseas students are embarking on their Western-based academic journey.

All of the interviewees were also strong in their arguments that supervisors should be prepared to spend extensive periods of time getting to know their students and getting a feeling for the difficulties which they were experiencing with their work. As one of them put it:

> S1: The most important things are the availability of the supervisor and that the supervisor gives you time.

While this is likely to be an excessive expectation from the point of view of most supervisors it is, nevertheless, one about which they should be mindful and also one about which some mutual understanding should be reached. Furthermore, it constitutes an area which, to some extent, could be capitalized on for the promotion of student growth. As Rowland (1984: 25) argues:

> If we ask ourselves which skills are needed to foster independent learning to help a student evolve his or her own goals, to develop nascent abilities and to share learning experiences, we are likely to come back to the supportive skills of questioning and listening and acting as a sounding board.

Within the present context, however, it appears that, apart from one interviewee, the students did not experience such an approach:

> S5: During the supervision we were scheduled for an hour. They had looked at my work beforehand. We looked through it page by page but then sometimes we were catching up with time. Sometimes we were rushing through because we could have gone beyond the hour. They would not go beyond the hour. I produced pages and pages of stuff and the one hour was not enough to look into the whole thing adequately.
>
> S.3: She was very busy and I had to make an appointment through her secretary every time I wanted to meet her. That is ok but at times you need things desperately as you are really stuck on a point.

The inhibiting effect of cultural isolation was also apparent in a hesitancy to contact supervisors outside of agreed-upon meeting times:

S1: People coming from different cultures find it very difficult in getting anything done. I should have been a bit more pushy and gone up to the lecturer and said 'Read this. This is what I want to do'. Students should be able to go and knock on a door and say: 'Please, I need help'. Because in a lot of cultures this is not acceptable. The student has to sit back and allow the lecturer to come.

In particular, students tended to regard contacting staff at home outside normal office hours as intruding on their privacy.

Teaching strategies of the supervisor

It would be wrong to conclude that the interviewees were not anxious to manage and self-direct their learning. They did demonstrate a realization of the need to seek out an issue for pursuit and to consider the most appropriate way to go about investigating it. What is instructive, however, are their notions of how, under supervision, this process should proceed. They definitely did not favour the engagement in broad and extensive reading in order to find a general area of interest which would, in turn, lead to the identification of a variety of research questions, a number of which could then be refined and possibly selected for investigation. Rather, it would seem that they wished to be focused from a very early stage and structure their reading towards identifying a problem area within narrow parameters:

S2: I think good supervision is when you are aware from the beginning of where you can get material on a subject to pursue.
S4: He was a good supervisor. If he found some material he would hand it over to me to look at to see if I could use it in my research. Sometimes he would give me titles of books which I would go to the library to check on. He also gave me the names of persons I could contact on the phone who knew about the area I was pursuing.

Associated with this was a desire on the part of all the interviewees that they should work to short-term goals:

S1: I need guidance to get started. I have no idea how to get started. My supervisor was good in this respect. He lent me copies of his articles and broke up my work into different sections and got me to concentrate on sections at a time.
S2: At last I have a good supervisor. He assures me that we will be meeting three times a week, he will correct my work at the rate of 500 words at a time, and get me to rewrite it while he is correcting the next 500 words.

At the same time, it would be fair to say that the students were not arguing for 'blind' directions. Rather, they felt that the setting of their goals should take place through a process of negotiation between themselves and their supervisors, and that this could be done if their supervisors were prepared not to rush them in meetings but to give them time to discuss their concerns at length.

Two of the interviewees were also adamant that their supervisors should have given them direct instruction where necessary and provided concrete examples of what was expected:

> S3: Masters students, like the other overseas students, should have to go through a preparation in English language for academic writing. I did a course in research skills but it only covered theoretical background. My supervisor should have given me specific instruction in research skills, library skills and the referencing of assignments.
>
> S5: There were lots of assumptions that I knew exactly what I was doing in quantitative and qualitative research and also that I knew how to put my research findings together. I got no instruction on how to put it all together. I was never given a thesis to look at as a model of what I was trying to achieve.

In this respect, institutions would do well to be mindful of Hodgkinson's (1980) and Campbell's (1980) recommendation that overseas students should undergo a research training programme even before entering a course requiring thesis preparation.

Continuity and consistency were also identified as important factors in supervision. This is well illustrated in the fact that one of the interviewees was, at the time of the interview, still greatly confused. She began the year believing that she was going to be allocated to a particular supervisor. After ten weeks, she was sent to someone else. However, by the end of the year she had made no progress, due, in her opinion, to the fact that her supervisor knew nothing about her topic. At the time of the interview her supervisor had yet again been changed.

Another interviewee expressed his frustration at the lack of continuity as follows:

> S5: I had a second supervisor along with my main supervisor. What I had was one hour supervision each week when I brought some of my assignment work to my supervisors for discussion. However, we did not meet every week. We met regularly in the first few weeks, then I was left to work on my own for about eight weeks.

This situation was compounded by the fact that occasionally when he met with both of his supervisors their interactions with one another in his presence were such that he became confused:

> S5: My dissertation is a combination of qualitative and quantitative data. One supervisor was on quantitive and the other on qualitative. I often found myself in the middle because of their uncertainties with regard to each other's area of research. They did not disagree but they had confusions with each other. They had uncertainties in certain areas. I tried to solve the uncertainties but not very quickly, over a period of time. Sometimes I was caught in the middle although we tried to arrive at a compromise.

While dual supervision is becoming the norm in many universities for a variety of reasons, this evidence suggests further exploration of whether there might be a good case for not recommending it for overseas students.

The supervisor's cultural understandings

Language is the prime medium of cultural transmission and therefore the key to enculturation. Accordingly, as an interviewee put it: 'one of the most important factors for supervisors of overseas students is to have an awareness of the student's difficulties with using English as a second language'. This becomes particularly clear when one comes to a realization that even for first-language speakers of English, academic terminology is a potential source of alienation.

In the case of some of the interviewees the encounter with academic discourse was problematic:

> S5: I gave them the work a week beforehand so that they could read it, then we met and we discussed it on the basis of the comments which they had written down. Sometimes I found the comments to be clear, yet to get around the technicality of the languages I had difficulty. I took that up with my supervisors but I was not usually happy with their response. I was still not absolutely clear at the end about what the comments meant.

It is likely that the situation for this student was compounded by his Melanesian background. Melanesians are not inclined to ask too many questions in seeking clarification of issues because to show ignorance is to experience shame (Epstein, 1984). Interestingly, however, he said he found it most helpful when, in the last few weeks prior to the conducting of the interview, a 'European academic friend came to the rescue' by going through the work with him page by page, reading it aloud and pausing at the supervisor's comments to discuss a variety of possible meanings which could be attached to them. Here it is instructive to consider Burns' (1991: 171) point that being able to articulate reactions and express opinions freely is difficult for most overseas students as 'they are not used to such freedom in either academic or social contexts'.

Some of the interviewees' reflections also suggest a lack of clear understanding on the part of supervisors of the culturally-based sensitivities of their students:

> S3: I was devastated when I got back my final assignment on Research Methods. The comments made by the lecturer showed that we had not communicated at all well. Some of the comments were 'I don't understand what you are doing', 'Who does these work experience programmes you want to study?' If he had read he would know that work experience programmes are taken by students who are going out to employers. That I found very dissatisfying. His comments showed that he had not read what I had written.

One can appreciate that the supervisor was simply trying to be helpful by using written questions to get the student to clarify his thoughts. However, he did not allow for the fact that what is perceived as helpful by Australian students is often perceived as hurtful by overseas students. One of the interviewees had come to terms with this matter and suggested:

> S4: Students should be made aware of the fact that learning is a process and making errors is just a part of learning. Students should be aware of this because they might have supervisors who are very critical. They should realize that the goal is to emerge as people who have learned something.

McLaughlin (1989: 8), however, argues that lecturers also need to develop strategies to deal with the matter, pointing out that in the case of Melanesians, for example, it is culturally insensitive to convey 'personal inadequacies' through the medium of impersonal written comments on assignments. This view endorses that of Samuelowicz (1987: 126) who argues for greater cooperation between staff and students and offers a series of strategies to facilitate the learning of all students 'through manipulation of learning contexts and... changing students' perceptions of learning'.

Conclusion

The process of transferring knowledge across international boundaries is no longer just a matter of educators travelling abroad to see what they can learn to improve the system at home. It is now also characterized by a variety of other activities, one of which is that of students being educated outside their home countries. Associated with this broadening of the process is an increasing emphasis on the need for all involved to develop an awareness of each other's cultural backgrounds. This chapter drew particular attention to this matter with respect to students from the developing world engaged in postgraduate study in a developed country.

Because of the small number of students involved in the study no claim is being made that one can generalize for a wider population. However, it is arguable that the study does have wider significance in that it goes some way towards 'giving voice' to the findings of studies like that of the National Liaison Committee for Overseas Students in Australia (1992) on the supervision problems being experienced by overseas students. The hope is that this in turn will interest potential researchers in the academic life of overseas students in developed countries, thus encouraging in-depth research into the area with the aim of contributing to the improvement of that life. The summary of responses is also offered to all supervisors of overseas students so that they might consider their practices. In particular, it appears that those involved in the supervision of overseas students need to:

- make it clear to those marketing the degree that they have a duty to spell out the intellectual demands involved in preparing and writing a dissertation
- be culturally sensitive with regard to the students' learning styles and also to the possibility of eliciting negative responses through the adoption of particular Western strategies of supervision
- appreciate that the students may not only have language difficulties but also differences in beliefs and value systems about the nature of knowledge and learning

- empathize with those students who expect a fairly clear prescription of the general area to be selected for their research, including the identification of a number of topics
- understand the desire of students to have a supervisor with whom they can feel comfortable not only intellectually but also socially and culturally
- understand students' expectations that there be continuity and consistency in the supervision, that time should not be a constraint in the relationship, and that the supervisor should play a teaching role when necessary.

Overseas students should, both prior to departure from home and also on arrival at university, be given the best possible tuition to prepare them for the academic culture in which they will have to operate. There seems little doubt that supervisors also require special preparation for working with overseas students. The contention is that case studies of this nature can provide a framework for developing enlightenment and guiding activity since they can 'speak' to other supervisors and provide them with 'material which could be of some use to them in sharpening their own perceptions' (Sultana, 1991: 62). There should not be surprise if in those universities which continue to adopt an unenlightened approach, the overseas student market goes into decline.

References

AIDAB (1992). *Cooperation—Australia's International Aid Programme*. Canberra: AGPS.

Apple, M. (1990). *Ideology and Curriculum*. New York: Routledge.

Australian Industry Commission (1991). *Export of Education Services (Report No. 12)*. Canberra: AGPS.

Baldwin, P. (1991). *Higher Education: Quality and Diversity in the 1990s*. Canberra: AGPS.

Ballard, B. and Clanchy, J. (1984). *Study Abroad: A Manual for Asian Students*. Malaysia: Longman.

Bilbow, G.T. (1989). 'Towards an understanding of overseas students' difficulties in lectures: a phenomenological approach'. *Journal of Further and Higher Education* 13(3): 85-89.

Brookfield, S. (1985). 'Self-directed learning: a critical review of research', in S. Brookfield (ed.), *Self-Directed Learning: From Theory to Practice*. San Francisco: Jossey-Bass.

Brown, G. and Atkins, M. (1988). *Effective Teaching In Higher Education*. London: Methuen.

Burns, R. (1991). 'Study and stress among first year students in an Australian university'. *Higher Education Research and Development* 10(1): 61-77.

Campbell, R.S.F. (1980). 'Educational difficulties of graduate students related to academic background', in *AIDAB Conference on Difficulties of Overseas Students*. Canberra: AIDAB.

Cohen, A.P. (1982). *Belonging. Identity and Social Organisation in British Rural Cultures*. Manchester: Manchester University Press.

Connell, R. (1985). 'How to supervise a Ph.D'. *The Australian Universities Review* **28**(2): 38-41.

Cox, R. (1988). 'Postgraduate research training', in *Reviews of Literature and Data Sources. The Characteristics of the Training Process and Those Undergoing the Research Training*. London: Institute of Education.

Crossley, M. (1984). 'Strategies for curriculum change and the question of international transfer'. *Journal of Curriculum Studies* **16**(1): 75-88.

Crossley, M. (1992). 'Teacher education in Papua New Guinea: a comment on comparative and international observations'. *Journal of Education for Teaching* **18**(1): 23-28.

Crossley, M. and Broadfoot, P. (1992). 'Comparative and international research in education: scope, problems and potential'. *British Educational Research Journal* **18**: 99-112.

DEET (Department of Employment, Education and Training) (1991). *Annual Report 1991*. Canberra: AGPS.

Delamont, S. and Eggleston, J. (1983). 'A necessary isolation?', in J. Eggleston and S. Delamont (eds), *Supervision of Students for Research Degree*. Birmingham: BERA.

Epstein, A. (1984). *The Experience of Shame in Melanesia*. London: Royal Anthropological Institute.

Field, S. (1987). 'Questionaire and interview schedules', in G. Guthrie (ed.), *Basic Research Techniques: Report No. 55*. Waigani: Educational Research Unit, University of Papua New Guinea.

Ginsburg, E. (1992). 'Not just a matter of English'. *HERDSA* **14**(1): 6-8.

Grace, M. (1992). *Student Perceptions of Supervision*. Brisbane: School of Curriculum and Professional Studies, Queensland University of Technology.

Halleck, S.L. (1976). 'Emotional problems of the graduate student', in J. Katz and R.T. Harnett (eds), *Scholars In The Making*. Cambridge: MA Ballinger.

Hansford, B.C. and Maxwell, T.W. (1993). 'A masters degree programme: structural components and examiners' comments'. *Higher Education Research and Development* **12**: 171-187.

Harris, D. and Holmes, J. (1975). 'Open to Martha, closed to Mary'. *The Times Higher Education Supplement*, 19 December, p. 74.

Hodgkinson, M.C. (1980). 'The English and study problems of overseas students', in *AIDAB Conference on Difficulties of Overseas Students*. Canberra: AIDAB.

Jones, C. (1992). 'Learning to exchange ideas'. *The Australian*, 25 November, p. 6.

Krebs, H.A. (1967). 'The making of a scientist'. *Nature* **215**: 1441-1445.

Louis, M.R. (1980). 'Surprise and sense-making: what newcomers experience on entering unfamiliar organisational settings'. *Administrative Science Quarterly* **25**: 226-251.

Lowenthal, D. and Wason, P.C. (1977). 'Academics and their writing'. *Times Literary Supplement*, 24 June, p. 2.

McLaughlin, D. (1989). *Matching Meaning and Message in Melanesia* (mimeo). Port Moresby: University of Papua New Guinea.

Makrotest, H. (1987). 'PhD submission rates — synopsis of results', in *The Background Papers, The Social Science Ph.D.* London: The ESRC Inquiry On Submission Rates. London: ESRC.

Marsh, A. (1972). *Postgraduate Students' Assessment of Their Social Science Training.* SSRC Survey Unit, Occassional Paper No. 2. London: SSRC.

Marton, F. (1988). 'Phenomeography: a research approach to investigating different understandings of reality', in R.R. Sherman and R.B. Webb (eds), *Qualitative Research in Education: Focus and Methods.* London: Falmer Press.

Mezirow, J. (1985). 'A critical theory of self-directed learning', in S. Brookfield (ed.), *Self-Directed Learning: From Theory to Practice.* San Francisco: Jossey Bass.

Moses, I. (1985). *Supervising Postgraduates.* Sydney: HERDSA.

National Liaison Committee for Overseas Students in Australia (1992). *Australian Education: Excellent or Dismal — A Survey.* Carlton: Overseas Students Department of the National Union of Students.

Powles, M. (1989a). 'Higher degree completion and completion times'. *Higher Education Research and Development* 8(1): 91-101.

Powles, M. (1989b). *How's The Thesis Going? Former Postgraduates And Their Supervisors' Views On Lengthy Candidature And Dropout.* Melbourne: University of Melbourne, Centre for the Study of Higher Education.

Rowland, F. (1984). 'Industrialised, individualised or independent?' Paper presented at the *5th Annual Study Skills Conference.* Geelong: Deakin University.

Rudd, E. (1975). *The Highest Education.* London: Routledge and Kegan Paul.

Rudd, E. (1985). *A New Look at Postgraduate Failure.* London: SRHE.

Samuelowicz, K. (1987). 'Learning problems of overseas students'. *Higher Education Research and Development* 8(2): 121-133.

Schön, D. (1987). *Educating The Reflectve Practitioner.* London: Jossey-Bass.

Schutz, A. (1964). 'The stranger: an essay in social psychology', in A. Brodersen (ed.), *Studies in Social Theory.* The Hague: Martinus Nijhoff.

Simons, H. (1982). *Conversation Piece: The Practice of Uttering, Muttering, Collecting, Using and Reporting Talk for Social and Education Research.* London: Grant McIntyre.

Singleton, J. (1974). 'Implications of education as cultural transmission', in E.G. Spindler (ed.), *Education and Cultural Process: Towards an Anthropology of Education.* New York: Holt, Rinehart and Winston.

Smart, D. and Ang, G. (1992). *Policy Paper No. 2. Medium Term Market Opportunities for Australian Higher Education: A Pilot Survey of Singapore.* Murdoch: Western Australia , Asia Research Centre, Murdoch University.

Smawfield, D. (1989). 'The supervision of overseas students: a bridge between two cultures'. *Supervision in Education* 39: 51-61.

Sultana, R.G. (1991). 'Research in teaching and teacher education: qualitative methods and grounded theory methodology'. *South Pacific Journal of Teacher Education* 19(1): 59-68.

The Times Higher Education Supplement (1991). Editorial. 6 December, p. 2.

University of Queensland Union (1983). *Supervision Survey: Preliminary Analysis.* St Lucia: University of Queensland Union.

Vulliamy, G. (1990). 'Case-study research in schools in Papua New Guinea', in G. Vulliamy, K. Lewin and D. Stephens (eds), *Doing Research in Developing Countries.* London: Falmer Press.

Wason, P.C. (1974). 'Notes on the supervision of Ph.Ds'. *Bulletin of the British Psychological Society* **27**: 25-39.

Welsh, J.M. (1979). *The First Year of Postgraduate Study.* Guilford: SRHE.

Whalley, A. (1982). *Postgraduate Education in Universities and Polytechnics.* London: Policy Studies Institute.

Williams, B. (1989). *Overseas Students in Australia: Policy and Practice.* Canberra: International Development Programme of Australian Universities and Colleges.

Wilson, A. (1980). 'Group sessions for postgraduate students'. *British Journal of Guidance and Counselling* **8**: 237-241.

Wright, J. and Lodwick, R. (1989). 'The process of the PhD: a study of the first year of doctoral study'. *Research Papers in Education* **4**: 22-56.

Zuber-Skerritt, O. (1988). 'What constitutes effective research? A case study'. *Higher Education in Europe* **13**(4): 64-76.

Zuber Skerritt, O. (1992). *Starting Research—Supervision and Training.* St Lucia: The Tertiary Education Institute, The University of Queensland.

Part Two

Educational Processes to Achieve Quality

Chapter 7

Improving the Quality of Postgraduate Supervision through Residential Staff Development Programmes

Ortrun Zuber-Skerritt

Introduction

This chapter assumes that the quality of postgraduate research in universities depends largely on the quality management and supervision of postgraduate degree programmes and theses, and demonstrates that quality management and supervision can be improved through a systemic approach to staff development programmes with a multiplier effect.

On the basis of principles of good supervisory practice derived from the literature and case studies at Griffith University, the chapter presents a model of staff development programmes on postgraduate research and supervision. The aims of these quality improvement programmes are to achieve professional development, effectiveness and efficiency in postgraduate supervision and to achieve a multiplier effect by 'training the trainers'. These programmes are residential in order to give participants every chance of having informal discussions, getting to know colleagues from other faculties and universities, and working in an environment which is conducive to a creative, pleasant and effective work atmosphere without the usual time stresses and other constraints.

Compared to studies in undergraduate learning and teaching, there is a dearth of published research and theory on postgraduate research and supervision. Yet there seems to be a great need for inexperienced supervisors to learn about and develop skills in supervising postgraduate research students; and for experienced supervisors to pool, exchange and conceptualize their practical experiences in a more systematic and collaborative way than has been done to date.

As a result of these residential staff development programmes, participants have gained a greater awareness of theoretical and practical issues, such as student needs, learning approaches and conditions, barriers to learning, 'the lonely researcher' syndrome, communication problems between supervisor and student, responsibilities on both parts, etc. The participating universities have realized that postgraduate supervision cannot be taken for granted, but that it is a legitimate and necessary area of academic staff development, and that postgraduate students have the right to be guided and trained professionally. Most of the participating institutions have established or reviewed their institutional and departmental documents and guidelines for supervisors and students, and workshop programmes are in place to help students in the process of research and writing.

Other universities may be interested in the outcomes, and may wish to adopt or adapt some of the ideas of this model, using the resource materials produced as a result of the programmes, such as books, manuals and video programmes.

Problems and strategies in postgraduate education

In recent years, government and funding bodies in many countries have exerted increasing pressure on higher education institutions to improve the quality and effectiveness of postgraduate research in order to reduce drop-out and late submission rates. This has implications for postgraduate supervision and, at least in Britain and Australia, institutional funding, since quality assurance audits have been introduced.

Moses (1981, 1984, 1985), Powles (1988, 1989a), Rudd (1975, 1984, 1985) and Zuber-Skerritt (1992a) have summarized the main problems identified in the literature on postgraduate education. For the purpose of this chapter the following areas of concern are important:

- inadequate supervision: supervisors' lack of experience, commitment and/or time
- emotional and psychological problems: students' intellectual and social isolation; their insecurity as to standards and lack of confidence in their ability to complete their theses within the specified time limit or at all
- lack of understanding and communication between supervisor and student
- students' lack of knowledge, skills, training or experience in research methods
- consequent late completion and high drop-out rates.

Various strategies have been suggested to overcome these problems by improving the single-supervisor model and students' research skills. For example, Moses (1985) provides a useful guide on *Supervising Postgraduates*. The Science and Engineering Research Council in Britain (SERC, 1989) has issued a publication for the guidance of supervisors, including a checklist on good supervisory practice. Similarly, the Economic and Social Science Research Council (ESRC, 1991) has produced guidelines on postgraduate training in the social sciences. All of the above problems are addressed in some detail and from various perspectives in Zuber-Skerritt (1992a), aimed at university administrators and academics, as well as students. There are other useful resources specifically designed for students, such as the reference books by Ballard and Clanchy (1984), Howard and Sharp (1983), Madsen (1988),

Phillips and Pugh (1987) and Powles (1989b).

I have described elsewhere examples and case studies which illustrate various approaches to help postgraduate students learn, e.g. Zuber-Skerritt (1992b, Chapter 2), where students' needs and problem areas were first identified at the beginning of a course or courses within a department and then met in a series of workshops for students with participation of several or all supervisors involved. This workshop model and other group supervisory models are described in Conrad et al. (1992) and were integrated in the design of a staff development model of postgraduate supervision. Before presenting this model, I outline the principles of good supervisory practice which have guided the development of the model.

Principles of good supervisory practice

An important factor for minimizing problems of attrition and late completion rates in postgraduate education is good supervisory practice based on sound principles derived from the literature and reflection on practical experience.

The following are procedures outlined by SERC (1989) on the basis of a national survey in Britain and intended to improve the traditional **single-supervisor model**:

- publication of a departmental document on good supervisory practice
- careful matching of supervisor and prospective student
- provision of a student reading guide for the summer holiday prior to commencement of research
- assessment of student's first year report by academics other than the immediate supervisor
- regular meetings between student and supervisor
- the student's record keeping to be checked to ensure it is systematic
- a mock viva to be held six to twelve months before submission of the thesis.

On the basis of case studies at Griffith University (Knight and Zuber-Skerritt, 1986; Zuber-Skerritt, 1987; Zuber-Skerritt and Knight, 1985, 1986; Zuber-Skerrit and Rix, 1986) and reflections on this experience, the following aims have proven to be effective for **group supervisory models**:

- to provide a supportive environment for learning and research through group discussion, group sharing of ideas, problem solving, mutual encouragement and motivation, overcoming the intellectual and social isolation of the 'lonely' researcher
- to identify and meet students' informational, motivational and social needs at the beginning of and during their degree programmes, through workshops with fellow students and supervisors apart from their own, so that they are exposed to a wide range of perspectives
- to save resources and time for supervisors who can cover topics and discuss problems with a group of students simultaneously, which also has advantages for

students; for example, topics are covered systematically, rather than accidentally or not at all
- to share resources and expertise among supervisors, which means that supervisors can specialize in certain aspects of postgraduate supervision and skills training and that everything can be covered by the best-skilled academics
- to help students be more responsible for their own and each other's learning; postgraduates are able to provide each other with advice, help and critique; for example, they can exchange literature surveys and copies of relevant articles and books, and can also critique each other's research proposals, draft chapters and theses, once a climate of trust, open communication and cooperation has been established
- to ensure that the key areas of postgraduate supervision (e.g. standards, expectations, requirements, roles, functions) are discussed, clarified and agreed
- to raise students' awareness of alternative approaches, epistemologies and research methods through discussion rather than lecture
- to focus and reflect on the **process** of learning and researching, rather than merely the content; this is achieved more easily and more effectively in a group.

The above conclusions and principles of good supervisory practice have been incorporated in the design of two government-funded residential staff development programmes on postgraduate research and supervision: the first in 1992 for 80 women representatives from all departments at the University of Queensland and from several Australian universities; and the second in 1993 for 127 male and female representatives (50 per cent of each) from all seven universities in Queensland.

A staff development model of postgraduate supervision

These two residential staff development programmes were very similar in design, content, method and outcome, except that the first had the additional aim to start with women as an affirmative action measure. This was considered to be justified because of the need to increase the number of professional women as leaders in research and higher education management.

The significance of both programmes is that they aimed to address the key issues arising from the literature and from the participants' own practical experience, and to focus on and improve the **process** of postgraduate training and supervision. The outcomes of these programmes in 1992 and 1993, funded by the federal government's Department of Employment, Education and Training (DEET), are described and discussed as one model.

The express purpose of this residential staff development model was 'training the trainers', that is developing academics as supervisors and/or as postgraduate students who would then run similar workshop programmes themselves in their own institutions. The programme was designed for representatives from academic departments, faculties and from the unions who had a special interest in postgraduate supervision and who, in turn, would be the role models and trainers of their colleagues and students in their own departments, faculties and institutions. In order to achieve this multiplier effect, the programme itself modelled the process of collaborative staff development in postgraduate supervision. We worked with concrete examples of postgraduate projects provided by academics enrolled in higher degrees and by representatives of the postgraduate students' unions.

Aims

The first aim was to initiate an effective strategy in all institutions of higher education in Queensland for improving staff competence in postgraduate research training and supervision. A second aim was to establish and foster a network through which participants could continue to focus on the quality of postgraduate research and researchers in their universities.

The residential programme

The conference proceeded in a workshop style with input from national and international experts in higher education who addressed key issues relating to postgraduate supervision. Topics in the programme included:

- Major Issues and Concerns (a needs analysis)
- Issues of Communication in Postgraduate Education
- Expectations and Standards, the Supervisor's Role and Functions
- From Thesis Writing to Research Application
- Induction into the Research Application Culture
- Creating a Supportive Environment
- Gender Issues
- The Design and Implementation of a Research Project
- Supervision of the Thesis Writing Process
- Getting Yourself Published
- Introducing a Workshop Programme on Postgraduate Supervision in Departments and Faculties
- Special Interest Group workshops, held on the last day:
  - The Reflective Literature Search
  - Giving Constructive Criticism
  - Collaborative Supervision and Research Training
  - Contracts and Checklists
- Reflections, Evaluation, Future Action Plans.

In the two workshops on project design and implementation and on supervising the writing process, participants worked in two main groups (with sub-groups), the Natural Sciences and the Social Sciences and Humanities, in order to address discipline-specific issues and concerns.

The last plenary session was a review of the conference proceedings in relation to the stated aims and objectives and to the participants' expressed needs and expectations before and at the beginning of the conference. The previous plenary session with workshop activities on how to introduce a workshop programme on postgraduate supervision in university departments and faculties specifically encouraged participants to design an action plan to address the issues of postgraduate supervision in their own institutions.

Action plans

These action plans have been monitored and evaluated to assess the impact of the programme on departmental practices. At this stage, participant feedback has indicated that many action plans are in place in departments, including workshops on supervision, compilation of handbooks for postgraduate students, increased access for students to facilities, the appointment of a research tutor or committee, and increased awareness of issues relating to postgraduate research and supervision.

As a result of the conference in 1992, monthly informal networking lunches at the University of Queensland Staff Club were initiated as well as a reunion dinner five months later, at which participants shared the developments of their action plans. This enabled the networking to continue. It provided a forum for participants to give feedback and to question the rest of the group about the changes that had occurred in their departments as a result of the conference. It was also a mechanism by which the effect/impact of the conference could be monitored and evaluated.

Some participants have conducted workshops on postgraduate supervision for supervisors and students in their departments. Some have formed groupings with other departments or institutions. For example, women from the University of Queensland, Gatton College and the University of Southern Queensland have formed a network for implementing their 'Staff Development Programme for Academic Women on Postgraduate Research and Supervision'. Other inter-departmental groups at the University of Queensland are the Bio-Medical Group (Physiology and Pharmacology, Anatomical Sciences, Pharmacy, Microbiology), the Engineering and Physical Science Group (Electrical Engineering, Mechanical Engineering, Chemical Engineering, Physics), the Health Science Group (Dentistry and Pathology), and the Agriculture and Veterinary Science Group. Conference organizers are in the process of receiving feedback on the implementation of these action plans for 1993-4 in the seven Queensland institutions.

In the final plenary session, participants showed a high level of enthusiasm for follow-up activities which would assist them and their colleagues in their institutions. Some of the responses are recorded below.

- I am hoping that I will also be able to go back to my own institution and help other people get some of the understandings that I have obtained from the conference.
- I welcomed very much the fact that the conference was addressing the issue [of postgraduate supervision] because this is something that is not often discussed. In many universities, it's rather a hit and miss business between the supervisor and the student and I think this is an issue that should be addressed. I hope that we will be able to continue this discussion because this is just the beginning.

A number of follow-up activities in departments and faculties were suggested in the concluding session. Participants' plans include:

- ways of generating and maintaining collaborative support networks for supervisors of postgraduate students using university email systems
- ways of generating and maintaining a collaborative support network for postgraduate research students
- follow-up meetings in individual institutions to continue planning for workshops on postgraduate supervision and research
- follow-up regional meetings and possible future regional conferences.

Evaluation and outcomes

The evaluation of the programme was conducted by means of:

- a pre-conference questionnaire survey (establishing participants' needs and expectations)
- reflection and feedback after individual sessions
- audio and video interviews during and at the end of the conference
- a final plenary discussion
- two post-conference questionnaire surveys, one at the end of the conference and one after six months.

Results of the evaluation

As a result of participants' feedback and their reports on the conference for their heads of departments (some of which were published in various newsletters) we have evidence that overall this programme was a great success in terms of the original aims and objectives and the personal, professional and departmental development in the area of postgraduate research supervision. Most departments have repeated all or part of the conference workshops with their staff and students using the materials provided by the Institute, such as the series of 12 videos entitled *Postgraduate Research, Supervision and Training* and the *Manual for Conducting Workshops on Postgraduate Supervision*. Thus the original objective of 'training the trainers' was achieved.

Participants appreciated the opportunity to learn from expert speakers and senior consultants chosen for their expertise in postgraduate education and their experience in leading workshop discussions. Participants also valued the opportunity of workshops to formulate ideas about postgraduate supervision and research, for example:

- to meet people from a wide variety of institutions to discuss the issues concerning old and new universities
- to discuss the issues raised by conference speakers
- to reflect upon their experiences and develop appropriate supervision strategies
- to develop their awareness about gender issues

- to access distributed materials for later use in follow-up workshops at participants' institutions.

The following are typical verbatim comments:

- In terms of a knowledge base, I have acquired a host of new ideas and new concepts that will further develop my thinking in the area of supervision, and this was acquired by listening to the keynote speakers and interacting with the group that attended in developing those ideas further.
- I welcomed hearing so many experts in their fields discuss the matters that are crucial to anyone dealing with postgraduate students in a supervisory role and I think it helped students who were here too.
- I found the lecture 'From Thesis Writing to Research Application: Learning the Research Culture' really interesting. Someone with access to the latest information on funding, the benefits of his experience of being a judge of the quality of proposals was helpful to me, as a new researcher. This will influence my supervision and the way I can provide greater guidance for students to help develop their careers in a more effective way.
- There is, in the distributed materials, a lot of information which can be used directly as overhead slides or updated to meet situations in particular institutions together with written or typed material that can have parts abstracted from it. I think that will be very useful in setting up a procedure for distributing the information at our home institutions.

Possible improvements

Some suggestions for improving future programmes include:

- holding a session on ethics and departmental guidelines
- giving information about an infrastructure that acknowledges the significance of research supervision in staff promotion
- including in the conference programme the perspective of higher degree students who are not members of academic staff
- inviting members of library staff from the various institutions to the programme.

On reflection, the feedback from many participants indicates that they would have preferred the traditional knowledge transmission model (one-way communication in lectures) and 'instrumental learning' to the more active, participative approach to 'generative learning' (by discovery and through discussion) which was used in this programme.

However, this latter approach needs to be included in staff development programmes for modelling best practice (based on recent research and educational theory on adult learning), so that participants may adopt this model in their own teaching and supervision (and shift from a spoonfeeders to a deep-enders approach) and, by doing so, help students shift from a surface to a deep approach to learning.

For future programmes, it would be more beneficial to participants and easier for organizers if the size of the programme were limited to about 50 participants, because it is difficult with over 100 people to address all individual needs in all sessions.

Although there were positive comments on the diverse target group (including experienced and beginning supervisors, as well as supervisors who themselves were enrolled in higher degrees), it would be interesting to work with more homogeneous groups, for example with those academics who have no PhDs but who are expected to attract and supervise postgraduate students.

It is interesting to note that we could not meet the great demand for places at the residential programme. There were many requests, especially from small universities such as the Australian Catholic University and the post-1987 universities, which expressed their urgent need for staff development in postgraduate supervision.

Benefits

Participants commented (on the questionnaire forms and on audio and video tape) that they had benefited personally and professionally from this programme; that they had gained a greater awareness and understanding of their students' problems and of the whole process of research supervision and thesis writing. In addition, participants viewed the opportunities for networking favourably and considered the distributed resources to be useful for future workshops in their own institutions. The following are typical responses.

•   I think probably the most positive aspect of the conference is the fact that we are at last discussing the requirements of good supervision. I think it was vital for me to see the need for improved communication at all levels of the process, both between the supervisor and student, and among supervisors.
•   The conference has given me lots of ideas about the ways in which I can improve my ability to assist students through the supervision that I am able to offer them. It has developed me at a professional level in terms of making contacts with a range of people from various different institutions working within different disciplines and different methodologies and that has challenged me to think about ways that I have practised in the past and to look at some of the alternative ways which I might be able to practise in the future.
•   The conference was impressively organized. I would like a copy of all that has been said.
•   One of the things that I thought would be valuable for people (although they may not have seen it to start with) was the development of an awareness about gender issues.

The DEET funding made it possible to provide:

•   a venue and forum for state-wide inter-institutional collaboration, networking and follow-up activities in the area of postgraduate education

- staff development for a significant number of academic staff, including those without PhDs who were supervising Masters and PhD students
- a coherent, but flexible programme making problem areas explicit and covering most issues in postgraduate supervision which would not have been dealt with otherwise
- the availability of resources and materials to participating and other staff and students in Australia and other countries so that they can access them and better understand the nature, processes and pitfalls of postgraduate studies.

It might be of interest to universities in other states and countries that the first programme cost approximately $70,000 (for 80 participants) and the second $100,000 (for 127 participants), including residential costs, a half-time research assistant, production costs for books and video programmes, and miscellaneous expenses. We believe that the results already justify the cost, and that cost-effectiveness will increase with time as more and more supervisors and students will benefit from the model process and practical outcomes.

Resource materials

There are three categories of resource materials: a book, a manual and a series of video programmes, arising from each of the two programmes. These are as follows.

In 1992:

1   Zuber-Skerritt, O. (ed.) *Starting Research—Supervision and Training*, Tertiary Education Institute, University of Queensland, Brisbane, 1992a. Cost: $10.
2   Zuber-Skerritt, O. (ed.) *Manual for Conducting Workshops on Postgraduate Supervision*, Tertiary Education Institute, University of Queensland, Brisbane, 1992d. Cost: $10.
3   *Postgraduate Research, Supervision and Training* — First series of 12 video programmes, produced by Ortrun Zuber-Skerritt and the TV Unit, University of Queensland, Brisbane, 1992c. Cost: $50 each or $450 for the full series.

In 1993-4:

1   A book entitled *Quality in Postgraduate Education*, edited by Ortrun Zuber-Skerritt and Yoni Ryan (with contributions from workshop leaders and participants — Kogan Page).
2   *Second Manual for Conducting Workshops on Postgraduate Supervision*, edited by Ortrun Zuber-Skerritt, published by the Tertiary Education Institute, University of Queensland, Brisbane (with workshop outlines, OHTs and materials), 1994b.
3   *Postgraduate Research, Supervision and Training* — second series of 7 video programmes, produced by Ortrun Zuber-Skerritt and the TV Unit, University of Queensland, Brisbane, 1994a.

The titles of videos and Manual chapters correspond with the titles of workshops and lectures in the residential programme (see above) and provide a resource package for staff developers and supervisors of postgraduate students.

Conclusions

Participants confirmed that the following intended outcomes of the conferences had been achieved:

1 for the participants: enhanced supervisory skills; a greater awareness of the processes, problems and effective strategies of postgraduate research training; competence to conduct workshops on postgraduate supervision for supervisors and postgraduate research students in their department; and hence the opportunity to become leaders and to be recognized and rewarded as excellent supervisors
2 for the departments: revision and improvement of postgraduate research supervision which may be expected to lead to better quality research and researchers, shorter completion time and lower attrition rates
3 for the universities: enhancing achievement of their goals and objectives and creating an environment for equity, affirmative action and the continuous improvement of high quality learning and teaching, at both the undergraduate and the postgraduate levels.

This idea of 'training the trainers' is considered to be exemplary because of the multiplier effect in the participants' institutions. The idea of a residential programme has also succeeded because of a more concentrated, yet relaxed and creative work atmosphere free of interruptions from other professional or private duties.

It is therefore proposed to design and implement a similar residential staff development programme targeted specifically for up to 50 representatives from all post-1987 university campuses in Queensland in 1995, with a potentially similar multiplier effect and similar outcomes.

References

Ballard, B. and Clanchy, J. (1984). *Study Abroad — A Manual for Asian Students.* London: Longman.
Conrad, L., Perry, C. and Zuber-Skerritt, O. (1992). 'Alternatives to traditional postgraduate supervision in the social sciences', in O. Zuber-Skerritt (ed.), *Starting Research — Supervision and Training.* Brisbane: Tertiary Education Institute, University of Queensland, pp. 137-157.
Economic and Social Research Council (1991). *Postgraduate Training: Guidelines on the Provision of Research Training for Postgraduate Research Students in the Social Sciences.* Swindon: ESRC.

Howard, K. and Sharp, J.A. (1983). *The Management of a Research Project.* Aldershot: Gower.

Knight, N. and Zuber-Skerritt, O. (1986). 'Problems and methods in research: a course for the beginning researcher in the social sciences'. *Higher Education Research and Development* 5: 49-59.

Madsen, D. (1988). *Successful Dissertations and Theses.* San Francisco: Jossey-Bass.

Moses, I. (1981). *Postgraduate Study: Supervisors, Supervision and Information for Students.* Brisbane: Tertiary Education Institute, University of Queensland.

Moses, I. (1984). 'Supervision of higher degrees students — problem areas and possible solutions'. *Higher Education Research and Development* 3: 153-156.

Moses, I. (1985). *Supervising Postgraduates.* HERDSA Green Guide No. 3. Sydney: Higher Education Research and Development Society of Australasia.

Phillips, E. and Pugh, D.S. (1987). *How to Get a PhD.* Buckingham: Open University Press.

Powles, M. (1988). *Know Your PhD Students and How to Help Them.* Melbourne: Centre for the Study of Higher Education, Melbourne University.

Powles, M. (1989a). 'Higher degree completion and completion times'. *Higher Education Research and Development* 8(1): 91-101.

Powles, M. (1989b). *How's the Thesis Going?* Melbourne: Centre for the Study of Higher Education, Melbourne University.

Rudd, E. (1975). *The Highest Education.* London: Routledge and Kegan Paul.

Rudd, E. (1984). 'Research into postgraduate education'. *Higher Education Research and Development* 3: 109-120.

Rudd, E. (1985). *A New Look at Postgraduate Failure.* Guildford: Society for Research into Higher Education.

Science and Engineering Research Council (1989). *Research Student and Supervisor. An Approach to Good Supervisory Practice.* London: SERC.

Zuber-Skerritt, O. (1987). 'Helping postgraduate students learn'. *Higher Education* 16(1): 75-94.

Zuber-Skerritt, O. (ed.) (1992a). *Starting Research — Supervision and Training.* Brisbane: Tertiary Education Institute, The University of Queensland.

Zuber-Skerritt, O. (1992b). *Action Research in Higher Education.* London: Kogan Page.

Zuber-Skerritt, O. (1992c). *Postgraduate Research, Supervision and Training.* A series of 12 video programmes, edited by A. Jardie, F. Howell, K. Hosking and T. Roe. Brisbane: Tertiary Education Institute, The University of Queensland.

Zuber-Skerritt, O. (ed.) (1992d). *Manual for Conducting Workshops on Postgraduate Supervision.* Brisbane: Tertiary Education Institute, The University of Queensland.

Zuber-Skerritt, O. (1994a). *Postgraduate Research, Supervision and Training.* Second series of seven video programmes, edited by F. Howell and G. Rice. Brisbane: Tertiary Education Institute, The University of Queensland.

Zuber-Skerritt, O. (ed.) (1994b). *Second Manual for Conducting Workshops on Postgraduate Supervision.* Brisbane: Tertiary Education Institute, The University of Queensland.

Zuber-Skerritt, O. and Knight, N. (1985). 'Helping students overcome barriers to dissertation writing'. *HERDSA News* **7**(3): 8-10.

Zuber-Skerritt, O. and Knight, N. (1986). 'Problem definition and thesis writing: workshops for the postgraduate student'. *Higher Education* **15**: 89-103.

Zuber-Skerritt, O. and Rix, A. (1986). 'Developing skills in dissertation research and writing for postgraduate coursework programmes'. *Zeitschrift für Hochschuldidaktik* **10**: 363-380.

Chapter 8

The 'Big Picture' about Managing Writing

Robert Brown

Introduction

'A man may write at any time, if he will set himself doggedly to it' (Samuel Johnson, quoted in Boswell's *Journal of a Tour of the Hebrides with Samuel Johnson*). There is a lot of truth in those sentiments, but good writing often requires more than doggedness; it requires a clear sense of **direction**. Unfortunately, when supervising the writing of a student, it is all too easy to get mired in trying to correct clumsy expression and verbosity and to lose sight of the need for direction. When this happens, the process often becomes one of attrition with both student and supervisor staggering across the finishing line, but without the lucid coherent document that both set out to produce.

The reasons that this happens are that most people try to manage writing from the bottom up, rather than the top down and that they fail to appreciate the emotional factors in writing and how fear can influence writing style.

This chapter sets out a top-down structure for writing and reviewing both individual chapters and whole theses which helps keep everyone focused on the overall direction. The structure is based on understanding that writing is an exercise in marketing. Thus clear writing comes from having a clear understanding of the benefit that a reader can expect to gain from reading a document. This means that a skilful writer crafts each document so that a reader cannot fail to see the benefit of reading it. The role of the academic supervisor becomes one of guiding the student to a distillation of whatever the benefit to the reader might be. The supervisor needs to manage for clarity and manage time, but often also needs to manage fear, because fear is often the root cause of missed deadlines and turgid writing styles.

Writing requires deliberate management

Paradoxically, writing is such an obvious and integral part of postgraduate study that we sometimes take it for granted and so fail to manage it as deliberately as we would manage, say, the data collection. That is unfortunate. Higher degrees are about thoughts, original thoughts, and as John Stuart Mill (1875) (cited by Barrass, 1978: 11) said:

> Hardly any original thoughts on mental or social subjects ever make their way among mankind, or assume their proper importance in the minds of their

inventors, until aptly selected words or phrases have, as it were, nailed them down and held them fast.

Getting those aptly selected words takes management and a lot of that management will fall to you as an academic supervisor. That is why this chapter is about **managing writing**.

I work in a state department of agriculture and manage the publication of research. I also lecture in research methods at two universities and I find that the three institutions have a lot in common: they are part of the information industry. That means that we grow, package and market information by doing original research and by publishing the results in dissertations and scholarly journals. Accordingly, the perspective I have adopted in writing this chapter is as one manager to another. I have not relied a lot on the published literature because management is much more an art than a science. I offer you a practitioner's perspective of things that I find help researchers get coherent thoughts onto the page and, as far as I can, some explanation of why I think these things work.

The essence of management = the essence of teaching

You will find that I seem to have a fondness for things that come in threes. I don't know why this should be so, but here is the first of them: 'Treating workers well — providing useful feedback, social support, and the room for self-determination — is the essence of good management' (Kohn, 1993: 60). This is as true for someone making widgets as it is for a scholar trying to produce a manuscript, but it may be a blindspot for universities. This came out clearly in a continuing survey of the reputational ratings of doctoral programmes:

> All the relationships discussed so far, however, confirm the popular notion that departments with high peer ratings are ones which value and reward research rather than teaching. Other doctoral programme characteristics are not closely related to peer ratings. For example, peer ratings appear to be unaffected by graduate student completion rates, student perceptions of the quality of teaching or degree of faculty concern for students, or the degree of departmental effort toward the career development of junior members of the faculty .... (Hartnett et al., 1978: 1313)

The authors went on to say that these results were highly stable over the 11-year period of the survey. Kohn's management trifecta of feedback, support and self-determination also seems to go to the very heart of what makes a good teacher, so it is worrying that quality of teaching seems to be a non-starter when it comes to evaluating whether a university's doctoral programme is a good one or not.

Hartnett et al.'s data are American and perhaps things are different elsewhere in the world, perhaps not. There is a blindspot in most professions: professionals often treat what they do as an entirely intellectual process and try to ignore the emotional component. To the extent that they acknowledge the emotional, it is usually perceived as something that people should not allow to happen. Of course, things might be a whole lot easier if emotions did not exist, but the fact is that they do and arguing that people should act as if they did not is about as rational as arguing with the rain. However, denying the validity of emotions opens the way to overlooking the need for social support and, to an extent, the need for self-determination. It becomes easy to assume that students just need to be directed in what to do without fully realizing that they also need to be free to make mistakes, to learn from those mistakes, and to be supported in that process. Moreover, if a commitment to support and self-determination is not in place, the feedback that is given can be compromised because it may be put in inappropriate forms and at inappropriate times.

Accordingly, in this chapter, I set out mainly to demonstrate an intellectual framework about how a document should be structured that will allow you to give better feedback but I also want to give you some insights into the fears that writers often have. It is important to understand and manage those fears because, as you will see, they can be the underlying cause of some of the faults that make documents unreadable.

A model for failure?

When I did my doctorate, I thought that the PhD was an institution that had been around for a long time, so it came as a surprise years later to find that I was mistaken. According to Nicholson (1993), it began in Germany in the early nineteenth century and was awarded for reasons that were not always well specified. For example, the famous German chemist, Justus Liebig, actually bought his PhD! The PhD came to England soon after the First World War. It was one of the changes to British scientific training and research that followed from the realization that the War had been so hard to win partly because of the superior education that the Germans gave their scientists and engineers. Hence the PhD is only a few generations old and its very newness probably explains the divergence in opinions about how it should be done, what constitutes an acceptable dissertation, and so on. It is important to understand that the ambiguity that results from this divergence of opinions is itself a problem and makes it more difficult to manage the writing.

So, rather than ask the question, 'How can we make sure that people write good theses?', let us turn the question around and ask, 'How can we make sure that people write poor theses?'. In that case, probably all we would have to do would be to ensure that students had (a) poor examples to follow; (b) conflicting advice; and (c) a poor understanding of the real purpose of writing a dissertation. This would make them confused, the confusion would create anxiety, the anxiety would reduce creativity, and, given that creativity is what research is all about (Bostian, 1986), any thesis that managed to emerge would probably be a miserable specimen.

The bad news is that that is pretty much the system we have now. When I wrote my doctoral dissertation, I learned how to do it by osmosis — I read and modelled on the theses of those a year or two ahead of me. It was a case of the blind leading the blind. That was in the 1970s, but nothing much seems to have changed since then (Rees, 1993).

So how did we get stuck with a system like this? I think it comes from a pair of common assumptions about writing and from losing sight of the purpose of writing.

The two assumptions are that (a) because postgraduate students are educated people, they know (or should know) how to write, and that (b) good writing is just a matter of making good sentences. These assumptions are rarely stated explicitly and that makes them all the more insidious because they are not out in the open where they could be challenged. Nevertheless, they help explain why books and training courses in writing tend to be 'back to school' exercises: heavy on grammar, jargon, spelling, punctuation, clear expression and how to get a pleasing layout on a page, but light on anything but the most general advice about how to get the thoughts onto the page in the first place. In essence, most of the advice that you will find is only 'small picture' advice about the trivia of writing (what is the point in having perfect punctuation and spelling in a sentence that adds nothing to the argument?) or else too general to be of any real use (for instance, it is hard to argue with advice like 'be concise', but does saying 'be concise' actually tell anyone how to do it?). I think we need to look more carefully at what we need to do to communicate well, and that is why this chapter is about the 'big picture' in writing.

Moreover, it is so easy to lose sight of the real purpose of writing a dissertation. This came home to me during an exchange at a recent workshop when someone asked, 'What's the purpose of a thesis anyhow?' and someone else instinctively shot back, 'To get the degree!' What worried me was that nobody in the room dissented. On the surface, the reply was correct but, deeper down, it missed the point. The same issue arises when people ask, 'Why publish' and the answer comes back, 'To gain tenure/ promotion'. Higher degrees, tenure, and promotion are by-products of the primary purpose of scholarly writing. That primary purpose is to crystallize original ideas and to nail them down in a form that others can understand and appreciate. In short, it is to transfer ideas from one mind to another. Getting the degree flows from this and is a by-product of the process, not the end-point. Losing sight of this just makes the degree harder to gain.

Creating clarity

The three axioms about having something worth writing

At this point, it is useful to understand that there are three axioms that guide the writing of any readable document.

First, writing comes much easier when you have something to say.

Second (a corollary of the first), what appears to be a sloppy or meaningless use of words may well be a completely correct use of words to express sloppy or meaningless thoughts.

Third, people don't buy products, they buy benefits.

Those three axioms all point to the one thing: clarity. All documents rise or fall on their clarity and that is the one thing you must manage above all. But to get clarity you must also manage time and fear. These three are integral to understanding the 'big picture': clarity is everything, but fear is the enemy of clarity, and time (or more precisely the wasting of time) is the tool of fear.

Bottom up or top down? Grammar focus or marketing focus?

It is no secret that most theses are hard to read, so let us look at what people do when a draft or chapter hits their desk.

There is a hierarchy of tasks that an author has to master to create a truly readable document and they are shown in Figure 1. At the bottom of the hierarchy are the least complex tasks for which rules are well established and which are easy to cover in books and training courses. Tasks higher in the pyramid are increasingly complex and increasingly ambiguous. Accordingly, they are increasingly difficult to teach and mastering them requires increasing amounts of judgement and insight the closer one gets to the top of the hierarchy. However, the almost universal response when commenting on a draft is to work at the lower levels to suggest changes that might be made. It is hard to argue against doing this, especially as some improvement seems to result, but working from the bottom up (by trying to correct the individual words and phrases) doesn't always get to the top. Even when all the typos and poor grammar have been corrected, there is still no guarantee of producing a coherent document and most remain capable of substantial improvement.

I prefer a top-down approach. It is less tangible but also gets more dramatic results. The top-down approach comes from getting your writer to understand that every document is a marketing exercise and the number one rule in marketing is that people don't buy products, they buy benefits. (They listen to W2I FM ['What's In It For Me?']). That means that there has to be a benefit for the reader. Readers do not read for the sheer privilege of being able to do so. Even a captive audience (like the two or three examiners of a dissertation) needs to be persuaded to the candidate's point of view and that means that candidates have to market their work. (For an excellent explanation of the essence of marketing, free of quantitative smokescreens and academic bulldust, read Ries and Trout, 1986).

This means that, sitting astride the document, there has to be a clear vision of the benefit that a reader will gain from reading it. That benefit dominates and shapes the document and is reflected in every section of it because the only reason for including a sentence becomes whether or not that sentence will add directly to the reader's appreciation of the benefit. Importantly, I find that when writers do this, a lot of their problems with clumsy sentences evaporate because they have a much clearer understanding of what they need to say.

The notion of marketing is strong medicine for some because they feel that marketing is unscholarly and that the truth will speak for itself. At best, that view is naive; at worst, it is arrogant. It also shows one of the blindspots that arise from the expert power of the scholar. Most scholars operate in their own niche of expertise without direct competition (if the competition is too direct, it becomes hard to sustain claims of originality). That makes scholars monopoly suppliers within their own niche. Unfortunately, monopolies have a long history of failing to keep sight of the needs of their customers and it is easy to unwittingly fall into the same trap. This happens by failing to realize that information needs to be pitched in ways that make

Figure 1: The hierarchy of tasks that both students and supervisors need to master

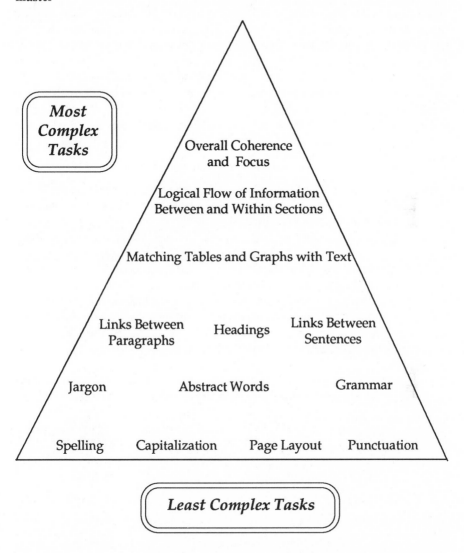

it easy for readers to understand. It is easy to think (often unconsciously, but sometimes you will hear it said aloud) 'if readers are really interested, they will wade through it and work it out' but the proportion of readers who will do this is far smaller than many people would like to believe. Once we tell ourselves that all we need to do is to present all the information we have and to leave it to the reader to do the rest, we start sliding down the slope that leads to impenetrable prose. This comes as a shock to some but facts do not cease to exist just because they are ignored. Thus your first task as a manager is to get students to understand that a thesis (or journal paper or any other document) is an exercise in marketing.

How to nail down the 'benefit'

Unfortunately, it is much easier to talk about benefits in general than it is to nail one down. By their very nature, benefits are intangible and that makes them elusive. (You can prove this to yourself if you like. Ask yourself what it is that Kodak markets. If you answered 'film', join the 99 per cent of the population who also answered incorrectly. If you answered 'memories', congratulate yourself on your insight because the difference between the two answers makes a huge difference to Kodak's profitability.) Nevertheless, elusive as benefits might be to define, there is a recipe you can use with your students to help them distil the benefit they need to market.

The recipe

First, get your student to list three to five scholars who might wish to read the thesis, then make sure that the names of these anticipated readers are placed prominently at the start of all drafts (except the submitted one). The names may change over time, but they must be there and in front of the writer at all times. Marketing is always done to flesh-and-blood people and the examiners will be flesh-and-blood people (perhaps not always warm-blooded, but that is another issue). Accordingly, the document written with real people in mind which takes account of the fact that different people know different things, will always outclass a document pitched at a faceless, nebulous 'them'. As far as possible, the assumed readers should be chosen to represent the full range of potential readers and not just cluster at one point of the spectrum. Fewer than three intended readers narrows the focus too much and more than five creates a mental overload.

The second thing to do is to get your student to write answers to the questions in Table 1 and to do it both separately for each chapter and for the document as a whole.

Table 1: Seven questions that provide a framework for writing the first draft

Question	Word limit
(1) What did you do?	50 words
(2) Why did you do it?	50 words
(3) What happened?	50 words
(4) What do the results mean in theory?	50 words
(5) What do the results mean in practice?	50 words
(6) What is the key benefit for the readers?	25 words
(7) What remains unresolved?	no limit

It does not matter if the answers are written before or after the text is written, because (as you will read below) they are part of an iterative process. The key thing is to ensure that the answers are written as an integral part of each draft.

The word limits are important and I suggest that you keep a tight rein on them, because they provide a discipline missing in the main text. They force the writer to state the essence of what has to be said, whereas the main text allows writers to orbit in a fog. They also provide an anchor for you when critiquing the draft.

When texts wander all over the place and leave the reader unsure of the destination, the changes that need to be made are often subtle and can be made only by the writer (it is usually impossible to edit in what a writer has not thought). That is why the answers to the questions are so valuable: they provide an explicit framework for a writer to compare what was actually written with what the writer **thought** was written. However, the gap between the two is not always apparent to the writer and that is where you come in. As supervisor, your role is to look for mismatches between the text and the answers to the seven questions and to feed those mismatches back to your student for them to be reconciled. Neither the answers nor the text should be taken as being set in concrete; they are both parts of a working document that cannot be considered to be finished as long as inconsistencies can be found between the two. As a corollary, the final draft is the one where the two of you agree that the answers to the questions are the best ones you can find and that they are faithfully reflected in the text.

That is how it is supposed to work in theory, but there are at least three places where you may strike difficulties. The first lies in applying the questions to some sections such as literature reviews. The key here is to get students to understand that they can treat published literature like any other data, the only difference being that it is not data they generated themselves. The second is that some students will give what is essentially the same answer for two different questions. That is a good indicator of muddled thinking, so act accordingly. The third difficulty is that some argue that they can answer about what their work means in theory but not in practice or vice versa. This is an indication that the writer has too narrow a perspective on the work.

The first five questions and the working abstract

If you have guessed that the answers to those first five questions add up to a working abstract, you are right. It is useful to get students to prepare abstracts for each chapter, and they can do it by building directly on the five answers. That also provides another check for the process: if you cannot see each answer clearly reflected in the working abstract, it signals that there is a gap in the student's perception of the work that needs to be filled. (It is often useful to mark on the abstract your own perception of which parts answer which questions as part of your feedback to your student.)

At the risk of labouring the point, ensure that you always look for explicit statements that answer those five questions. The great danger for both supervisor and student lies in being able to read between the lines and to assume (wrongly) that others will be able do likewise. This is more common than you might think. Salager-Meyer (1991) sampled abstracts in the published medical literature and found that over half met only one or two of four basic criteria (similar to the first five questions above) for adequate communication. In this regard, I doubt that the medical literature is either much better or much worse than any other.

Relationships between the first five questions

There is a relationship (Figure 2) between these first five questions that ties them together and brings us back to the concept of marketing. 'What was done' and 'what happened' are models of things that exist only in the writer's reality. As such, those things are of limited interest to a reader because the reader was not present when the events happened. On the other hand, researchers often get preoccupied with them (as Salager-Meyer (1991) showed), simply because they were there when the events under consideration happened and so those events are part of their lives. For readers to benefit from the answers to 'what was done' and 'what happened', they have to extrapolate to their own reality to see how they might use the information with their own problems. This leaving the reader to find the benefit unaided is a hit-and-miss approach that misses more often than it hits, and that is why it is important to attend to the other three questions.

'Why it was done', 'what it means in theory', and 'what it is good for in practice' provide the planks that bridge the author's reality and the reader's reality and that is why it is essential that they be answered explicitly and not left to the reader to infer. If that bridge to the reader is not built, then it is unlikely that a reader will see the full benefit of what the author has to say, and the author will have failed.

The last two questions

The question about the key benefit is the central one (Brown et al. 1993, 1994), but it is also the most slippery one and the one most likely to evolve with the document. This evolutionary aspect is part of the reason for keeping an explicit statement of the key benefit in front of both student and supervisor.

The question about what remains unresolved has no word limit. Whereas the other six questions are about what the student knows, the last one is about what the student doesn't know, and, of course, the biggest learning comes from exploring what we don't know rather than from parading what we do know. Used wisely, the answers to this question become the anvil on which students can shape their text and which will also help pinpoint the gaps in the answers to the first five questions. Expect students to understand this in their heads but not in their hearts, because our education system is largely punitive and it can be threatening to expose what remains unknown or unclear. Your best strategy is to decline to accept an incomplete answer, but do so with gentleness and subtlety.

A whodunnit or a journalist's pyramid?

Scholarship has its origins in letters and some journals still have letters as their mainstay. The scholarly paper is a highly stylized and expanded letter and the dissertation is an expanded and stylized paper with extra 'bells and whistles'. There is a logical progression, but it is a pity that someone did not manage to call 'halt' before things got as far as they did.

The reason I say this is that the letter is a perfectly sensible format by itself, but it becomes progressively less sensible the longer it gets. By the time it gets to thesis length, it is in serious danger of collapsing under its own weight. This is because a letter is basically a whodunnit. It follows a suspense format in that it starts off with what was done and why it was done, then moves to what happened, and ends with what the writer thinks it means. That is a good strategy to despatch small parcels of information, but it is like juggling: the more items there are to juggle, the harder it becomes.

Students seem to be hard-wired with the suspense format. This is probably because it is embedded in what they learn at school and expanded in undergraduate courses, so that by the time they become postgraduates it has become second nature.

The 'facts' may mean a lot to a writer, but they mean little to a reader until they are focused into the reader's reality by passing them through the lenses of why the work was done and what the results mean in both theory and practice. Only then does an author project the benefit to be gained from the work into the reader's reality.

Figure 2: Communication comes from overlapping realities

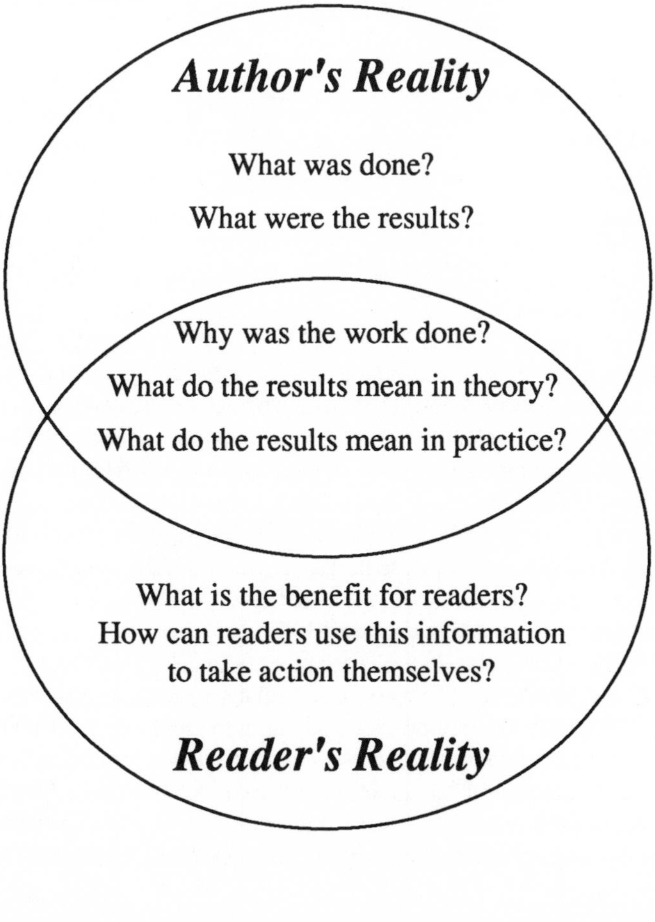

Author's Reality

What was done?

What were the results?

Why was the work done?
What do the results mean in theory?
What do the results mean in practice?

What is the benefit for readers?
How can readers use this information
to take action themselves?

Reader's Reality

The suspense format starts at Genesis and ends at Revelations (so it is also known as the Biblical format). It makes the reader labour up the incline to reach the punchline (and hence most readers routinely skip to the end). In contrast, the journalist's pyramid comes straight to the point by telling the reader the most important point and layering the other information underneath it in descending order of importance. Skilful scholarly writing folds the journalist's pyramid into the traditional IMRAD structure (Introduction, Materials and Methods, Results, and Discussion).

Figure 3: The suspense format and the journalist's pyramid

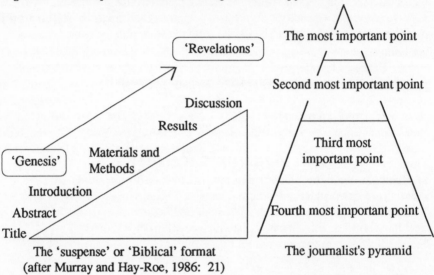

The 'suspense' or 'Biblical' format   The journalist's pyramid
(after Murray and Hay-Roe, 1986: 21)

As a supervisor, you will do everyone a favour if you learn to say 'stop' and the way to do that is to get your students to focus on their key benefit and to craft documents around it. Unless you do this, your students will keep right on writing to build up to that knockout punch at the end where all is revealed for the world to marvel at — except that practically everybody falls asleep before they get to the end.

Writing is not like boxing. Victory does not go to the player who delivers a triple whammy at the end; it goes to the player who carefully telegraphs every punch so that the reader knows exactly what to expect and when to expect it. Many examiners' criticisms would not be made if the candidates took more care to ensure that the examiner knew exactly why each piece of evidence was being introduced at the point it was introduced. (This is as true within a sentence as it is within a chapter. Gopen and Swan (1990) provide useful advice at the sentence level.) Without clear signals about the context in which each piece of evidence is to be interpreted, some pieces get overlooked and others are misinterpreted, sometimes with unfortunate consequences for the candidate. I learned this one back in the Dreamtime, when one of my examiners recommended that a chapter in my doctoral dissertation be substantially redrafted. I was reluctant to do this because it was already bound, so I re-read the chapter very, very carefully. Eventually, I found where the examiner had gone wrong and it was my fault. At a critical point, I had failed to provide the signpost that would have said 'fork in the road'. The examiner, quite understandably, had not realized that there was a fork in the road had taken the low road instead of the high road and, by reasonable means, came to an unreasonable conclusion. Since then, I have lost count of the writers who have made the same sort of error.

The thing that telegraphs the punches and says where to put the roadsigns are those key benefits that your student identified for each chapter and for the thesis as a whole. Once they are there, reviewing the text that follows is largely a matter of ensuring that every part of the text stands clearly to support the relevant benefit. At a minimum, you should be able to find the key benefit reflected clearly in the title, abstract, introduction, and discussion (both with individual chapters and with the dissertation as a whole).

This is where the journalist's pyramid comes in: Murray and Hay-Roe (1986) and Blicq (1987) provide comprehensive descriptions of the journalist's pyramid and its uses. Journalists write stories as layer cakes. They put the most important point at the top, the next most important point underneath it, the third most important point under that, and so on. The journalist's motivation comes from knowing that putting the main point at the end (as so many scholars seem to think they have to do) means that it will rarely get read, either because the sub-editor cuts it off to make it fit the available space or because the reader gets bored and never reaches the end (with scholarly works, most readers flip to the end to get the punchline, but I think that just tells us how much we have grown accustomed to accepting an inferior model of communicating). I find that intellectual snobs have difficulty in accepting the value of the journalist's pyramid, but that is their problem. Conversely, good writers nearly always use it, but their use is often instinctive and so may not be apparent to others.

If you can review a chapter and find that the title gives you a clear understanding of the key benefit to be found in that chapter, that the abstract gives you a clearer understanding of it, that the introduction also refers to the key benefit and that the discussion elaborates on it (probably several times, but each time from a different perspective), then your student will have successfully planted a journalist's pyramid within the chapter. The process needs to be repeated for the whole document, but if it is done well at the level of individual chapters, bridging any gaps between chapters will often be largely only a matter of adding strategic sentences or paragraphs.

Saying that the key benefit should appear in several places also reminds me of another myth that seems to be common among researchers, namely, that it is unscholarly to repeat oneself. Intellectual snobs are big on this one too and it defies reality. I have yet to meet the person who understood and remembered everything they were told the first time they were told it. Given that those same people are going to be the audience, the only logical strategy seems to be to repeat things wherever an author thinks that a reader may need to be reminded, especially as not doing so leaves a reader free to go down an unseen fork in the argument.

On developing a readable style

Books about how to improve one's writing style are probably almost as common as books about cooking and there is no shortage of published articles that complain of turgid style by researchers (for example Dixon, 1993;   Doniger, 1992; Fey, 1978; Fielden, 1964; Gopen and Swan, 1990; Mack, 1992; Maddox, 1983; Mitchell, 1993; and Rees, 1993 to mention just a few). If they made much difference, I wonder why we have so many of them? Moreover, they also tend to obscure the fact that it is easy to get tangled up in arguing the minutae of style — at which point writing becomes a lot like trench warfare (and about as productive).

It certainly will not fix everything, but if I can do only one thing to help someone improve their writing style, I get them to read their words aloud. This is a more holistic approach than the traditional grammarian approach, but it fixes a lot of problems in one pass.

Moreover, I cannot emphasize 'read aloud' too much. Lots of people think that reading to themselves does the same job, but it doesn't. The eye is far more forgiving than the ear and glosses over pompous complexity and ambiguity. On the other hand, with the words coming out of the mouth, writers soon start to understand whether what they have written sounds natural or not. If you have trouble in convincing someone to do this, try reminding them that the written word is merely a substitute for the spoken word and that writing is just a way of ensuring that there is an agreed version of what was said and is not an end in itself.

As a corollary of this, if your student gives you a draft and you find you can hear that student speaking to you inside your head (you will hear the voice almost as you would hear it in conversation), you can be assured that the style is good.

Managing time

Do not let your student 'write up'

Writing is not something to be done when the research is finished: it is an integral part of the research itself. Leaving the writing until the end nearly always means that the job is rushed and that is not the way to develop the insights needed to build a good dissertation. 'No great thing is created suddenly, any more than a bunch of grapes or a fig. If you tell me you desire a fig, I answer you that there must be time. Let it first blossom, then bear fruit, then ripen' (Epictetus, *Discourses*, cited by Walen et al., 1980: 22).

'Writing up' is an insidious term. It implies that writing is something separate from the research and that it is appropriate to do it at the end. In reality, writing is an integral part of sorting out thoughts and we always teach ourselves as we write. 'The toil of writing and reconsideration may help to clear and fix many things that remain a little uncertain in my thoughts because they have never been fully stated, and I want to discover any lurking inconsistencies and gaps' (H.G. Wells, 1913, cited by Barrass, 1978: 11). Failing to find those inconsistencies and gaps until the end (when it is too late to do much about them) is a good way to do second-rate research.

Both of you must keep deadlines

Manage the writing as a project. Set a submission date and then work backwards with your student to identify the steps that need to be done from reading the literature through to the time needed to get the volume bound, and the time each is likely to require. The more detailed the analysis the better, because people often oversimplify the task and so underestimate the time required, with the usual outcome being either a rushed and poorly written effort or missed submission dates or both. Make a flow-chart of what needs to be done and by when, and extract the relevant deadlines for each step.

The next task is to keep to the deadlines and that is where supervisors fail as much as students. By temperament, I am inclined to be flexible about most things but I have learned that flexibility is inappropriate with writing deadlines. When I work with a writer and we agree a deadline, that deadline becomes inviolate. The secret is to understand that the matter cuts two ways — your time is involved as much as your writer's and that gives you both rights and responsibilities. You have a right to expect to be given what the two of you have agreed on (i.e. a draft document or part of a draft document on a given date), but you also have a responsibility to deliver your part of the bargain as well (usually detailed and considered feedback on the document by an agreed date).

I often find that, where deadlines are not being met, both parties have contributed to the problem: the student who is having trouble getting the writing done is often paired with a supervisor who has trouble in finding the time to read and fully digest what is written. Some supervisors take the line that their students are responsible adults and that it is not their job to chase up a student who is running behind schedule. That is true, but it can also be a cop-out.

Managing fear

Writing is a mix of emotion and intellect

Writing my own doctoral dissertation was a lot like banging my head against a brick wall — it felt so good when I stopped! Others have expressed similar sentiments and I think they reflect the emotional energy that goes into preparing a dissertation. Unfortunately, it is something that we easily lose sight of because the research itself is a highly intellectual affair. Nevertheless, losing sight of the fact that writing is an emotional experience for many (most? all?) writers is one of the more serious errors to be made when supervising writing.

Why should writing be threatening?

Lack of motivation ranks high on the list of hazards researchers face when they try to write (Penaskovic, 1985). There are at least two levels of threat that we need to consider. The more superficial level is the one where your student will be worrying about whether the work itself is good enough and whether there is enough of it to get the degree. On a deeper level is what a friend and colleague calls 'intellectual streaking'. This is the feeling of vulnerability that most of us feel when our ideas are exposed to the rest of the world for judgement. This is all the more insidious because it arises when we equate the value of what we do with our self-worth. The extension of this is that things that threaten the value of what we do also threaten our self-esteem, and the usual reaction is one of defensiveness. This becomes sand in the gears of scholarship, because defensiveness obscures rather than reveals the truth.

Unreadability comes from distorted reality

It is tempting to assume that people write clumsily because they are ignorant of the rules of grammar, punctuation and allied topics, and most writing courses have this as one of their core assumptions. However, it is a red herring. Postgraduate students are demonstrably not illiterate. The reasons they write poorly have more to do with psychology than with their understanding of the language.

Words reflect a writer's reality, so if you want to know why a writer uses distorted words, look for distortions in the writer's reality.

I can think of at least three types of writers who have problems with readability: 'Slippery Sam', 'Masked Marauder', and 'Intellectual Snob'. Slippery Sams write turgid text because they don't want readers to understand. Either they know that there is a flaw in their arguments or (more usually) they fear that there may be a flaw and do not want to risk discovery.

Masked Marauders think that they have to write in a particular style to be acceptable. Unfortunately, that style is nearly always the clumsy, turgid one that dominates most theses and most of the published literature. They hide themselves behind a mask of 'professional objectivity' and do regrettable things to their text as a consequence.

> ['Intellectual Snobs'] want to believe that they are so unusually learned and/or intelligent that only a small elite could possibly be capable of appreciating their writings. They seem to believe that the average IQ of their readers is a ground-zero sum, a sum reached by dividing some constant by the total number of all the readers, the individual IQ falling in direct proportion to the number of readers. (Doniger, 1992: 5)

All three types have made the error of linking their deeds with their own self-worth. This is socially acceptable and is even encouraged by most parents and schools, but it is disastrous. All three types are driven by personal insecurities and you may or may not be able to help such students, either because their resistances may be too strong or because most (all?) of us share the same insecurities and differ only in degree. Nevertheless, understanding the problem is the first step to finding a solution. In this context, it means understanding that writing is only partly an intellectual activity and that there is an emotional dimension that cannot be overlooked.

Of the three, Masked Marauders are the easiest to deal with. They write the way they do because of what they read. As Perry (1993) pointed out, there is more guidance available to postgraduates about setting margins than there is about how to decide the content of a thesis. Faced with this problem, the logical solution for a student is to copy a successful example. This usually comes down to 'let's see what old Dave did', which means reproducing the mediocre thesis of your 26-year-old postgraduate who submitted last year (Rees, 1993).

This is a cycle that will repeat itself unless you intervene. Intervention means helping students develop an understanding of what is good and what is bad in both theses and published literature. This is not something that universities do well. For example, I recently gave a group of researchers a short paper to criticize. All but one of them decided that the paper was so badly written that it was not fit to be published (Brown, 1992). Much of their reasoning was based on the fact that is was short, written in simple direct language, and did not strictly follow the format they expected. Because of these preconceptions, they could not see that the paper was well written and they were surprised when I told them that it had been cited over 600 times. (I subsequently repeated the experiment five times with different groups, each time with similar results.) Most of these researchers had higher degrees and, if anything, were a bit more experienced than the average postgraduate. I think this shows a hole in our approach to education: we focus on the content of documents and take for granted the process of how the arguments are made. Unfortunately, this ignorance of process eventually feeds back into creating clumsier content. As a supervisor, you can help students to write better by making a deliberate effort to help them understand what is well written and what is not so well written amongst what they read. By doing this, they may become more discriminating in the styles they choose to copy.

Encourage the use of the first person

One of the most destructive myths in scholarly writing is that it is unacceptable to write in the first person.

> If an author insists on using the passive voice for fear that he might otherwise occasionally be forced to use a first-person pronoun, ... he will deaden what he has to say .... 'Evidential support for this hypothesis has been provided by ...' is more and not less pompous than 'I have found support'. (Maddox, 1983: 478)

'Regardless of what anybody else tells you, it's okay to use first person in the scientific literature' (Cassel, 1993: iv). (Keith Cassel and John Maddox are both editors of prominent journals.) Watson and Crick (1953: 737) took a Nobel Prize with a paper that began 'We wish to suggest a structure for the salt of deoxyribose nucleic acid ...' and there are plenty of similar examples. Maddox is 100 per cent right: the dullest writing comes from those most reluctant to use the first person.

So why are so many scholars unwilling to use the first person? The answer is simple: fear! Writing in the third person creates an intriguing double-think. Because words like 'I' or 'we' are not used, it creates an impression that the words are written by some unseen observer who is at arm's length and therefore objective, rather than somebody close by who is presumably subjective. Of course, that is bunk, but we human beings are adept at cognitive distortion (that is psychojargon for 'kidding ourselves', but I thought I ought to put it in so that you could be confident that I knew what I was talking about!). Unfortunately, the bunk often goes even further. It extends along the lines of thinking that if the words are written by a third party and there happens to be an error in them, the error must be the responsibility of that third party and not the author. This then allows the author to say dopey things but not have to take responsibility for them — I know that doesn't make sense, but it is often how people think. Given that we live in a society that conditions us to treat errors as things that diminish our own intrinsic worth, this can be a neat way of side-stepping threats to self-esteem (it doesn't really work, but it is enough if people just **think** that it works). So if you have a student who insists on preparing a thesis entirely in the third person even after you have explained that it is acceptable to use the first person occasionally, take that as a clear signal that you have a student who is scared to accept responsibility for his or her words. Treat it seriously because good scholarship cannot be divorced from personal responsibility and poor scholarship is a luxury that none of us can afford.

Other things to manage

How do I know what I think until I see what I have written?

People are often reluctant to write because they have only part of the story and they feel they should wait until things are clearer and they can give a fuller account. This is nearly always a cover for insecurity and causes opportunities to be lost. It is neither necessary nor desirable to wait for total clarity before starting to write (note that I am talking about clarity at the start, not clarity at the end). The most clear-cut example of this was given to me by Gordon Wills, a Marketing Professor, when he remarked:

> Writing is my think therapy. I can't beat it. Every time I am really confused, I go away and write an article about it. ... I got into the habit when I first left university and went to work in market research at ICI and didn't understand a thing I was doing. So I spent the first year and a half making notes and writing down what I thought I was trying to do. I sent it off to Robert Maxwell as a book and he published the bloody thing! It was called *Marketing Through Research*, was published in seven languages and is the best selling book I ever wrote — and it all came out of my trying to find out what I was trying to do!

There is a lesson there for all of us. We so easily concentrate on what we know that we lose sight of how the real learning comes from confronting what we **don't** know. Had Gordon waited until things were clearer, he would never have written his best book. He knew instinctively what experienced writers eventually discover and what inexperienced writers often find hard to accept: that documents take shape as they are written. Only rarely does an author pour a document fully formed from some mental mould. Far more often, the very process of putting words on the screen or onto paper calls forth other words and thoughts which weren't there at the start but which give substance to the document.

Your students may have to accept this on faith and some will be reluctant to do so. In that case, push them to write and keep doing it until they discover that it works. You may even get more than you bargained for. In a retrospective analysis of the work of 56 researchers, Daft et al. (1987) found that the more significant work was associated with less clarity and more uncertainty at the start whereas the opposite was true for the not-so-significant research. So lack of clarity at the start may actually be an asset!

A thesis from published papers?

Doctoral candidates are essentially apprentice researchers. If they show that they can make an original contribution to knowledge, they pass the test and are deemed to know enough about the discipline to teach it (remember that doctor also means teacher). There is a parallel here with journals. The main test editors apply in deciding whether or not to publish a paper is its contribution to knowledge. On that basis, it should be possible to collate some published papers with appropriate review text to support it, call it a thesis, and have it accepted. The bad news is that things don't seem to work that way (Halstead, 1988), except in Sweden and Japan (Breimer and Mikhailidis, 1991), and I think that tells us something about the neuroses that have developed in higher education.

The collated paper approach has a lot to recommend it, not least being the fact that formal publication is likely to create far greater clarity than most people achieve in a thesis. The sticking point seems to be the presumed burden of proof, with examiners wanting a greater level of proof than journal referees (Halstead, 1988), even though the same people do both jobs at different times. Perversely, this greater burden of proof for a dissertation seems to express itself in a more verbose document that probably obscures more than it clarifies and so becomes self-defeating.

This is not the place to debate whether the burden of proof for higher degrees has been set correctly or otherwise, except to point out that it does limit the options you have with students. Most students want to publish their work and your job extends to helping them do this. In a perfect world, the student would read widely and critically, do the research, publish it, prepare a dissertation, and do it in that order. In the real world, time is the problem. All up, six months from first scribblings to acceptance letter is a pretty good time and it can often take longer, not least because some journals take four or five months just for the initial review. Seen in that context, it becomes a big slice of the three or four years allowed for a doctorate. Nevertheless, it is possible to publish before submitting the dissertation. At the Royal Free Hospital School of Medicine in London around 35 per cent of theses contained published papers (Breimer and Mikhailidis, 1991).

Thesis to papers — the impossible dream?

Practically all postgraduates proclaim that they are writing their dissertation so that certain chapters can go on to be published as journal papers with minimal change. I am sometimes tempted to ask if they also believe in the tooth fairy, because I have yet to see that approach work well. In my experience, the papers that do eventuate are unfailingly waffly and turgid and scream 'thesis' before a reader gets past the first two pages. Even if they get published (and some do), they usually get ignored because they are so poorly written.

Keep copies, always

Once the words are on the page, the last thing to manage is their physical survival. Copies are insurance policies. Strictly speaking, keeping copies of all parts of a thesis in preparation (preferably in different places) is your student's responsibility, but your time goes into the project so you have an interest in the insurance policy and are entitled to insist that spare copies are made routinely. Nobody ever plans to lose a copy, but it happens just the same. Rrecently, I read of a Californian music student who sent his thesis and performance tape to his supervisor through his university's internal mail system only to have it exploded by police when mail-room staff thought it might be a bomb. A good manager ensures that duplicate copies make the loss an inconvenience rather than a catastrophe.

And so we reach the end

The bottom line is that getting it on paper is 90 per cent of the battle. Writing is not a colour-by-numbers process, it is a creative one. If you can help your students to see the 'big picture' in their writing and to understand and manage the fear that so often blocks or clouds writing, you will unlock their creativity and take them a long way down that first 90 per cent. After that, helping them to iterate between their text and their answers to the key questions discussed in this chapter will help them to find and fix the lurking gaps and inconsistencies that make mediocre dissertations, and, in so doing, will help take care of much of the remaining 10 per cent of the battle.

Acknowledgements

This chapter owes a lot to the many conversations that I have had in recent years with my two invaluable colleagues, John Rogers and Tony Pressland.

References

Barrass, R. (1978). *Scientists Must Write: A Guide to Better Writing for Scientists, Engineers and Students*. London: Chapman and Hall.
Blicq, R.S. (1987). *Writing Reports to Get Results: Guidelines for the Computer Age*. New York: IEEE Press.
Bostian, L.R. (1986) 'Working with writers'. *Scholarly Publishing* 17: 119–126.
Breimer, L.H. and Mikhailidis, D.P. (1991). 'A thesis for all seasons'. *Nature* 353: 789–790.

Brown, R.F. (1992). 'Recognising good work'. *Nature* **338**: 534.

Brown, R.F., Pressland, A.J. and Rogers, D.J. (1993). 'Righting scientific writing: Focus on your main message!' *Rangelands Journal* **15**(2): 183–189.

Brown, R.F., Rogers, D.J. and Pressland, A.J. (1994). 'Create a clear focus: the 'Big Picture' about writing better research papers'. *American Entomologist* (in press).

Cassel, K. (1993). 'Become a more successful author'. *Soil Science Society of America Journal* **57**(1): iv- v.

Daft, R.L., Griffin, R.W. and Yates, V. (1987). 'Retrospective accounts of research factors associated with significant and not-so-significant research outcomes'. *Academy of Management Journal* **30**: 763–785.

Dixon, B. (1993). 'Plain words please'. *New Scientist* **137**(1865): 40–41.

Doniger, W. (1992). 'The academic snob goes to market'. *Scholarly Publishing* **24**(1): 3–12).

Fey, C. (1987). 'Engineering good writing'. *Training* **24**: 49–54.

Fielden, J. (1964). 'What do you mean I can't write?' *Harvard Business Review* **64**: 144–156.

Gopen, D.G. and Swan, J.A. (1990). 'The science of scientific writing'. *American Scientist* **78**: 550–558.

Halstead, B. (1988). 'The thesis that won't go away'. *Nature* **331**: 497–498.

Hartnett, R.T., Clark, M.J. and Baird, L.l. (1978). 'Reputational ratings of doctoral programmes'. *Science* **199**: 1310–1314.

Kohn, A. (1993). 'Why incentive plans cannot work'. *Harvard Business Review* **71**(5): 54–61.

Mack, T.P. (1992). 'Common problems of writing style in entomological publications'. *American Entomologist* **38**: 207–211.

Maddox, J. (1983). 'Must science be impenetrable?' *Nature* **305**: 477–478.

Mitchell, D. (1993). 'On the origin of theses'. *New Scientist* **138**(1868): 41–42.

Murray, M.J. and Hay-Roe, H. (1986). *Engineered Writing: A Manual for Scientific, Technical and Business Writers*, 2nd edn. Tulsa, USA: PennWell Books.

Nicholson, J. (1993). 'That contemptible German degree'. *New Scientist* **138**(1873): 49–50.

Penaskovic, R. (1985). 'Facing up to the publication gun'. *Scholarly Publishing* **16**: 137–140.

Perry, C. (1993). *A Structured Approach to Presenting PhD Theses: Notes for candidates and their supervisors*. Mimeograph, Faculty of Business, Queensland University of Technology.

Rees, A. (1993). 'Morphology of theses'. *New Scientist* **139**(1891): 45–46.

Ries, A. and Trout, J. (1986). *Positioning: the Battle for Your Mind*. New York: McGraw-Hill.

Salager-Meyer, F. (1991). 'Medical English abstracts: how well are they structured?' *Journal of the American Society for Information Science* **42**: 528-531.

Walen, S.R., DiGuiseppe, R. and Wessler, R.L. (1980). *A Practitioner's Guide to Rational-Emotive Therapy*. New York: Oxford University Press.

Watson, J.D. and Crick, F.H. (1953). 'Molecular structure of nucleic acids: a structure for deoxyribose nucleic acid'. *Nature* **171**: 737–738.

Chapter 9

Supervising the Writing of a Thesis

Nanette Gottlieb

Introduction

Non-completion or delayed completion of a research higher degree, in particular the PhD, is an ongoing problem in the humanities and, to a lesser degree, in the social sciences. Not a lot appears to have changed in this regard since the 1950s in Oxford, when there was a 55 per cent wastage rate in the 1953-4 cohort of candidates for the DPhil and BLitt degrees, compared to a wastage of only 20 per cent in the sciences (Hancock, 1967). This issue of completion rates has become a matter of concern for many Australian Pro-Vice-Chancellors of research and/or postgraduate studies since DEET's decision to tighten up funding for higher degree students so that the universities now receive no funding for students after five years of full-time study. Scholarships, of course, run out much earlier.

There are many possible explanatory contributing factors to the marked lack of on-time completion in humanities, among them the fact that the typical student works in isolation rather than as a member of a team as in the sciences. Gottlieb and Edwards (forthcoming) identify some of the major problems contributing to longer completion times in the humanities at the University of Queensland as isolation from other students and staff (other than supervisors), which leads to almost total dependence upon the knowledge, skills and whims of the supervisor; lack of coordinated training in research methodology skills common to all departments; and the unreasonable amount of time spent easing into the topic at the beginning of the candidature.

A further factor is that humanities students as a rule have a much greater amount of writing to do than science students. It cannot be assumed that they are by virtue of their undergraduate training already equipped with the confidence and ability to write a cogently-argued, well-structured thesis. Many students come to the task unprepared and apprehensive. The role of the supervisor in directing the development of confidence in writing in this situation is extremely important. As Whittle tells us in this collection, 'the quality of supervision is one of the main factors which influence the quality of research theses and the ability of candidates to complete their degrees on time'. The 1983 SERC document *Research Student and Supervisor: An Approach to Good Supervisory Practice* identifies the second function of the supervisor, after that of selecting problems and advising and stimulating students, as ensuring that the student makes good progress. Part of this entails seeing, by asking for the regular submission of written work, that any deficiency in the student's writing is corrected before it becomes a major problem. Instead of viewing his or her primary role as assisting the development of the research, with the responsibility for writing resting solely with the student, the supervisor should regard helping the student to develop assurance in producing written work as one of the most important aspects of the process. A confident supervisor who assists the student to work out a carefully structured programme of writing for which feedback can be obtained from a variety of sources can do much to keep that student on track.

This chapter will suggest some strategies which the supervisor can employ to help build confidence in the student by breaking down the task of writing the thesis into manageable parts. A balanced and cumulative approach to writing from the very earliest stages of the candidature will go a long way toward improving completion times. It may also help prevent students from dropping out where their motivation for doing so does not stem from external factors but from a failure of confidence in their own ability to complete the task.

Planning from the beginning

The importance of helping the student plan out the research from the very beginning is widely recognized in the literature (Allen, 1973; Mauch and Birch, 1989; Moses, 1985, 1992; Rudd, 1985; Watson, 1970; Zuber-Skerritt and Knight, 1992) and cannot be overestimated as a tool for inspiring confidence in the beginner. There are various approaches to the preliminary organization of research: it is variously called research mapping, concept charting and research design. Watson (1970) advocates the same thing in the form of devising a table of contents in the early stages to give students a feel for the eventual organization of the thesis and to direct the collection of data and structuring of the writing process.

Whatever name it goes by, a research map takes away the fear of the monolithic nature of the task ahead by segmenting the project into manageable sections. A coherent plan sorts out the student's thinking and helps develop a systematic approach to the task from initial chaos. In addition, it helps identify priorities and eliminate the peripheral or irrelevant. That is not to say, of course, that it is always immediately obvious at the beginning exactly what will turn out to be peripheral or irrelevant; further along in the research something not originally considered important may turn out to play a bigger part than realized at the start of the project. A good research map lays the basis for the structure of the thesis in terms of chapters, which in turn can help with the writing of the introduction and conclusion. It can also help identify limits in terms of time, size of the project, funds needed to complete it (if applicable) and any foreign language dependency in terms of sources. In humanities departments focusing on the study of European or Asian countries and languages, for example, it may be necessary to travel to the target country for fieldwork — how will this be achieved? How many of the relevant primary sources in the target language are available in Australia, and how are they to be read if they are not? Early devising of a research map or plan concentrates attention on these matters while there is still ample time to plan ahead for the best outcomes.

Devising a good research map requires two simple steps: initial brainstorming and then rationalization of the results into a logical plan. For brainstorming, the student needs only a large sheet of paper with the topic written squarely in the middle. He or she then writes down on the paper any idea, however insignificant or seemingly tenuously related, which occurs during an hour or so spent considering the topic. The usual result is a web of squiggles resembling an explosion in an inkpot. The next step is to consider carefully each of the ideas on the sheet in terms of its relevance to the proposed project as far as can be seen at the moment. By removing what seems to be marginal at this stage, the student can then focus attention on the main points which emerge and move on to assigning them rank order in terms of mooted chapters of the thesis or stages in the research. What has been eliminated in these early stages may prove on further investigation to be relevant in ways not previously envisaged, but the purpose of the research map in the early stages of the project is to identify what is of immediate value in order to indicate the direction in which data collection should initially move — to identify those issues crucial to the examination of the topic which ought to take priority in the research. This in no sense puts a cap on creativity or precludes later changes to the plan; it simply gets things going and prevents unreasonable loss of time at the beginning.

The importance of time management

The other great advantage of having the student do a research map/concept chart in the early part of the first year, apart from clarifying thinking on how the topic is to be approached, is that it makes an invaluable aid for time management. Poor planning and poor time management contribute significantly to lengthened candidatures in the humanities (Moses, 1985; Rudd, 1985), and this is one area where a supervisor can and should suggest simple strategies to keep on track. Attitudes to time management with a research project vary: Anderson et al. (1970), for example, advocate a three-way split of 60 per cent – 20 per cent – 20 per cent between problem definition and data collection, first draft writing and final draft preparation respectively. Others, myself among them, support a more sustained *ab initio* approach to first draft writing, and this will be discussed in more detail in the following section. Regardless of individual approaches to the structural issues, a supervisor should always assist the student at the earliest feasible opportunity to devise a proposed schedule for activities to be undertaken, and ensure as much as is possible that the schedule is respected. Producing a well-considered research map is one way to do this.

Time management is important, then, as an aid to completing the thesis within the stipulated time before financial support or motivation run out. By extension, it is also relevant to the student's future career plans, particularly if those include entrance to academe. The PhD is usually a step in a planned career progression; many universities stipulate the possession of a doctorate in the relevant field as a minimum requirement in their advertisements for faculty positions. It is therefore very much to the student's advantage to have already submitted the thesis before beginning on the round of applications. It is even better if a publication or two, produced during candidature, can be added to the CV.

Successful time management, of course, depends heavily on early specification and definition of the parameters of the research. If the nature and scope of the topic are not clarified in the early stages, then it will not be possible to construct a clear research map and programme of activities and time will be unnecessarily wasted in going down blind alleys in data collection (Zuber-Skerritt and Knight, 1992). After six months at the most, the student should be able to encapsulate in one long sentence the central question which the research is addressing. Once this is decided to the satisfaction of both student and supervisor, and preferably enshrined on the wall where it will meet the student's eyes every time he/she looks up from reading, it is then possible to work out a timetable of activities to give structure to the remainder of the candidature. In what order will different activities be undertaken? Approximately how much time will be needed for each, e.g. the literature review, the drawing up of a research map? Can some be done simultaneously, or must they be consecutive? What has to be completed at each stage before the next can be begun? Will it be necessary to spend some time on fieldwork overseas, and if so, when would be best? What are the deadlines for scholarship applications for funds to travel? and so on.

Most departments have some sort of document setting out requirements for the converting of a provisional PhD candidature to full status (after the first year of full-time study or the second year of part-time study) which is given to beginning candidates and can help to further focus attention on the necessity of good planning in the early stages. In the Department of Japanese and Chinese Studies at the University of Queensland, for example, a student is required to submit at the end of this time a substantial paper (minimum of 20 pages or 6,000 words in length) outlining: the objectives of the thesis; the 'state of the art' in the chosen field and why the proposed project would represent an original contribution; the outcome of the literature search and a preliminary bibliography; a detailed outline of the methodology and a statement of hypotheses; a tentative outline of the argument of the thesis (including chapter structure); and a schedule of research and writing activities that will lead to completion of the thesis (including any anticipated problems and proposed travel). Such a document acts as a beacon which in conjunction with planning advice from the supervisor helps to keep the issue of time management in the forefront of the student's mind.

The role of the supervisor

In addition to encouraging effective time management practices and research mapping in the early stages, there are several other useful ways in which the supervisor can assist with the writing process. First and foremost among them is to provide a role model by being an active researcher and publisher. The strong connection between supervisor-as-model and completion times is well documented in the literature (Baird, 1990; Girves and Wemmerus, 1988; Katz and Hartnett, 1976; Mauch and Birch, 1989; Moses, this volume; Powles, 1989; Rudd, 1985). A supervisor who publishes regularly not only sets an example in practical terms but is also able to engage in the sort of frank discussion of the problems he or she has faced in writing which does much to reinforce the atmosphere of collegiality important to the postgraduate supervision process. Mauch and Birch (1989:33) recommend 'that one of the criteria for the appointment of doctoral research advisers from among the general faculty be evidence of high-quality research and writing', and such a requirement is laid down as part of supervisor qualifications in some Australian institutions (Keeps, 1989; Whittle, this volume). Baird (1990) reported a positive correlation across disciplines between duration of doctoral study and both the reputational ratings of faculty scholarship and the number of publications attributed to departmental faculty, a finding which further emphasizes the importance of the supervisor as role model.

As already mentioned in connection with time management, there is heavy stress in the literature on the importance of asking for regular submission of written work from the very beginning of the candidature (Allen, 1973; Moses, 1985, 1992; Nightingale, 1992; Rudd, 1985; Watson, 1970). This strategy is particularly useful for students in the humanities. Unlike their counterparts in science faculties, they are not restricted by the need to wait until their experiments are finished before writing up the results but can begin almost at once on tasks such as writing a couple of pages on how and why they came to be interested in their topic, what their main ideas are at present, how they plan to approach the collection of data on their topic, and so on. It is a simple matter for the supervisor to request such written pieces at, say, every second meeting. Frequent sessions with the pen or computer keyboard help accustom the student to writing about topics relating to the area of research. They also enable the supervisor to pinpoint early any possible difficulties with the mechanics of writing itself which may need to be remedied by referring the student to appropriate courses offered by the counselling services unit of the university. Committing ideas to paper on a regular basis not only develops the technical skills of academic writing but also functions as a means of checking the development of the critical inquiry which is being undertaken, revealing the depth to which particular issues have been investigated and the direction the study is taking. Watson (1970: 31) tells us that 'it is only after one has begun to write, as any author knows, that one begins to understand what the questions really are'.

An initial activity might be to have the student write a think-aloud account of how they arrived at their topic. It is especially important to insist on regular written material in the cases of students who are spending part of their candidature overseas and communicating by mail, as often happens in the humanities. All written work should, of course, be returned in good time with appropriate feedback. It is particularly important that feedback should include written comments from the supervisor even where there has been face-to-face discussion, as often comments on important aspects can be forgotten or their significance diminished in the mind by the time the student is able to be alone again to consider the work being returned.

Hints as to methods by which supervisors might encourage frequent writing abound. Moses (1985), for instance, suggests asking for regular written progress reports, including written documentation of problems encountered which may have led to revision of the research plan, as well as such written items as the initial research proposal and literature review, the introductory chapter, tentative conclusions to direct the writing, a thesis outline, summaries of all data analyses, and even written reflections and insights or day books. Nightingale (1992: 173) discusses a suggestion made by Zubrick (1985) that students keep reading logs in which to record their personal reactions to the literature they are studying, and further suggests that a diary of the progress of the research should be maintained wherein is entered 'not only what they did and what happened, but why they chose to do things one way rather than another and what questions are coming up at each stage of the work', including the things which did not work out as hoped.

Where a problem is revealed to exist with the mechanics of writing itself, in addition to encouraging the student to attend remedial on-campus courses, the supervisor can also keep a file on useful computer software which can help in this regard. The supervisor should insist on the regular use of the spell-check function if the student is not too confident with spelling, and should also stress the importance of meticulous proofreading when it comes to the final (or indeed, to any previous) draft. The rules for presentation and preparation of a PhD thesis at the University of Queensland, as presumably at any other, explicitly state that it is the responsibility of the candidate to ensure that all typing and other errors have been corrected and that the spelling, grammar, punctuation and choice of language are of doctoral standard. Given that these issues are borne in mind by examiners, the supervisor does the student no favours by allowing the submission of sloppy work, and should insist on high standards in this regard from the beginning. The student should be made aware of any particular discipline-specific requirements regarding referencing and general presentation and trained to use these at all times to avoid loss of time later in reformatting bibliographic citations. In larger departments it may be possible to run regular writing workshops for postgraduates, so that they can participate in interactive sessions to make them proficient in specific skills such as writing an abstract, writing introductions and conclusions, or writing literature reviews. Supervisors from the same department could cooperate in this and/or invite other departments to take part as well.

What of the student who procrastinates, or worse, suffers periodically from the dreaded writer's block? Allen (1973) lists good reasons for not putting off starting: the supervisor may leave the university for a period or for good; what was originally a hot topic becomes less so the more time passes; other scholars working in the same field may pre-empt the student by finishing first; and the longer writing is put off the harder it is to begin. Moses (1985) advocates that if perfectionism on the student's part is the cause of procrastination, the supervisor should insist on seeing frequent drafts of successive sections and impress on the student the importance of committing thoughts to paper even if not in polished form. Students at Macquarie's Graduate School of the Environment are advised to break writer's block by adopting a stream of consciousness technique, spending a maximum of ten minutes blocking out a draft in point form and later filling in some detail. This is then consigned to a drawer for a few days and later exhumed to form the starting point for writing the section properly (Fairweather, 1993). A useful technique to suggest for those whose writing is frequently interrupted and who find it difficult to pick up the thread again is the use of 'pick-up points' (Nightingale, 1992), little memos to themselves at the point where they left off to remind them of what should come next. The best thing a supervisor can do is pass on hints of this kind gleaned from personal experience, discussion with others or reading in the area, to remind the student that he or she is not alone in this situation and that others have successfully overcome the same difficulties.

The supervisor should make the student aware from an early stage of the candidature what the institution's criteria for examination of research theses are and what exactly they mean (see Nightingale, 1992, for an illuminating discussion of the traps unwary players may encounter in interpreting such criteria). In the case of the University of Queensland, the criteria for examination of PhD theses are that the candidate's thesis should:

- provide a contribution to knowledge with a level of originality consistent with three to four years full-time study and supervised research training after a bachelors degree with honours
- reveal a capacity to relate the research topic to the broader framework of knowledge in the disciplinary area in which it falls
- be clearly, accurately and cogently written and suitably documented.

Examiners are also asked to comment on whether they consider the thesis to be of publishable standard. Of the three criteria listed above, the one likely to prove problematic is the first, the most all-embracing and least clearly defined. Nevertheless, the student must know what the people who ultimately assess the results of his or her research will be looking for, in order to produce a thesis which meets their expectations.

Finally, the supervisor can help a student develop experience and confidence as a writer by encouraging publication during candidature. Opinions differ as to the wisdom of this. Some, such as Allen (1973), advise against taking time away from the task of producing the thesis because of the risk of extended completion time involved while at the same time acknowledging the usefulness of publications to a subsequent job search. Others (Moses, 1985; Sadler, 1990) do advocate publishing during candidature, which can be a means of gaining feedback on written work from people other than the supervisor and of establishing academic credentials. Since one criterion examiners are asked to address in their report on the thesis is whether the work is of publishable standard, it is obviously helpful to have attached to the submitted thesis an offprint of a chapter, say, which has already been published in an internationally refereed journal. The danger is, of course, that if an article is submitted and rejected the student may become discouraged and take that one rejection to reflect a general condemnation of the quality of his or her entire body of work.

An experienced and sympathetic supervisor can help here by recounting personal experiences of similar rejections and pointing out that they are experienced by all scholars along the way, be they graduate students or professors. The editorial comments on the article submitted can be a valuable source of feedback from the viewpoint of another person, or of two other people depending on the number of readers it was sent to, so that the student can be encouraged to take note of the comments where appropriate and revise the manuscript with a view to either resubmission, if appropriate, or submission elsewhere. In the happy event of acceptance, the boost to self-confidence can be enormous. Whittle (1992) reports that University of Adelaide students found that having their work published was one of the most satisfying aspects of their postgraduate years and that their self-confidence was greatly improved as a result; further, the experience of becoming published authors helped the development of colleague-type relationships between students and their supervisors. Handled judiciously, then, the encouragement of submission of parts of the work for publication can only benefit the students in terms of increased growth as a scholar.

Sources of feedback

The major source of feedback is of course the supervisor, who should be conscientious in providing written comments on work submitted. It should be made clear to the student, however, that he or she is at liberty to seek feedback from the department at large where appropriate. Many students believe that they may only approach their own supervisor or associate supervisor, when in fact there may be other staff members interested in the same field who could also provide useful comment if approached. Students are usually reluctant to do this, not wanting to 'burden' busy staff with extra reading, but in an environment where research is valued and postgraduates supported and encouraged, most people would be happy to take on the task if given a reasonable amount of time to do so. The staff member's network is usually more developed than the student's, so that he or she may know of someone else outside the department who could also be approached. Phillips and Pugh (1987) point out that supervisors expect their students to seek advice and comments on their work from others, and that this can be an effective tool in overcoming the sense of isolation so often mentioned by humanities postgraduates and identified as a contributing factor in postgraduate failure (Rudd, 1985; Whittle, 1992).

Fellow students are also excellent sources of constructive criticism (Mauch and Birch, 1989). This is particularly so in the humanities because, unlike in the sciences where graduate students may work in a team focusing on different aspects of one problem, other postgraduates are usually removed from the topic under discussion. Coming to it without much prior knowledge of the subject, they can thus focus on whether the main points are coming through clearly, whether the argument is unfolding in a logical progression, and whether there are any glaring gaps which need filling and which may not have been noticed by the person wrapped up in the topic and too close to the work for objectivity. 'If it is not clear to another person of good intelligence', Mauch and Birch (1989: 176) tell us, 'it is probably not fully clear to the writer'. The opportunity for this sort of collegial feedback can be given by having postgraduates present seminars on their work, or circulate sections of written work for comment, or meet together for informal discussion sessions of their progress. When a student is experiencing a problem with the work, it can be valuable to call a brainstorming session where other students and staff listen to the problem and then try to suggest solutions.

The other main source of feedback, if the student is attempting to publish during candidature, is the comments returned from readers of the manuscripts submitted to journals. Good journals have editorial boards or on-call readers who are among the top scholars in their field; whether or not the article is accepted, the student has the benefit of their comments which would otherwise not have been accessible. (That is assuming the journal is among those who send readers' comments back with rejected manuscripts, of course; few things are more infuriating than to receive a flat rejection notice with no indication of what might have been unacceptable about the paper). Where the work submitted forms part of the thesis, it can be rewritten in the light of the comments where appropriate, with the result that it just gets better and better. Rejections are hard to take, but if the supervisor points out the value of the feedback from the extended readership of the work, something positive can be salvaged from the wreckage.

Conclusion

In sum, the supervisor's task is not only to assist with the training of a scholar in terms of research methodology and content of the thesis. It also encompasses the affective and practical elements involved in producing a scholar who can confidently and skilfully communicate ideas in writing. By encouraging the use of writing as a voyage of discovery and by imparting the simple techniques of planning and time management, the supervisor can provide postgraduates with skills which will stand them in good stead in their future publishing careers.

References

Allen, G.R. (1973). *The Graduate Students' Guide to Theses and Dissertations: A Practical Manual for Writing and Research*. San Francisco: Jossey-Bass.

Anderson, J., Durston, B. and Poole, M. (1970). *Thesis and Assignment Writing*. Brisbane: John Wiley and Sons.

Baird, L.L. (1990). 'Disciplines and doctorates: the relationships between program characteristics and the duration of doctoral study'. *Research in Higher Education* 31(4): 369-385.

Fairweather, P. (1993). 'Tips on writing', in P. Fairweather (ed.), *Notes for Student Researchers*. Macquarie University Graduate School of the Environment, pp. 34-38.

Girves, J.E. and Wemmerus, V. (1988). 'Developing models of graduate student degree progress'. *Journal of Higher Education* 59(2): 163-189.

Gottlieb, N. and Edwards, L. (forthcoming). *Facilitating Institutional Change: The Problems of Being Change Agents*. Brisbane: Tertiary Education Institute: The University of Queensland.

Hancock, Sir K. (1967). 'Ordeal by thesis', in K. Hancock, P.H. Partridge and R.W.V. Elliott. *Postgraduate Studies in the Humanities in Australia*. Sydney: Sydney University Press, pp. 2-12.

Katz, J. and Hartnett, R. (eds) (1976). *Scholars in the Making: The Development of Graduate and Professional Students*. Cambridge, Mass: Ballinger.

Keepes, B. (1989). 'Institutional responsibilities to postgraduate students: the Sydney CAE approach'. *HERDSA News* 11(1): 3-5.

Mauch, J.E. and Birch, J.W. (1989). *Guide to the Successful Thesis and Dissertation, Conception to Publication. A Guidebook for Students and Faculty*, 2nd ed. New York and Basel: Marcel Dekker.

Moses, I. (1985). *Supervising Postgraduates*. HERDSA Green Guide No.3. Sydney: Higher Education Research and Development Society of Australia.

Moses, I. (1992). 'Research training in Australian universities — undergraduate and graduate studies', in O. Zuber-Skerritt (ed.), *Starting Research—Supervision and Training*. Brisbane: Tertiary Education Institute, The University of Queensland, pp. 3-24.

Nightingale, P. (1992). 'Initiation into research through writing', in O. Zuber-Skerritt (ed.), *Starting Research — Supervision and Training*. Brisbane: Tertiary Education Institute, The University of Queensland, pp. 166-179.

Phillips, E.M. and Pugh, D.H. (1987). *How to get a PhD*. Buckingham: Open University Press.

Powles, M. (1989). 'Higher degree completion and completion times'. *Higher Education Research and Development* 8(1): 91-101.

Rudd, E. (1985). *A New Look at Postgraduate Failure*. Surrey: SRHE and NFER-Nelson.

Sadler, D.R. (1990). *Up the Publication Road*, 2nd ed. HERDSA Green Guide No.2. Sydney: Higher Education Research and Development Society of Australia.

Science and Engineering Research Council (SERC) (1983). *Research Student and Supervisor. An Approach to Good Supervisory Practice*. London: SERC.

Watson, G. (1970). *The Literary Thesis: A Guide to Research*. London: Longman.

Whittle, J. (1992). 'Research culture, supervision practices and postgraduate performance', in O. Zuber-Skerritt (ed.), *Starting Research – Supervision and Training*. Brisbane: Tertiary Education Institute, The University of Queensland, pp. 86-107.

Zuber-Skerritt, O. (ed.) (1992). *Starting Research — Supervision and Training*. Brisbane: Tertiary Education Institute, The University of Queensland.

Zuber-Skerritt, O. and Knight, N. (1992). 'Helping students overcome barriers to dissertation writing', in O. Zuber-Skerritt (ed.), *Starting Research—Supervision and Training*. Brisbane: Tertiary Education Institute, The University of Queensland, pp. 180-188.

Zubrick, A. (1985). 'Learning through writing: the use of reading logs'. *HERDSA News* 7(3): 11-12, 24.

Chapter 10

The Postgraduate's Journey —
An Interplay of Roles

Pam Denicolo and Maureen Pope

Introduction

> *I have been hiding things from myself, trying to ignore them, but now I must do something about them before they get worse.*

This *cri de coeur* is from a postgraduate student who was one of the participants in the research study discussed later in this chapter. We present it at this point because we wish to argue that quality in postgraduate education would require the supervisor to be concerned not only with the formal content of postgraduate training programmes, but also to have empathy with the personal learning which the postgraduate student undertakes when embarking on the PhD journey.

The decision of the research councils in Britain to make their support for research studentships dependent on completion rates of institutions (Winfield, 1987) has given impetus to the development of a growing body of literature on postgraduate training; see, for example, Murray (1988), Young et al. (1987), Zuber-Skerritt (1992). There have also been a number of texts aimed at helping the postgraduate student come to terms with what might be expected when embarking on a PhD (Phillips and Pugh, 1987; Rudestan and Newton, 1992). Much of the literature has either been concerned with problems which arise if organizational or interpersonal factors in supervision are inadequate, or if the content of training programmes has received scant attention. Whilst these are important issues, we would argue that there is also a need for research on personal factors involved in postgraduate education and that consideration should be given to the quality of the process adopted within training programmes.

Students' personal construing

The action research presented here is an attempt to give voice to a cohort of postgraduate students, particularly with respect to how they see the postgraduate role in relation to other roles that they may view as important and possibly competing with the student role. As personal construct psychologists we find that our practice as teachers, postgraduate research student supervisors and researchers has been influenced by the writings of George Kelly (1955). He proposed that people choose between alternative roles that are created for them by their personal constructs. Personal constructs are implicit networks or systems which people use to structure their thinking and make sense of their experiences. The content and structure of a person's construct system will be unique to that individual. Kelly drew parallels between the process he adopted in his clinical work and how he saw the process of postgraduate supervision. In both endeavours the conversation was often aimed at helping the person articulate at least part of his or her individual construction. This articulation is important on two counts:

- it allows the clinician/supervisor to have some understanding of the personal models the client/postgraduate student is currently using to impose meaning on the world
- the process of articulation may help the client/postgraduate student to clarify thoughts, recognize the significance of the power of these thoughts and form the basis for reflection about potential avenues for change.

For Kelly these aspects were vital if the encounter between the clinician/supervisor and client/research student was to be fully effective. This is the essence of his sociality corollary within his theory. Diamond (1991: 70) stresses the importance of role relationships between teachers and students: '... if teachers do not understand their students, if they do not construe their developing understandings, they may do things to them, but they cannot relate to them'.

We would contend that the personal understandings of postgraduate students are often neglected by their tutors. Whilst considerable steps have taken place within institutions (often due to the impetus of the need for ESRC recognition of training programmes) to provide formal training, relatively little attention has been given to the quality of the interpersonal encounter between those engaged in the process of research student supervision. A starting point must be the concerns of the postgraduate students themselves. Discussions with supervisees confirmed this view and these discussions formed the genesis of the current research.

Approaching the problem

Elton and Pope (1989) drew attention to the fact that earlier research on research supervision has, in the main, used quantitative survey methods with interviews at times providing supporting evidence. Lincoln and Guba (1985) acknowledge the similarities of philosophy between naturalistic enquiry and that of personal constructivism. We share their concern regarding the need for more qualitative enquiry and we have also suggested (Pope and Denicolo, 1993) that, by combining techniques such as the repertory grid with other techniques consistent with personal construct psychology (e.g. the self-characterization sketch and the use of 'snakes') such triangulation enhances the rigour of constructivist enquiry. This commitment was followed in the current study into postgraduate students' personal construing.

It is commonly accepted that research towards a higher degree is, *inter alia*, demanding, time consuming and requires a high degree of motivation. Yet especially in social sciences and education studies, a large number of research students are mature, and hence have many roles and responsibilities, personal and professional, which compete with their research student role. Salmon (1992), in the introduction to her excellent and moving book *Achieving a PhD*, noted that when PhD students are the focus of public concern, their variety is ignored while a single stereotype is referred to — full-time, funded and typically young. For her, too, the reality is that the average doctoral student is part-time, self-funded and mature, but neglected by the research literature: 'Becoming a PhD student means entering a peculiarly complex and private situation: it is a world about which few people have spoken' (Salmon, 1992: 1).

In her book she tells the stories of ten PhD students as well as revealing in depth how she construes the role of supervisor. We hope that this research provides further complementary first-hand evidence, for many parallels can be drawn between the reflections of the participants in both studies.

Previous interest and research (e.g. Pope and Denicolo, 1989) guided a focus on the multiple roles held by such students. For the purposes of this study the dramaturgical model of 'role' (Goffman, 1959) provided a foundation for interpretation of the term although acknowledgement was given to Gergen's (1968) and Brittan's (1973) criticisms that this model underestimates individual variability and places too much emphasis on social rules of behaviour. (This discussion is pursued in greater detail in Hammond and Denicolo, 1993.) Thus, 'role' is understood as encompassing a set of standards, certain rights, obligations and duties which the person occupying the role may be expected or encouraged to perform in a given social situation. Each role played by an individual, and the interactions it has with other roles, is seen as having a range of psychological effects on that individual's sense of self and identity. The person's constructs define these roles.

The rationale underpinning a commitment to undertaking the development of constructive action through research which incorporates both a personal construct psychology and an action research approach has been well rehearsed in previous papers (cf Denicolo, 1994; Pope and Denicolo, 1991). However, it is pertinent to emphasize here agreement with Popkewitz (1984) that all data collection and analysis emerge from some theory about what the world is like and how information about that world is to be given coherence. Further, the words of Barton (1988: 91) have some salience: 'Research is not a value-neutral activity. It is a social experience in which the subjects of research can suffer and perceive particular forms of study as oppressive'. He suggested that this can only be avoided or mitigated if those subjects are involved in decisions about deliberations with students throughout the research process and the caveats pronounced along the way did not make it a totally painfree process for all the participants, as will be demonstrated by the quotations presented later in this chapter.

Methods used

One of the authors (PD) wrote to all of the 70 students currently registered on the doctoral programme in Educational Studies in her department. She explained the research purpose, i.e. to explore and collect evidence about common benefits, opportunities and constraints that the research student role affords, especially in relation to the many other roles that students inhabit. A brief description was given of the form of the research, the use to which the data would be put and in what way, including the confidentiality of the data, and the flexibility of the engaging in/opting out system. Then, in order to check our 'intuitive theory' that each had many and various roles and to check the consistency of role definition, students were asked to volunteer a list of roles they were engaged in and to indicate if they would like to take part.

For the second stage, volunteers (some 30 in total) were sent a pack containing instructions/explanations about how to:

- complete a concept map of up to ten key roles which were particularly relevant to them as individuals but to include the research role
- construct a repertory grid with two family, two social, two professional, two individual, two community roles and the research student role as elements (a generic grid form was provided)
- draw up a 'snake' or 'winding river' chart in which 'bends' denote the critical incidents in their lives which led to them taking up the research student role
- write a narrative in the third person describing themselves and their reactions as research students.

It was intended that the annotated concept maps (after Novak, 1988) would provide some information about how the different roles interact with each other and influence lifestyle. The purpose of the grid (Bannister and Fransella, 1986) was to explore the ways in which different roles are construed in relation to each other and to provide an indication of the construct poles used to describe being a research student. The snake charts (Denicolo and Pope, 1990) would focus attention on recurrent themes, pervasive influences on development towards becoming a research student and, indeed, while being a research student. This would be complementary to the narratives (Mair, 1977) which may reveal influences on lifestyle that being a research student generates, and cognitive, emotional and behavioural reactions to them. An example of a concept map, a grid and a snake chart can be found in the Appendix as Figures 1, 2 and 3 respectively. The personal detail disclosed in the narratives, in conjunction with the 'confidentiality clause', precludes the provision of an example at this stage.

This range of techniques allowed for a study of the problem space from a variety of perspectives for each individual, each contributing something unique to the picture, while also allowing cross reference by methodological triangulation for each individual and across the group of participants. It also takes account of the possibility that individuals will be more comfortable and articulate through different media. These techniques provided the warp and weft upon which each participant worked their own part of the rich tapestry, in some places using elaborate stitches, for others plain thread, while other sections are yet left unembroidered.

The picture so far

The initial letter of invitation to participate was posted close to Christmas 1993. We were overwhelmed not merely by the returned data but, more importantly, by the trust shown by all those who have provided a wealth of detail and shared great depth of personal reflection.

The students varied in stage of study and were drawn from all four years of the postgraduate programme. Full- and part-time students were represented and one student was working part-time collaboratively at a distance. The age range reflected the normal span of intake for the department, with most being in their late 30s, early 40s. However, one was not yet 30 and one had passed 60 years of age.

The foci of their research were equally diverse, with contexts spanning school to higher and professional education, dealing with philosophical to pragmatic problems, using a variety of methodological approaches.

In some ways they were less isolated in their studies than has been reported (Phillips and Pugh, 1987) for most such students, for the department provides a research methods programme and a variety of opportunities to meet as interest groups. Many of the students not only took full advantage of this, but were also proactive in establishing support groups themselves. Elton and Pope (1989) drew attention to this important aspect of collegiality.

The responses to the first stage of the enquiry revealed an even greater diversity of roles than was expected. Different people also used the term 'role' to embody different levels of activity. Thus, for the second stage of the research, in order to accommodate two different objectives, that of being able to review the data for comparability between individuals while allowing participants to communicate in a way which was personally meaningful, guidance was given about selecting/naming personally salient role titles from within the following overarching categories derived from the original role lists:

- Family (e.g. parent, partner, sibling)
- Social (e.g. friend, neighbour, confidante)
- Community (e.g. voluntary worker, fund raiser, group member)
- Individual (e.g. artist, pet owner, sportsperson)
- Professional (e.g. manager, consultant, teacher).

The figures in the Appendix demonstrate how participants could interpret this advice and serve as illustrations for the kind of data derived. (NB Some details on these examples have been edited out to preserve confidentiality. Indeed, the selection of examples was made solely on those which could readily be so edited. We have deliberately chosen a grid, a concept map and a snake from different postgraduate students as a further attempt at protecting identity. This we felt particularly important given the fact that we have been open regarding the department of origin of students.)

For each participant lists were compiled of comments, issues, etc. from the concept maps, snakes and narratives and of the constructs from the grids, with the pole most relevant to the research student role noted. These lists from the group of participants were amalgamated and frequently recurring themes from each technique/

activity identified. 'Frequently recurring' in this context means 'mentioned in some form by at least 75 per cent of participants'. These have been summarized onto a chart to allow comparisons to be made. This is presented as Table 1, in which themes deemed to be similar or linked in some way are grouped together.

As an interesting comparison, a selection from Salmon's (1992) work of descriptions about the experience of researching for a PhD are provided here:

- pp 10/11 — creativity, imaginative boldness, ownership of direction, transformative, requiring courage and vision
- p 13 — personal immersion
- p 14 — suffused with feeling, real excitement
- p 15 — arduous, lonely, challenging
- p 23 — passionate commitment.

Table 1: Frequently recurring themes about the student role

Grids	Narratives	Snakes	Concept Maps
Concerns self-development Is stimulating, rewarding, challenging.	Involves intellectual and personal growth; is a bid for sanity and preservation of self	Self-esteem low in earlier years; a need to challenge the 'authorized' version; an interest in 'finding out'	Personal interest roles enhanced
Solitary Time-consuming Absorbing	Loners, isolation; guilt about selfishness of pursuit; losing touch with family and friends; obsessive, takes over mind and life; importance of supportive partner	Need for independence or to be committed to an activity; passionate involvement	Social roles neglected; domestic roles are restrictive; need for an understanding partner/ colleagues; sometimes made to feel guilty
Professional importance	Enhancement of professional status	Frequently 'late developers' in traditional academic terms	Enhancement of professional skills and attitudes
Need for self-discipline, control, organization; taking responsibility	Need to organize, prioritize; recognize own priorities	Need to demonstrate achievement to self and others	Conflicts of duties; pressures from other roles; distraction from 'real' interests
Creative; intellectual activity, mental challenge	Different perspective on life; tolerance increased for different ideas/perspectives	Always trying to find out, asking questions	
Confidence developing	Enhancement of confidence, though insecurity early on, common	Self-esteem enhanced by accepting challenges; humiliations in early years frequently reflected on	Empowerment of perform- ance in other professional roles

Discussion

Like the students in Salmon's study, the raw data from the volunteer students exemplified here reveal each as a distinct individual. Each has led, and continues to lead, a complex life in which some facets are harmonious while others cause dissonance. Like Chaucer's pilgrims, or knights seeking the Holy Grail, each has a fascinating story to tell and, though they have some commonality of purpose, each pursues that aim in a unique way. There is little evidence in the complete data for attributes which denote 'an average doctoral student', apart from rather predictable ones which probably formed the basis of their selection for the group anyway, such as 'demonstrating perseverance/courage', 'having a questioning, challenging approach to life'. It is interesting that so many had low self-esteem, and/or suffered humiliations early in life, and/or were late developers academically, and we may speculate that a complex interaction between these and early educational experience has resulted in their demonstrating the aforementioned characteristics now. However, we would be no wiser to suggest that people who have had such experiences would necessarily make successful doctoral students than we would to insist that prospective students had followed a traditional educational route culminating in a highly classed degree (Research Councils please note!). Neither would appear to be necessary or sufficient conditions for predicting ability to cope with the challenges of doctoral study.

We have only been able to present some of the richness in the data to hand. It was clear to us that the students revealed a wide diversity of concerns regarding their roles as postgraduate students as they connect with other personal and professional roles. Whilst we do not intend to generalize the findings, we would suggest that the data clearly indicate that we could alert prospective students and supervisors to the likely personal and professional benefits which can derive from engagement with such a form of study (over and above the attainment of a title and whatever that may entail): self-development, stimulation, confidence development, priority recognition, skill development, etc. Equally strongly, some possible costs could be more overtly reviewed and emphasized: the neglect or loss of some previous roles, particularly social ones, and the consequent feelings of guilt; the pressures of conflicting duties or distractions and the anger that this can generate in self and others. Significantly, it seems that very personal relationships may be put under stress or at risk; given the timespace of a PhD, i.e. four to five years on average for a part-time student, and its nature, a partner or friend has to be tolerant for a considerable time of some degree of neglect, and would be unwise to wait patiently for the attention of the student.

Since we are discussing responsible adults, it is our contention that they must make their own choices, when study quality itself is unquestioned. However, we should help students more in making an informed choice when weighing the other costs and benefits about embarking on, suspending or terminating their studies. Such advice/information should not be restricted to the rehearsal of the institution's policy and regulations about completion rates, nor is it sensible to await the evidence of deteriorating quality of work before recognizing that crises do occur.

Few academics would disagree that students should make decisions regarding their 'private' lives. What is contentious is how much and what kind of support should be provided to 'responsible adults' during domestic, social or other professional crises which have been at least exacerbated if not stimulated by the MPhil/PhD process. Some supervisors would feel themselves remiss not to be alert to incipient problems and not to be able to provide willing and professionally skilled support. Others, notably novice supervisors, are surprised that such crises are so common and so are unprepared, if not unwilling, to provide support. More experienced colleagues may have become alert and concerned but are untrained in providing adequate support. Yet others can justify taking a more distanced stance by demonstrating that their institution engaged them for the academic — not personal — support of their students.

Implications for supervision

The research has shown that students are able to reflect upon and articulate their views on the postgraduate role. Some participants have taken advantage of the optional personal feedback and support offered; many want to meet as a group to discuss the results and decide on the next stage. Supervisors should encourage more such group activity amongst postgraduate students.

> This has been a fascinating activity — many things are becoming clearer for me now.
> I can't believe how much I have told you here, things I haven't even shared with my nearest and dearest.
> This hasn't been an easy exercise. If we had done this earlier, I would have made different choices.
> Revelatory!!! The more I got into an activity, the more I wanted to stop doing it but the less able I was to.

The quotations above indicated that the students who participated in the research had found the process illuminating. It has been our view that participation in research can be emancipatory for those involved. The various tools used within the enquiry can be taken further to form useful conversations within the process of supervision itself. We illustrate this with just one example.

Figure 2 in the Appendix shows the focus grid from one of the students. One can see from the dendograms that she has clusters of constructs regarding the various roles reflecting issues of confidence, satisfaction and restriction of personal development. There are some roles she feels take up a lot of time, and some without which she feels she would not be living fully. It is interesting to note that she sees her role as a research student as one that helps her grow, gives her enjoyment; she feels confident about herself in this role, despite the fact that she gets exhausted, it takes a lot of time and she recognizes that she is less in control in this role than, for example, in the role of neighbour, gym member, hostess/cook. There is a variety of roles that she clearly feels that she could survive without, but being a research student and a wife are not included in these. A major current concern is that she feels that she would like to be more active and give more in her role as a wife than her role as a research student allows. Her role as a research student she sees as exhausting, whereas she does not feel the same about her role as a wife. These very personal concerns can be addressed within supervision.

We have indicated earlier that we do not wish to present generalizations with respect to the specific results of this study. However, our experience as supervisors, in addition to the data found in this particular study, would lead us to suggest that the balancing of roles and the choices and dilemmas faced by many mature female postgraduate students in particular (such as indicated in the example above) are not uncommon. Whether one uses tools such as the grid, concept map, snake or narrative is a matter for negotiation between the student and the supervisor. We have found that some students prefer the snake, others the grid, whilst others prefer the freedom of the narrative form. Kelly (1969: 135) maintained that 'humanistic psychology needs a technology through which to express its humane intentions. Humanity needs to be implemented and not merely characterised and eulogised'.

Kelly offered the repertory grid as one such technology. We have tried to develop other techniques consistent with this philosophy for use both in research and in our role as supervisors of research students.

Conclusion

We suggest that it is not sufficient to pay lip-service to the need to understand the perspectives of students. A systematic attempt throughout the period of registration to address such personal concerns is required. This is in addition to our duties to inform students regarding the niceties of design and the writing of theses. Individual students may have more need than others for regular periodic reviews about how they are coping with the balancing of roles.

We have used a number of tools to aid conversations. Some supervisors may not have the training in such techniques nor the inclination to use such tools. We have helped a number of our colleagues to develop expertise in the methods used. However, we would suggest that the main issue is not which tool to use, if any. Rather the emphasis should be on the responsibility of the research supervisor to recognize that conversations with their supervisees regarding such personal issues are a legitimate focus of attention. The quality of the relationship between the supervisor and supervisee should be such that a climate is engendered which will allow free expression of these lived experiences.

Appendix

Figure 1: Concept map

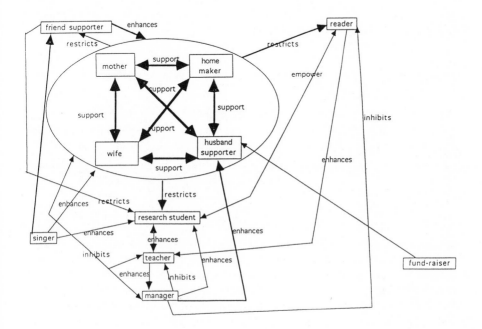

Figure 2: Focus grid

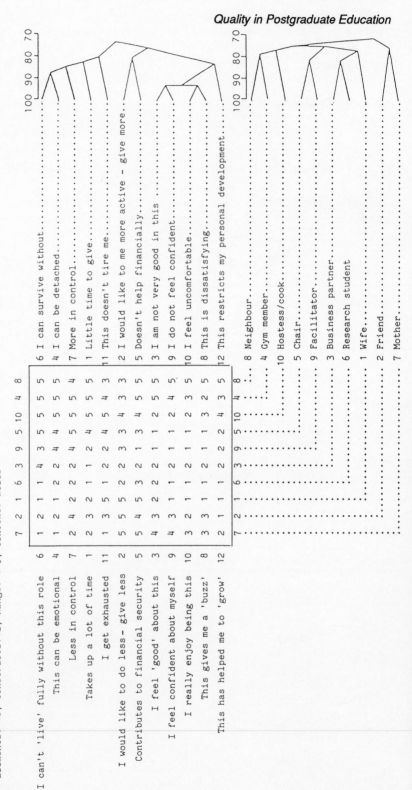

FOCUS: Role Comparison
Elements: 10, Constructs:12, Range: 1-5, Context: Roles

Figure 3: Snake (as drawn by a student in the study)

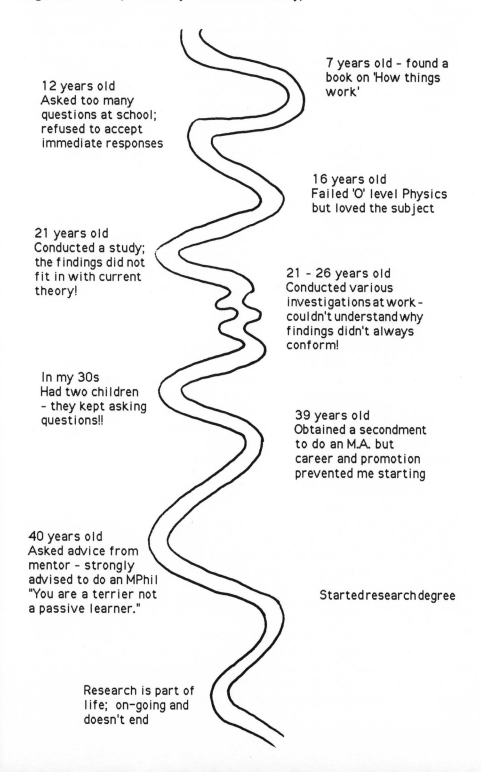

7 years old - found a book on 'How things work'

12 years old
Asked too many questions at school; refused to accept immediate responses

16 years old
Failed 'O' level Physics but loved the subject

21 years old
Conducted a study; the findings did not fit in with current theory!

21 - 26 years old
Conducted various investigations at work - couldn't understand why findings didn't always conform!

In my 30s
Had two children - they kept asking questions!!

39 years old
Obtained a secondment to do an M.A. but career and promotion prevented me starting

40 years old
Asked advice from mentor - strongly advised to do an MPhil "You are a terrier not a passive learner."

Started research degree

Research is part of life; on-going and doesn't end

References

Bannister, D. and Fransella, A. (1986). *Inquiring Man*, 3rd edn. London: Routledge.

Barton, L. (ed.) (1988). *The Politics of Special Educational Needs*. London: Falmer Press.

Brittan, A. (1973). *Meanings and Situations*. Boston: Routledge and Kegan Paul.

Denicolo, P. (1994). 'Activating active learning — confining constructions reconstrued', in R.A. Thomson and R.A. Cummins (eds), *European Perspectives in Personal Construct Psychology*, selected papers from the inaugural conference of EPCA. Lincoln: EPCA.

Denicolo, P. and Pope, M. (1990). 'Adults' learning — teachers' thinking', in C. Day, M. Pope and P. Denicolo (eds), *Insights into Teachers' Thinking and Practice*. London: Falmer Press.

Diamond, P.C.T. (1991). *Teacher Education as Transformation*. Buckingham: Open University Press.

Elton, I. and Pope, M. (1989). 'Research supervision: the value of collegiality'. *Cambridge Journal of Education* **19**(3): 267-276.

Gergen, K.J. (1968). 'Personal consistency and presentation of self', in C. Gordon and K.J. Gergen (eds), *The Self in Social Interaction*, Vol. 1. New York: Wiley.

Goffman, E. (1959). *The Presentation of Self in Everyday Life*. Harmondsworth: Penguin.

Hammond, J. and Denicolo, P. (1993). 'Actors' constructions of self and identity'. Occasional Papers, University of Surrey.

Kelly, G.A. (1955). *The Psychology of Personal Constructs*, Vols. 1 and 2. New York: W.W. Norton.

Kelly, G.A. (1969). 'The language of hypothesis: Man's psychological instrument', in B. Maher (ed.), *Clinical Psychology and Personality. The Selected Papers of George Kelly*. New York: John Wiley, pp. 147-162.

Lincoln, Y.S. and Guba, E.G. (1985). *Naturalistic Enquiry*. Beverley Hills, CA.: Sage.

Mair, J.M.M. (1977). 'The community of self', in D. Bannister (ed.), *New Perspectives in Personal Construct Theory*. London: Academic Press.

Murray, R. (1988). *Training Needs in the Social Sciences and the Effectiveness of Current Provision in Meeting these Needs*. London: ESRC.

Novak, J. (1988). 'Constructively approaching education: towards a theory of practice'. *International Journal of Personal Construct Psychology* **1**(2): 169-180.

Phillips, E. and Pugh, D. (1987). *How to Get a PhD*. Buckingham: Open University Press.

Pope, M. and Denicolo, P. (1989). 'Connecting threads in teachers' role perceptions', paper presented at 3rd conference of European Association into Learning and Instruction (EARLI), Madrid.

Pope, M. and Denicolo, P. (1991). 'Developing constructive action: personal construct psychology, action research and professional development', in O.

Zuber-Skerritt (ed.), *Action Research for Change and Development*. Aldershot: Gower.

Pope, M. and Denicolo, P. (1993). 'The art and science of constructivist research in teacher thinking'. *Teaching and Teacher Education* 9(5/6): 529-544.

Popkewitz, T.S. (1984). *Paradigm and Ideology in Educational Research*. London: Falmer Press.

Rudestan, K.E. and Newton, R.R. (1992). *Surviving your Dissertation*. London: Sage.

Salmon, P. (1992). *Achieving a PhD — Ten Students' Experience*. Stoke on Trent: Trentham Books.

Winfield, G. (1987). *The Social Science PhD: the ESRC Enquiry on Submission Rules*. London: ESRC.

Young, K., McRae, S. and Fogarty, M. (1987). *The Management of Doctoral Studies in the Social Sciences*. London: Policy Studies Institute.

Zuber-Skerritt, O. (ed.) (1992). *Starting Research — Supervision and Training*. Brisbane: Tertiary Education Institute, The University of Queensland.

Chapter 11

Avoiding Communication Breakdown

Estelle Phillips

Introduction

Communication breakdown is rampant amongst students and their supervisors (Phillips and Pugh, 1994). Whether difficulties are caused by the nature of the power relationship, as Grant and Graham suggest in this volume, or by systemic ambiguities, as might be inferred from Gottlieb's chapter, problems of communication exist regardless of the model of supervision being used. This means that whether it is the one–to–one supervision model that is being discussed, joint supervision, or even a supervisory panel made up of several supervisors, there is still a requirement for supervisors to check with students (and each other) that what has been said has been understood, i.e. that there are nomisunderstandings.

The research from which this chapter originates has been conducted over a period of 15 years; many papers have already been published on different aspects of the student and supervisor relationship (see for example Phillips, 1983, 1992, 1994). This research has contributed to a PhD and to learning to conduct and supervise academic research (Phillips, 1985, 1989, 1991). These data are now being used to illustrate a) how communication breakdown occurs, and b) potential areas of communication breakdown which may be avoided given sensitive action on the part of supervisors.

All of the early research was primarily concerned with the one–to–one model of supervision. However, it cannot be too strongly emphasized that, if there is more than one supervisor, it is absolutely vital that communication occur between all the participants. Hence if there are two supervisors there must be three-way communication — not just between the student and one supervisor, and the student and the other supervisor, but also between all three of them, and between the two supervisors themselves. The same is relevant to any panel of whatever size. The main message contained within this chapter is: 'do not assume that anything is understood'.

Following a brief description of how the information contained in this chapter was obtained, I provide a few examples of 'simple' communication breakdown together with some commentary. Later in the chapter different kinds of communication breakdown are discussed and an argument is presented concerning the importance of making things explicit. This is vital, even if there is a basic assumption that there are no communication difficulties, that student and supervisor/s are completely on the same wavelength. Beware!

The comments which follow derive from Phillips (1983) when student and supervisor pairs were speaking in separate confidential interviews on the same topic. Participants were aware that they would receive no feedback and that no action for changing their particular situation would be taken as a result of anything that was said during the course of the interviews.

Each interview was very relaxed and informal. The method was for the student to have a friendly chat with the interviewer who then interviewed the supervisor. This 'supervisor' interview was equally friendly and informal. Both student and supervisor said something about the various topics being discussed. These interviews were then compared topic by topic.

Some examples of communication breakdown

Paired comparison no. 1

> Student: It's important to get good guidance. I feel my supervisor is doing this. Whenever I get a few results I discuss them with him but otherwise I work on my own.
> Supervisor: On his own he'd be a complete flop, but with guidance and pushing he'll probably do a good PhD if my colleague and I put enough effort into it.

In this first paired comparison of quotations taken from the interviews, we see that the student is actually quite happy — it is the supervisor who is not really content. The problem of course is: should the supervisor tell the student that he considers that this student would be a complete flop, that the student has been spoonfed, and that the supervisor really feels quite irritated at the amount of effort he is having to put into this particular student?

It was only at the very end of the student's period of research that he realized that he had not become an autonomous researcher. This was after he had experienced great difficulty in getting his PhD, having been offered a Master of Philosophy which he refused, and having spent a very long time rewriting the thesis. The problem is, of course, that becoming an autonomous researcher is what working towards a PhD is all about.

It seems obvious that the supervisor should have spoken to his student and told the student directly about some of the points that he was making in the interview. Unfortunately, he did not. If the student had been told by the supervisor that he had to try to do some work on his own, it might have had the effect of preventing him from leaning so heavily on the supervisor. This, in turn, could have resulted in the gradual development of autonomy as the student became more deeply involved in his research.

Paired comparison no. 2

> Student: My supervisor is not going to be a help to me. He doesn't read what I write. So I've realized I'm going to have to get on without him.
> Supervisor: I wish all my students were as good as he is. I'm really happy with him, he's produced five or six short papers about his work, all exploring various aspects.

In the above example we have a slightly different situation. Here, the supervisor is happy but the student is not. In fact, this supervisor, who had been supervising for about 25 years, commented that this particular student was probably one of the best students he had ever had. Unfortunately, he did not tell his student that.

The student was very frustrated and, although he ended up with a good PhD in reasonable time, he believed that this was despite the neglect he had experienced. He went on to get a job in the department in which he had worked as a research student, but avoided the Professor who had been his supervisor. The Professor never understood why.

This student really believed that he had never had adequate supervision. However, he did not tell the supervisor how unhappy he was, and the supervisor believed that, as the student was doing so well, it would be better if he did not interfere. He did not want to push his student in any way or make him feel unsure of himself. So, as long as the student progressed, the supervisor stood back and unobtrusively monitored his progress.

An example of what was happening between them was that the student said the supervisor did not read what he wrote. However, the strategy that the supervisor had adopted for dealing with the student's work was as follows. The student would give the professor a piece of writing six weeks before a tutorial meeting. The Professor would read it, think about it, be concerned that some parts of it went off at tangents that would delay the research (if they were to be followed up) and could be seen as relatively irrelevant. However, there was a core that was quite exciting and could be explored and developed.

The supervisor did not want to make his student feel in any way demoralized or unconfident because he considered this student to be exceptionally good — a self-starting student. So he decided that the best thing to do was not to give the student any negative criticism but to focus on the part that he, the supervisor, thought was worthy of development and encourage his student to work on that. He did this by talking about that specific part of the work in order to get the student excited about it.

By adopting this particular strategy the supervisor ensured that the student was continually receiving positive feedback. This is a good strategy if the student is aware of what is going on. But nothing was explained to the student so what the student thought was happening was that the writing, over which he had laboured so long, sat at the bottom of the supervisor's work pile for the six weeks. Further, the student believed that half an hour before the meeting, the supervisor had thought, 'Oh my goodness he gave me something, where is it?' and had a quick look at it. One paragraph jumped out at him so he spoke about this paragraph the whole time, in the hope that the student would think that he had read it all and was not aware that he had not. That was a misunderstanding. The student never challenged him and the supervisor never explained, 'this is what I am going to be doing with your work'. Consequently this unfortunate result has had long-lasting after-effects.

Paired comparison no. 3

Student: He really over-supervises, he's in twice a day to see what results I've got.

Supervisor: We don't meet as often as we should — about once a month. He has plenty of ideas and it's very much a shared meeting.

These statements were rather puzzling, as the student was complaining of claustrophobia due to lack of trust from his supervisor. He was being asked all the time what he was doing, how he was getting on, what results he had to report. However, during his interview, the supervisor was very embarrassed to speak about the amount of time that he gave to the student. In fact, it took quite a while for him to answer the question and his hesitation intensified the idea — originating from the student — that he was actually going to say he saw the student about twice a day.

How he could have afforded such time for this one student was a mystery as, apart from being head of department and active on the international conference scene, he also had several other research students. When he finally said that they met about once a month he also said, 'but I intend to do better next term and I am going to try and increase that'.

What was happening here was that the student was working in the same laboratory as the supervisor. The supervisor did not want the student to feel that he was working on something that was of no interest to anybody, or that people had forgotten he was there. For these reasons, whenever he was in that part of the lab, he would stop and have a quick chat with the student, just a few words usually, saying: 'How's it going? Any results yet?'

The student counted each of these interactions as 'supervision', whereas the supervisor only counted as 'supervision' the formal tutorials in his study. On these occasions they spoke only about how the work for the thesis was progressing, as opposed to the day-to-day work that the student was doing in the laboratory — not all of which was directly concerned with his thesis.

Once again, this misunderstanding was not discussed. Nothing was made explicit. The kind of arrangement recommended in Phillips and Pugh (1994) where a student and supervisor, at the very beginning of their relationship, discuss how often they should see each other, when the next meeting should be, and arrange at each tutorial when they should next have a tutorial meeting, had not been established. The process was not discussed and therefore we have ambiguity about what constitutes supervision.

Paired comparison no. 4

Student: The supervisor gets all the credit for the student's work and my supervisor should realize he's lucky I've got this far, given the way he supervises.
Supervisor: He suffers from periods of depression and I feel he hasn't put all the energy he might have into his work recently.

In this instance, we have a rather frustrated student and a supervisor who is aware that there is something wrong. He has not asked the student why he is feeling depressed or what is going wrong with his work. They just do not discuss such matters. This is a great mistake. It cannot be emphasized too strongly how important it is to talk about the **process** of the research, as well as the **progress** of the research.

By now it should be apparent that one of the ground rules to be established when a student and supervisor first agree to work together is that the process will form part of the on-going conversation. Once that has been accepted, then many of these topics will come out automatically because, during a tutorial discussion, it is customary to talk about the work. There is a lot of responsibility on both partners to do so: it cannot be all one-sided.

Nevertheless the supervisor is the one who has the experience. Although it is not easy to talk personally about this relationship, if it is on the agenda it can be agreed between them as they move through the tutorial discussion. It will avoid later problems when students might want to change their supervisors or when students even disappear completely, avoiding meeting with their supervisors at all. So putting process, not only content, on the agenda from the very start is essential.

Paired comparison no. 5

> Student: I can see now that, from a supervisor's point of view, if he thinks you have something to do he leaves you alone to get on with it.
> Supervisor: He's become an independent research worker, he's doing original work all the time, but he wouldn't have got very far without the supervision. But that's all part of the game.

These paired comments arose after the student had completed his PhD and was feeling more relaxed. He reflected that he thought that this method of supervision was possibly correct because he had been successful. Also, the supervisor thought that although he had put in quite a lot of effort with this particular student it was his job as a supervisor to do so.

In this example, we have a happy ending. But it was not happy all the way. The student only thought retrospectively that his way was effective. In fact this student, who had been quite unhappy during most of the time that he was a research worker, said that when he attained an appointment at a university and had research students of his own, he was going to do the same — he would treat his students as he had been treated. This was really surprising because he had been so unhappy and had wanted to give up on several occasions. One wonders how he could contemplate inflicting such unhappiness on other people.

He explained that he did not want to be responsible for not giving future PhD students any of the experiences necessary for them to be successful. As he had been successful, he thought that the best model for success was the model he had experienced. There is an obvious danger here.

Strategies for avoiding communication breakdown

The five paired comparisons above all come from work carried out some years ago, before supervision was discussed as openly as it is today. At the start of the research, experienced supervisors (i.e. academics whose students had been very successful and were now well-established in their professional fields — some even having become professors) were asked to conceptualize their supervisory role, as opposed to their academic role. They did not understand the question in those days. So we have come a long way, even though we still have some distance to go.

The information which follows is from more recent research and focuses on other topics that need to be made explicit. These issues should be opened up for communication in order to avoid the kinds of misunderstandings outlined above.

The concept of originality

The first topic is originality, because the PhD is awarded for an original contribution to knowledge. Further, in the statements which most universities have to guide examiners on the grading of theses, there is usually some reference to 'unaided work', 'significant contribution' and 'originality'. However, we do not really know what we mean when we talk about originality.

The main problem is that there is little or no discussion between students and their supervisors of what constitutes originality in the PhD. Although students and staff use the same word to describe a range of different concepts they do not discuss with each other the definitions to which they are working.

Phillips (1992) listed a number of different definitions of originality collected from students, from supervisors and from examiners, some of which are reproduced below. They show that there is a range of different ways in which people might be interpreting originality.

- Carrying out empirical work that hasn't been done before.
- Making a synthesis that hasn't been made before.
- Using already known material but with a new interpretation.
- Trying out something in this country that has previously only been done in other countries.
- Taking a particular technique and applying it in a new area.
- Bringing new evidence to bear on an old issue.
- Being cross-disciplinary and using different methodologies.
- Looking at areas that people in the discipline haven't looked at before.
- Adding to knowledge in a way that hasn't been done before.

A professor of hydraulics working in the area of civil and mechanical engineering, observed a variety of ways in which students may be considered to have shown originality (Francis, 1976). Six of these are:

- setting down a major piece of new information in writing for the first time
- continuing a previously original piece of work
- carrying out original work designed by the supervisor
- providing a single original technique, observation, or result in an otherwise unoriginal but competent piece of research
- having many original ideas, methods and interpretations, all performed by others under the direction of the postgraduate
- showing originality in testing somebody else's idea

making a total of 15 different definitions of originality from those involved.

Unfortunately, there does not appear to be any kind of understanding that originality is being defined in different ways. Students, supervisors and examiners merely assume that originality is originality.

Although initially originality appeared to be a problem, it now seems an escape avenue for students. This is because students are very worried about their work being original enough; but if there are many different ways in which their work can be said to be original, perhaps they will realize that it is much easier to be original in at least one of 15 possible ways than it is to be singularly original.

Students think that they have to be enormously original: that they have to take a seven-league stride and completely recreate everything. However, supervisors know that it is not too difficult to be original because it is not necessary to have a whole new way of looking at the discipline or the topic. In fact a very small step is sufficient. Unfortunately, supervisors do not usually tell their research students this and their students only discover it at a later stage of their research.

Supervisors, therefore, need to have a discussion with students about the concept of originality quite early, as it is something not usually discussed until later in the candidature. Supervisors should set their students' minds at rest and talk about the various ways in which they might be able to be original.

My on-going research shows that postgraduates' thoughts on originality do change as they progress through their period of registration. Initially research students tend to say things like, 'I'm worried about that — I don't know how creative I am'. But by the time they get into their third year they are more likely to say, 'Now I know it can be just a small advance in everyday life; before I knew this I was worried about being original enough'. So eventually, as part of their academic development, students acquire a similar grasp of what is expected in the way of a small step forward, but do not seem to be helped toward this realization by their supervisors.

When students spoke of originality they said that they had been worrying about it and that they might have spoken about it to other research students, but they never spoke about it to members of staff. Hence originality must be discussed at a very early stage. Students must be told of the many ways in which it is possible to be original and, in addition, it is essential to find out from them what they think originality means. Then it is up to the supervisor to explain the limits of the concept.

The PhD/thesis

Supervisors: 'The PhD is partly a piece of research and partly an examination'.

Turning now to the topic of what it is that students think they are doing when they are aiming towards the PhD (and what it is that university staff are supervising and examining), we discover that people tend not to talk about that either. Generally, supervisors said that the PhD was partly a piece of research and partly an examination (Phillips, 1994). They very quickly spoke about the thesis and the PhD synonymously as though they were one and the same thing.

They said that in the thesis there should be three key elements — technical proficiency, originality, and well-executed design, thought and explanation. They confirmed that they did not speak to their students about these things because they were taken for granted.

Students also had great difficulty in separating out the PhD from the thesis. They spoke about the thesis rather than the PhD. They said that there was a great deal of limitation on their freedom to express themselves in the way they wanted. This was because, irrespective of which subject area they were working in, they were convinced that theirs was one of the only theses ever that would not fit into the kind of structure either laid down by the university or the structure they thought they should be following. In fact it was not unusual for students to be confused about just what this structure should be and, often, supervisors had not discussed it.

So once again, we find an area that is not discussed as often or as early as it should be. Students however feel both constrained and concerned: 'There is a limitation on the freedom to express yourself'. Students speak of this lack of freedom relating to lots of different areas which have to be forced into one section. Supervisors say that a successful thesis means 'making a string of sausages into a small salami' which seems to be a useful analogy. Looking closer, it appears that perhaps the supervisors and students are saying the same thing. The difference is that students see it negatively while supervisors see it positively.

Students have great difficulty in discarding any of the enormous amount of data, information and background reading they have done over the years in order to pull it all into the shape of a coherent, well-structured thesis that hangs together, follows a line of argument and tells a story. The supervisors who described this process said that when students are successful, they have 'got the hang of it' and the idea of what is required for a successful, well-constructed thesis. Once again it is necessary to have these kinds of discussions with students to allow them to express their hesitations and their concerns.

Conclusions

As we have seen, research that covers a period of approximately 15 years reveals that there is much that is taken for granted with the student and supervisor relationship. This 'taken for grantedness' often results in stress for students who lack vital information, and frustration for supervisors who are unaware of the ignorance of their students with regard to certain matters.

In order to resolve such a situation and, by so doing, avoid communication breakdown, it is essential first not to assume that anything at all is understood, then to ensure that all significant topics have been made explicit, and finally to check that what has been said has been understood. By these means the kinds of misunderstandings that have been given in the examples outlined above will be avoided.

More specifically, issues such as the concept of originality and the PhD/thesis need to be introduced into the discussion very early in the candidature of the student. It is not good enough for supervisors to assume that everyone knows what a thesis is and that originality is originality. The different definitions of originality need to be confronted, together with the information that the original aspect of the research does not have to be anywhere near as extensive as their students think it has to be.

Similarly, students are not always sure what is required with regard to the thesis but do not mention this to their supervisors. Whether their reticence is due to the fact that they do not know that they do not know, or because they feel that they should know and will look foolish if they admit that they do not, it is up to the supervisor to ensure that such issues are raised in a very matter-of-fact way and also to make it possible for their students to be able to express their hesitations and their concerns.

It is also very important that the context and process within which the research will take place is clearly on the agenda. As demonstrated above, when the process is not discussed any communication breakdown and/or ambiguity that has occurred remains invisible and misunderstandings grow out of all proportion to their meagre origins. Overall, there is a need for supervisors to feel empathy with the inhibition and lack of freedom that students complain about in order to begin to work with them ... making the string of sausages into a salami.

References

Francis, J.R.D. (1976). 'Supervision and examination of higher degree students'. *Bulletin of the University of London* **31**: 3-6.

Phillips, E.M. (1983). 'The PhD as a Learning Process'. Unpublished PhD thesis, University of London.

Phillips, E.M. (1985). 'Supervising postgraduates at a distance'. *Teaching at a Distance* **26**: 23-31.

Phillips, E.M. (1989). 'Institutional responsibilities to postgraduate students'. *HERDSA News* **11**(1): 5-7.

Phillips, E.M. (1991). 'Learning to do research', in N.C. Smith and P. Dainty (eds), *The Management Research Handbook*. London: Routledge.

Phillips, E.M. (1992). 'The PhD: Assessing quality at different stages of its development', in O. Zuber-Skerritt (ed.), *Supervising Beginning Researchers*. Brisbane: Tertiary Education Institute, The University of Queensland.

Phillips, E.M. (1994). 'Quality in the PhD: points at which quality may be assessed', in R. Burgess (ed.), *Postgraduate Education and Training in the Social Sciences: Processes and Products*. London: Jessica Kingsley Publishers.

Phillips, E.M. and Pugh, D.S. (1994). *How to Get a PhD: A Handbook for Students and their Supervisors*, 2nd edn. Buckingham: Open University Press.

Chapter 12

Supervising Literature Reviews

Christine Bruce

What is a literature review?

The remark 'You know one when you see one', encapsulates the ill–defined nature of what actually constitutes a literature review (Cooper, 1985: 6). In recent years, however, literature reviews have been described by Cooper in terms of their content and intent:

> First, a literature review uses as its database reports of primary or original scholarship, and does not report new primary scholarship itself. The primary reports used in the literature may be verbal, but in the vast majority of cases are written documents. The types of scholarship may be empirical, theoretical, critical/analytical, or methodological in nature. Second, a literature review seeks to describe, summarize, evaluate, clarify and/or integrate the content of primary reports. (1985: 8)

In the context of postgraduate study literature reviews may also be described in terms of process and product:

> The process of the literature review involves the researcher in exploring the literature to establish the status quo, formulate a problem or research enquiry, defend the value of pursuing the line of enquiry established, and compare the findings and ideas with his or her own. The product involves the synthesis of the work of others in a form which demonstrates the accomplishment of the exploratory process. (Adapted from Bruce, 1994)

The process

When engaged in higher degree research, students are usually required to 'do a literature review'. The process of reviewing the literature, however, has a number of purposes and therefore should be on-going throughout the research programme. These purposes include:

- becoming familiar with the 'conversation' in the student's area of interest
- identifying an appropriate research question
- ascertaining the nature of previous research and issues surrounding the research question
- finding evidence in the academic discourse to establish a need for the proposed research

•   keeping abreast of ongoing work in the area of interest.

In very practical terms, the literature review process is an integral part of research planning (Moses, 1985). It provides a foundation for the student's research (Phillips and Pugh, 1987), and triggers creative thinking (Connell, 1985). The literature review process also assists in identifying appropriate research methods and techniques, and helps in formulating a discussion about the implications of the research.

The product

It is also usual for students to have to write a literature review as part of their thesis. This is normally a chapter appearing early in the thesis, but, in some styles of thesis, may appear throughout the work. (In fact, as the above discussion of the process of the literature review suggests, this process can contribute to all sections of the thesis.) The product of the literature review also has specific purposes which reflect those relating to the process:

•   demonstrating professional competence in the area of research (Phillips and Pugh, 1987)
•   establishing a theoretical framework for the research being reported
•   justifying the need for the research being reported.

Writing a literature review clearly both assists students to gain mastery of their field and demonstrates that they have mastered an important research skill. Writing literature reviews has not only been a long-standing tradition in research and scholarship, it continues to be a vehicle through which credibility is established. Literature reviews are required when writing grant applications, research reports and journal articles, as well as being sought after by journals for publication in their own right. Writing a literature review is therefore an important part of undertaking higher degree research.

Unfortunately academic interest in the literature review as an object of research has been limited. The existing body of literature is varied, however, and includes explorations of techniques and methods (Glass, 1976; Jackson, 1980), literature searching strategies (Cooper, 1987), and the influence of computers (Brent, 1986). More recent contributions have been an exposition of the literature review process (Cooper, 1989), a description of teaching interventions to facilitate the writing of literature reviews (Poe, 1990), and reflections on the objects of, sources for and common deficiencies found in the literature review (Afolabi, 1992).

Institutional support for literature reviews

The need for students to complete literature reviews early has been a matter of concern for some time. The Science and Engineering Research Council (1989: 11) recommends that students should carry out literature surveys in the early stages in order to facilitate timely submission of the thesis. This strategy is endorsed by Zuber-

Skerritt (1987: 85) who proposes workshops to help students find a research focus, thus ensuring that their reading and notetaking is also focused.

Literature searching skills and writing skills are both critical to reviewing the literature effectively. While students generally want help in developing skills for literature searching (Bruce, 1990), some supervisors do not feel that they have the skills to help their students (Zaporozhetz, 1987). In order to overcome this, a three-way partnership between the student, the supervisor and a librarian is sometimes established (Bailey, 1985).

Assistance with 'the world of information' is an area of growing concern to student researchers; a range of specific strategies for inducting students into this world is discussed in HERDSA's Green Guide Number 13: *Developing Students' Library Research Skills* (Bruce, 1992). Students who need most assistance in this area are usually mature age, often part–time students, unfamiliar with the electronic environments which are a large part of today's academic libraries. As an expression of institutional commitment to supporting higher degree research students, many university libraries now offer teaching programmes for postgraduates in various forms:

- workshops integrated into research methods courses (Kingston and Reid, 1987)
- subjects dedicated to information retrieval, management and evaluation (Bruce, 1990, 1991)
- workshops integrated into induction programmes (Phillips, 1989).

The programmes offered by libraries usually foster a range of skills needed for information searching. (An example of such a programme is described later in this chapter.) These may include planning and evaluating literature searches, familiarity with manual and electronic information sources, developing a current awareness strategy and developing bibliographic file management systems. These literature searching skills will then need to be implemented, together with a second set of skills required for effective writing and communication. These writing skills include:

- being able to outline the argument, i.e. establishing the aims and goals of the literature review
- planning the structure of the literature review
- interrogating sources for relevant information
- evaluating the quality of information
- synthesizing information.

I usually recommend four strategies to assist students to get started on their literature review. Essentially the idea is to encourage students to articulate ideas about their research before embarking on their literature search; this will help prevent them from feeling overwhelmed by information later on. These strategies are therefore critical beginnings to both the literature searching and writing processes:

- structuring the literature review as early as possible in terms of headings and subheadings; these can always be revised and amended as time goes on

- drawing concept maps
- writing as much as possible, whenever possible, about aspects of the research area; writing can always be restructured later
- formulating questions that the literature review will address.

Programmes designed to introduce students to literature searching and writing should not neglect the context within which these skills are to be used. To focus on students' understanding of literature reviews could only enhance their subsequent experience of these dialectical processes. One way of coming to understand the form of the literature review is to read through examples. Examples can be readily found by:

- identifying theses written by previous research students and examining the literature review chapter
- searching indexing and abstracting databases. Databases will respond to a subject search combined with the phrase 'literature review'; many now use the term 'literature review' as a subject heading. The term also often appears in the title of relevant articles.

Naturally, examples found should be critically approached to identify strengths and weaknesses.

How can supervisors assist students working on literature reviews?

The literature review has been put forward as the 'largest problem area' the student encounters in the research process (Hernandez, 1985). Not only are students unsure of what constitutes an adequate review (Hernandez, 1985), they may also consider the literature review section of their thesis as 'an unnecessary appendage to their real goal' (Leedy, 1974: 61). The need for emphasis on this aspect of research work is supported by the findings of a longitudinal study at the University of Reading. Here, it was found that more than 30 per cent of students had not 'largely completed' their literature review by the end of their first year of study (Wright and Lodwick, 1991). Wright and Lodwick (1991: 35) also report that students who attend supervisory meetings more regularly are more likely to have largely completed their literature review at the end of the first year. The most common way in which these students learn about information sources is by themselves or through their supervisor; other students are also reported as an important source (1991: 36). Some students reported that they needed more help with information sources (1991: 39).

Clearly students need to be challenged to complete aspects of the literature review early in the research process. As a literature review encompasses the processes of literature searching, analysis and synthesis of previous work, supervising for the literature review should address all of these. Strategies for helping students include:

- monitoring students' literature review achievements
- exploring students' conceptions of the literature review
- dealing with the problem of the scope of the literature review

- encouraging a reflective approach to literature searching
- encouraging them to bridge the gap between literature searching and writing.

Monitoring students' literature review achievements

An important aspect of supervision involves helping students determine the extent of their achievement in the literature review process. Familiarity with a 'hierarchy of literature review achievements' (Prosser, 1985) may assist with this. The hierarchy reproduced below was based on Alan Prosser's observations of and discussions with research students. Although he believes it to approximate a hierarchy, he also believes that in some instances the achievements may be observed slightly out of order. Interestingly, Prosser also comments that in his experience most students were only 'about two-thirds of the way down the list by the time they submitted their PhD theses'. He also comments that many students have difficulty with judging the value of other people's contributions, needing considerable help from their supervisor with making critical comparisons. Prosser's hierarchy is reproduced below:

- restatement of the author's conclusions in the student's own words
- condensation of information relating to the same specific aspect from different papers
- effective selection of information relevant to the student's project
- critical comparison of information from different sources
- summary of the state of knowledge for each specific aspect
- recognition of deficiencies for each specific aspect
- collection of information not directly relevant but indicative of what could be achieved
- authoritative statements about what has been achieved and what remains to be done in the area of the student's project
- putting the prior knowledge and the project into the context of the sub-discipline.

Exploring students' conceptions of the literature review

Students have been found to have a range of conceptions of the literature review whilst engaged in the early stages of higher degree research (Bruce, 1994). Students' attitudes towards their literature reviews, their apparent diffidence or reluctance to complete this aspect of the research process, may be influenced by particular conceptions of the review which they have adopted. Asking them what they understand by a literature review is a simple opening for exploring their understanding of what is required of them. The various conceptions that students have conveyed include seeing, or experiencing, the literature review as:

- a list of bibliographic citations, possibly supplemented by abstracts and/or lists of important journals in the field
- a search, in which a range of bibliographic tools and personal contacts are used to identify pertinent literature
- a survey, in which documents are read for the purpose of outlining existing

knowledge in the field
- a vehicle for learning, in which the student uses the literature to learn as much as possible about the area being explored
- a research facilitator, in which the literature supports, influences, directs, shapes or changes in some way, the student's research
- a report in which the student frames a written discourse about the literature interrogated.

Although all the conceptions held by students may be appropriate for particular stages of their work, they need to understand early that a literature review is not an annotated bibliography, an understanding which underlies the conception of a literature review as a list. It is also important that they regard the literature review as an important contributor to shaping their research, ultimately an integral part of their thesis, and that they work with this in mind.

Dealing with the problem of the scope of the literature review

The problem of the scope of the literature review, that is, 'What should I include in it?' would be familiar to many supervisors. There are varying approaches to dealing with this problem. Cooper (1988) outlines four possible alternatives: a) exhaustive coverage, citing all relevant literature; b) exhaustive coverage with selective citation; c) representative coverage (discussion of works which typify particular groupings in the literature); d) coverage of pivotal works.

Students themselves have been found to be concerned with a range of factors when considering the scope of coverage of their literature reviews (Bruce, 1993):

- comprehensiveness — they want their review to cover all existing and past knowledge in the area
- specificity — they want to confine their writings to those on a particular topic
- authority — they want to ensure they have identified the authoritative authors
- currency — they want to include current thinking and writing in the field
- availability — they are interested in material which is readily available
- relevance — they are interested in 'relevant' material
- exclusion — they have some idea of material which is to be excluded from their review.

The range of options suggests that supervisors need to clarify with students appropriate approaches to the scope of their literature review in relation to the question being studied. It may be necessary to discuss the scope of their literature review in its various phases. The appropriate coverage of the literature review is likely to differ in early exploration, say in rummaging for a problem, in conducting a literature search and reading around the problem identified, and in writing the review.

One criterion which is often considered, for example, is the need for the review to be 'up to date'; a more specific criteria would be to specify the time period of interest. This characteristic of the literature review is highlighted in Prytherah's definition of the genre: 'A survey of progress in a particular science over a given period (e.g. one, five, or ten years)' (1990: 378). Different time spans may be relevant to different portions of writing in the case of the dissertation literature review.

Supervisors may also wish to encourage students to abandon the attempt to be comprehensive in their approach. Not only is it usually an unattainable goal, but if a student's desire to be comprehensive conflicts with the supervisor's views, then this issue needs to be addressed early. A study of education supervisors reports that the group investigated were more concerned that students identify representative literature than that they be comprehensive (Zaporozhetz, 1987: 133).

Removing a student's goal of comprehensive coverage may however leave them somewhat uncertain as to the scope of the literature review. At this point it may be the supervisor's role to help the student determine what should be included in the literature review and to define criteria of relevance. Again, such criteria need to be formulated at various stages of conducting a review.

Zuber-Skerritt (1987) suggests that as students clarify their understanding of their topic, they will have less difficulty in determining what is relevant, and will be more efficient in their reading, note-taking and writing. Perversely perhaps, focusing on criteria of relevance may in turn create a need to encourage students to be more divergent in their reading from time to time in order to keep abreast of the work of the broader research community, in their own and related disciplines.

Encouraging a reflective approach to literature searching

Researchers have different information-gathering styles (Palmer, 1991). Neophyte researchers who appreciate this are less likely to be overwhelmed when confronted with the ever-growing world of information in their field of research. Palmer describes a range of categories to which information-gatherers may belong: the information overlord, the information entrepreneur, the information hunter, the information pragmatist, the information plodder and the information derelict. Becoming comfortable with your own information-gathering style is the first step in adopting a reflective approach to literature searching. Students who consider themselves to be information derelicts should, however, urgently seek help. The second central element is maintaining a regular log, or journal of information-gathering activity. This involves keeping records of personal contacts, correspondence, and material acquired through the Internet as well as keeping records of activity in more formal information networks such as libraries. Adhering to the cycle of reflective literature searching (see Figure 1) should then assist the student to make useful headway in literature searching. It will also provide records of their work if help is required from supervisors or librarians.

Figure 1: Reflective literature searching model (Bruce, 1992: 16)

Design a search strategy
PLAN

Redesign the strategy

Implement the strategy
ACT

Think about the outcomes
REFLECT

Record the results
RECORD

Encouraging students to bridge the gap between literature searching and writing

Given the need to encourage students to write in the early stages of research, suggesting strategies for linking literature searching to writing processes can be useful. Bruce (1994) suggests that a reflective approach to the literature review can act as a useful bridge. Using this approach students reflect regularly on various aspects of their literature searching and writing, preferably as part of a regular programme of maintaining a journal or day book. The following are suggested as appropriate trigger questions to which students could respond:

- What is the present state of my list of references? Is it up-to- date in the areas of present interest? Is it adequate?
- What literature searching have I done this fortnight? Are there any new areas in which I have become interested that I may need to search?
- What have I read recently? Have I found time to read recently?
- What have I learned from the literature this fortnight? Have I changed in any way my understanding of the area in which I am working?
- Is what I have read going to influence my research in any way? Has it given me any ideas which I need to consider and incorporate?
- Have I been writing about what I have read? Do I need to reconsider how what I have been reading fits into my research?

Critically reviewing the literature review

In reviewing their own writing for the literature review students need to be encouraged to evaluate their work against a range of criteria. The form of the literature review, qualities of good literature reviews and common deficiencies need to be taken into account, in addition to general criteria of using correct grammar and appropriate writing styles.

Reviewing the form of the literature review involves assessing whether key decisions have been made by the writer in each of the following areas (Cooper, 1988):

- **Focus** What are the focal elements of the review? These may include research outcomes, methods, theories.
- **Goals** What are the goals of the review? There may be more than one goal such as synthesising previous research, identifying key issues and critically analysing previous research.
- **Perspective** What perspective has been adopted? Does the writer assume the role of 'honest broker' or that of an advocate, arguing for a particular position?
- **Coverage** What extent of the literature is covered? Pivotal works only, works representing particular groupings in the literature, or is an attempt at exhaustive coverage made?
- **Organization** Is the review arranged conceptually, historically or methodologically? Perhaps more than one organizational technique is used?

The literature review should make it clear to readers what approach has been taken in each of the above areas.

Good literature reviews should include current literature as well as material of historical interest. The aims of the review should be clearly stated as well as the range of resources from which literature has been gathered, that is which databases were searched and what other sources were interrogated (Cooper, 1989). A breadth of knowledge of the area being studied should be demonstrated (Phillips and Pugh, 1987), and a strong argument developed justifying the nature of the original contribution made by the thesis. Above all, the review should be interesting to read!

Areas in which literature reviews are commonly deficient (Afolabi, 1992) include:

- exclusion of landmark studies
- emphasis on outdated material
- adopting a parochial perspective
- not being critical
- not discriminating between relevant and irrelevant material
- lacking synthesis.

Hansford and Maxwell (1993: 180) cite the literature review as the second most frequent chapter of the thesis to be criticized by examiners. These criticisms targeted at candidates of Masters degrees are also relevant to the PhD context. Common criticisms identified by Hansford and Maxwell (1993: 179) include the failure to use recent literature, lack of critical assessment, not relating the literature review to the research questions or hypotheses, and incorrectly interpreting sources. These criticisms are not unlike Afolabi's common deficiencies and could be largely avoided if students were alerted to them.

A model programme for assisting students working on literature reviews

Mentioned earlier in this chapter was the role of university libraries in assisting students through the literature review process. Since the late 1980s the Queensland University of Technology (QUT) library has offered a subject (IFN 001 Advanced Information Retrieval Skills), designed to support students across the university with this aspect of their research. The subject was offered as an expression of institutional support as a result of discussion between the university librarian and the Chancellery. A survey of postgraduate students and supervisors conducted in 1989 substantiated the need for the proposed service (Bruce, 1990). Advanced Information Retrieval Skills comprises seven modules (Bruce, 1990: 225):

- **Using QUT Library and Other Resources.** The title of this module reflects its intention to expose students to the wide range of information networks available to them, with special attention to university libraries. Workshops are structured to introduce students to search strategies, processes of scientific communication, controlled vocabularies, the database structure of online catalogues and effective ways of accessing these. (2 hrs) As an outcome of this module students have begun to analyse their research topic and to identify areas of interest for which 'information' is required. They have also begun to compile a list of authors, important sources, keywords, and have conducted searches of local and international library catalogues.
- **Accessing Information through Indexes and Abstracts.** Here students become familiar with the major print indexes in their fields and various means of identifying alternative services which may be useful. Different indexing techniques are discussed and students are encouraged to understand the disparate ways in which a single citation may be handled by different services. A major focus of this module is the use of citation indexes. (2 hrs) As an outcome of this module students begin to search CD-ROM and print indexing and abstracting services relevant to their topic. They also identify key references for tracing in citation indexes.
- **Computerized Information Retrieval.** This module equips students to use computerized bibliographic databases (other than library catalogues). They are introduced to the various types of information which can be accessed and the storage media which they are likely to encounter. Students learn to search an online system relevant to them under the guidance of a reference librarian familiar with the system and subject area. (3 hrs) As an outcome of this module students search at least one commercial online system and identify other systems and databases which need to be accessed.
- **Specialized Resources.** Workshops in this module are developed according to the needs of the student group. Emphasis usually falls on developing current awareness strategies, and the electronic communication methods available through AARNet (Australian Academic Research Network) and the Internet. Product information, electronic journals, statistical sources, government

documents, maps, etc. may also be included. (2 hrs) This is an important module for emphasising the significance of 'pre-published' information in the research process. Journal clubs, attendance at conferences and seminars and other strategies for communication amongst scholars are all considered. In this module students are encouraged to develop personal strategies for networking and keeping up-to-date with research in progress in their field.

- **Thesis Presentation.** Students are introduced to abstract writing, referencing systems and the many resources available for guidance on thesis writing. Students also engage in discussion about aspects of writing literature reviews in this module. (2 hrs) As an outcome of this module students begin to structure aspects of their thesis with special attention to the literature review. They draft a possible abstract, identify and use an appropriate referencing system and structure their literature review.

- **Organizing Information.** Researchers unable to effectively manage information are severely handicapped. This module introduces students to strategies for maintaining personal bibliographic files, including both manual and electronic systems. Strategies for notetaking and recording citations are also discussed. (2 hrs) Students are expected to design and implement a system for their own use as a result of this module.

- **Evaluating Information.** In this module students establish a range of criteria by which to evaluate information retrieved. They are encouraged not to depend upon a subconscious or intuitive assessment of information but to be able to articulate reasons for accepting items as valuable or otherwise. Finally, the literature search process itself is subjected to evaluation. (2 hrs) Work related to this module contributes to the development of the writing of the literature review.

The rationale underlying the subject is based on the need for new researchers to develop sound information literacy skills, and the need for postgraduate students to be adequately supported through the early stages of literature searching for and writing a literature review. The immediate goal is for students to complete thorough and systematic literature searches for their literature reviews, through formal networks and personal contacts. In the longer term students have the skills to keep up-to-date in their area of research interest, independently complete literature searches in other areas of research, and work intelligently and comfortably with a librarian.

Conclusion

The process and product of the literature review provide a significant opportunity for learning about substantive and methodological interests and the continually changing world of information. Adequate supervision of the literature review and attention on the student's part to this process will, therefore, impact not only on the quality of the thesis but on the quality of the graduating candidate.

References

Afolabi, M. (1992). 'The review of related literature in research'. *International Journal of Information and Library Research* 4: 59-66.

Bailey, B. (1985). 'Thesis practicum and the librarian's role'. *Journal of Academic Librarianship* 12: 79-81.

Borg, W.R. and Gall, M.D. (1989). *Educational Research: An Introduction*, 5th edn. New York: Longman.

Brent, E.E. (1986). 'The computer assisted literature review'. *Computers and the Social Sciences* 2: 137-151.

Bruce, C.S. (1990). 'Information skills coursework for postgraduate students: investigation and response at the Queensland University of Technology'. *Australian Academic and Research Libraries* 21: 224-232.

Bruce, C.S. (1991). 'Postgraduate response to an information retrieval credit course'. *Australian Academic and Research Libraries* 22: 103-110.

Bruce, C.S. (1992). *Developing Students' Library Research Skills*. HERDSA Green Guide No. 13. Kensington, NSW: HERDSA.

Bruce, C.S. (1993). 'When enough is enough: or how should research students delimit the scope of their literature review?' Paper presented to the HERDSA National Conference, University of Sydney, July 1993.

Bruce, C.S. (1994). 'Research students' early experiences of the dissertation literature review'. *Studies in Higher Education* 19: 217-229.

Connell, R.W. (1985). 'How to supervise a Ph.D.'. *Australian Universities Review* 28: 38-41.

Cooper, H. (1985). 'A taxonomy of literature reviews'. Paper presented at the *Annual Meeting of the American Educational Research Association, March 31st – April 4th, Chicago, Illinois.*

Cooper, H. (1987). 'Literature searching strategies of integrative research reviewers: a first survey'. *Knowledge* 8: 372-383.

Cooper, H. (1988). 'The structure of knowledge synthesis: a taxonomy of literature reviews'. *Knowledge in Society* 1: 104-126.

Cooper, H. (1989). *Integrating Research: A Guide for Literature Reviews*, 2nd edn. Newbury Park: Sage.

Glass, G.V. (1976). 'Primary, secondary and meta-analysis of research'. *Educational Researcher* 5: 3-8.

Hansford, B. and Maxwell, T. (1993). 'A master's degree program: structural components and examiner's comments'. *Higher Education Research and Development* 12: 171-187.

Hernandez, N. (1985). 'The fourth, composite 'r' for graduate students: research', ED 267671.

Jackson, G.B. (1980). 'Methods for integrative reviews'. *Review of Educational Research* 50: 438-460.

Kingston, P. and Reid, B. (1987). 'Instruction in information retrieval within a doctoral research program: a pertinent contribution'. *British Journal of Academic Librarianship* 2: 91-104.

Leedy, P. (1974). *Practical Research: Planning and Design*. New York: Macmillan.

Mauch, J.E. and Birch, J.W. (1989). *Guide to the Successful Thesis and Dissertation*, 2nd edn. New York: Marcel Dekker.

Moses, I. (1985). *Supervising Postgraduates*. HERDSA Green Guide No. 3. Sydney: Higher Education Research and Development Society of Australasia.

Palmer, J. (1991). 'Scientists and information: using cluster analysis to identify information style'. *Journal of Documentation* **47**: 105-129.

Phillips, E.M. (1989). 'Institutional responsibilities to postgraduate students: the Birkbeck College approach'. *HERDSA News* **11**: 5-7.

Phillips, E.M. and Pugh, D.S. (1987). *How to Get a Ph.D*. Buckingham: Open University Press.

Poe, R.E. (1990). 'A strategy for improving literature reviews in psychology courses'. *Teaching of Psychology* **17**: 54-55.

Prosser, A. (1985). 'A hierarchy of literature reviews', personal communication to the author 20/7/92.

Prytherah, R. (1990). *Harrod's Librarian's Glossary of Terms Used in Librarianship, Documentation and the Book-crafts*, 7th edn. Vermont: Gower.

Science and Engineering Research Council (1989). *Research Student and Supervisor: An Approach to Good Supervisory Practice*. London: SERC.

Wright, J. and Lodwick, R. (1991). 'The process of the PhD: a study of the first year of doctoral study'. *Research Papers in Education* **4**: 22-56.

Zaporozhetz, L. (1987). 'The Dissertation Literature Review: How Faculty Advisers Prepare Their Doctoral Candidates'. Doctoral Thesis, University of Oregon.

Zuber-Skerritt, O. (1987). 'Helping postgraduate research students learn'. *Higher Education* **16**: 75-94.

Chapter 13

Contracts and Checklists: Practical
Propositions for Postgraduate Supervision

Yoni Ryan

Introduction

The recent interest in postgraduate supervision in tertiary institutions is as much a consequence of the types of students undertaking postgraduate studies over the last few years as it is of the sheer explosion in their numbers.

As Ingrid Moses points out in her chapter, nearly 103,500 students were enrolled in postgraduate courses in Australian universities in 1992 — 18.5 per cent of the total enrolments within institutions. (Moses' figures indicate that this is an increase of just over 2 per cent from 1982, not a huge percentage increase — but the number of actual postgraduate enrolments is nearly double that of 1982.)

I have asserted that the nature of students now undertaking postgraduate studies has contributed to current inquiry into supervision issues. It is my contention that postgraduate students are increasingly mature age, and hence likely to have substantial family and social responsibilities, as well as work commitments (see also Chapter 10). In consequence they are likely to be more instrumentally oriented (Ferrier, 1992). They are likely therefore to be more critical of the 'postgrad process' — departmental procedures and practices and the quality of their supervision — than previous cohorts of postgraduate students, who generally progressed into a higher degree immediately on completion of an Honours/Masters Preliminary year, as preparation for an academic or research career, still suspended in that indeterminate (because financially dependent) adulthood which characterizes the 20-24-year old full-time student. Young adult full-time students are generally less demanding of their departments and supervisors, partly because they lack the experiential knowledge of other institutional cultures, and therefore have little basis of comparison, and partly because they have the emotional and social support of other full-time young adult students.

By contrast, mature age **postgraduate** students share the usual mature age **undergraduate** characteristics:

* high time commitments outside the study arena
* part-time 'studenthood'
* experiences which are often disjunctive with the theoretical constructs they are learning at university
* a knowledge of an organizational culture which is generally very different from university culture (i.e. corporate culture, small business, government department)

- a lack of deep confidence in their ability to meet the required standards of the institution, paradoxically coexisting with a knowledge of personal competence in other areas of life — what might be termed the 'I don't think I'm good enough. But I know I'm as smart as some of them' syndrome.

(See also Knowles, 1990.) The mature age postgraduate student poses additional perplexities for staff and tertiary institutions. Except in certain programmes (the MBA is the most common), where no undergraduate degree is required for entry, the mature student has a basic degree and probably an established learning style preference. The student may, however, have had no research skills preparation, such as an Honours year. He or she is less likely to be tolerant of supervisors' eccentricities and distractions and any departmental inefficiencies, as a consequence partly of time pressures and partly of experience with other organizational cultures. Equally, supervisors suspect often an instrumental approach by the mature student ('I must get this piece of paper'), which is considered alien to the nature of university higher degree study (although a vocational orientation is tolerated at undergraduate level).

To my knowledge, no major attitudinal or motivational study has been undertaken to clarify differences between the two age groups in postgraduate education, but once again Moses' study (in this collection) is useful: Table 3 of her paper indicates that of her students, 22 per cent of PhD and 20 per cent of Masters students were seeking 'an extension of knowledge for their current profession', and 30 per cent of PhD and 35 per cent of Masters students wanted 'to develop high level research skills for their current profession', which lends further empirical support to the argument that currently employed adults form an increasing proportion of our postgraduate students — and see also Whittle's comments here on the changing nature of postgraduate students. Moses' study also points to a high motivation for 'personal satisfaction to be gained from research and discovery', which replicates what we know of the complex motivational pressures for decision making in adults, and suggests the need for more research in this area.

Further — though I would not wish to make too much of this — a goodly number of these currently employed students are themselves academics, products of the college/new university sector where until recently industry or teaching experience was the primary criterion for promotion or tenure, but where higher degrees are now a requisite. One might expect such students to be acutely aware of any deficiencies in relation to supervision; one might also expect them to be less well-motivated because of the extrinsic pressure to gain additional qualifications, which is not to deny the strength of extrinsic motivation.

At the same time, one might posit that from the institutional point of view, they might be considered 'difficult' students because they are part-time and progress irregularly because of their work patterns, which are governed by the same semester/term-based times as those of their supervisors.

Apart from the immediate difficulty of rejigging departmental teaching priorities and resource allocation to cater for the more labour-intensive practices of postgraduate teaching, departments face other problems associated with the general increase in postgraduate numbers. Many university staff have had little experience with postgraduate supervision; they are also used to a rather compliant student group, not with negotiating with adults their own age or older who differ in attitude and experience from the eager, diffident mature students in their undergraduate classes (see Ryan, 1979). The potential for disaffected students and disgruntled supervisors in this situation seems obvious.

If we add to this potential the common concerns of postgraduate students and supervisors as revealed in studies like those of Phillips and Pugh (1987), or in student newsletters such as those put out by the Queensland University of Technology's Student Guild (which warns students to beware of the supervisor who publishes a student's report under his or her own name — *Expose* Semester 2, 1993: 18), we can readily perceive that postgraduate supervision is problematical, not merely for the institution, but for the individuals — staff and students — involved.

Institutionally, postgraduate supervision has been characterized by adhocery: by skimpy procedural mechanisms, beginning with the casual choice of supervisor ('Who has any spare capacity?') and continuing through a two-page progress report at six monthly intervals ('How many hours of consultation have occurred in the last six months?'). Only two years ago at one of the top research universities in Australia, it was possible to write 'six hours' for two consecutive semesters without any alarm bells sounding at departmental or institutional levels. Another common institutional problem with consequences for postgraduate students is the sort of decision making which allows professional development/study leave to be announced so late that postgraduate students are given as little as two months' notice of a six months' absence by their supervisor.

What possible responses can we make at institutional level which might alleviate, if not prevent, the problems inherent in the current 'postgrad process', and which might take account of the changing nature of the student population?

Practical propositions

I suggest that two procedures which might be useful are contracts and checklists, for departments, supervisors and students. Both contracts and checklists should cover pre-enrolment and enrolment procedures, as well as the practices and understandings pertinent to candidature, and the usual specific full documentation regarding production of the thesis and submission procedures. (It is surely ironic that most tertiary institutions have detailed specifications for the binding and copying arrangements, but so little in the way of specified expectations and understandings of the study process itself — see also Perry (1993).)

The checklist of questions supplied as the conclusion of the British Science and Engineering Research Council's *Research Student and Supervisor* (1983) provides a starting point; Parry and Hayden (1994) recommend general practices in supervision based on their Australian survey. The latter provides an excellent basis for departments wishing to customize contracts or checklists for their particular needs and approaches.

A contract can be interpreted as a fully negotiated document establishing the services each of several entities will undertake for other entities, taking cognizance of the needs of each entity. Such negotiation implies individualized and time-consuming activity on the part of each entity — student, supervisor and department. As Gagné points out, a contract

> ... solves the problem of the wide range of backgrounds, education, experience, interests, motivations, and abilities that characterize most adult groups by providing a way for individuals ... to tailor-make their own learning plans (quoted in Knowles, 1990: 139).

In an ideal world, such negotiation might be preferred in the matter of a relationship as significant and intense as postgraduate study implies, but totally negotiated contracts are obviously impossible for each of the 103,000 postgraduate enrolments in Australia.

There are shortcuts which could be employed by utilising items covering the issues of concern to the institution, the department, the supervisor and the student. For instance, the department might decide that all students should make an initial contact with a postgraduate coordinator who would then present to the prospective student the department's contract in relation to pre-enrolment and enrolment procedures. These might include that the department undertook to submit a proposal to a postgraduate committee which would decide, on the basis of the proposal, whether the student could beneficially be accommodated in the department, and with what supervisor and, if not, that the department would (or would not) provide advice to the student about other avenues, based on the student's potential to undertake a higher degree. The student contract, at this stage of the process, might encompass the provision of a specific proposal along the lines of that outlined in Moses (1985: 12ff), or a more general proposal substantiated by some level of literary review, such as is typical of humanities candidature, where it is often only in the course of the study that the topic is refined.

Contracts would be formally reviewed by the supervisor and student every six months and informally every three months, in line with the student's progress and the stage of the research. This would allow for the different rhythms of the study — data gathering, reading, writing, etc. Built into the contract would be the procedures for dealing with the sensitive matters of the personal and professional relationship between supervisor and student: for instance, an arrangement that encourages and allows a student access to a postgraduate coordinator if he or she feels uncomfortable or poorly treated should be spelled out and understood as a prerogative of candidature. A similar arrangement should be in place for a supervisor who has difficulty in dealing with a particular student. The postgraduate coordinator should also review the contracts of both supervisor and student formally at six monthly intervals, with the committee reviewing them every 12 months. This would in large measure subvert the unequal power relationship which is currently perpetrated by the six-monthly progress report, a scant two-page proforma which the student completes, the supervisor reads, comments on and sends on to the institutional postgraduate committee, often not to be seen again by the student.

Some departments might prefer a checklist, devised at departmental level, to cover the same areas of concern. We might define a checklist as a more prescriptive instrument, a proforma which does not imply negotiation, but obligations which must be verified by a party to the checklist as having been undertaken. A checklist implies a defined set of requirements, an observable set of procedures, which **may** — and only may — be more appropriate to the climate of the sciences, or even the social sciences. A pre-enrolment checklist for a department might include the following:

- Has the student been given a detailed outline of what the proposal must contain?
- Has assistance been given (will it be given?) in relation to compiling the proposal?
- Is a supervisor available
    - with the necessary expertise?
    - with the time capacity?
    - with the personal skills to deal with this student?
- Does the department have the requisite resources in the area? Can it obtain them?
- Does the general proposal fit the department's priorities and interests?
- Does the student appear to have the skills required — research or practical (computer skills, statistical packages, etc.)
- If not, can the student be directed to undertake any courses before enrolment? During enrolment?
- Are there any inhibiting factors in the candidature (departmental, student, supervisor)?
- If so, are there obvious solutions?
- Who will take responsibility for these?
- Has the student read at least two relevant theses before the final decision regarding enrolment?

Both contracts and checklists must be detailed, for it is the lack of clearly articulated detail in current procedures which leads to so many less-than-satisfactory candidatures. It is not the intention of this chapter to provide a proforma, because each department must commit itself to the notion of adopting either of the procedures, and should then devise its own items based on identified matters of concern to the discipline. However, the items above are indicative of minimum considerations, and the level of detail which must be included. I append a sample contract and checklist, but do not contend that these are exhaustive, or that they encompass every situation. Even a proforma adopted by a department must be capable of particularization if the individual situation warrants, as might for instance be the case if the student were not a native speaker and required extra assistance, or dual language supervision.

I now turn to the question of departmental, supervisor and individual student style, and the appropriateness of either contracts or checklists. It seems to me that the preliminary and partial checklists suggested in the early literature (e.g. Connell, 1985; Moses, 1985) fail to take account of the nature of disciplinary differences in approaches to teaching and research, or of the nature of the supervisor or student. Moses (1985) for example speaks of the 'writing up phase' at the end of the study, as does the SERC (1983), whereas my own experience in the humanities and social sciences has been continuous writing and rewriting, as both Gottlieb and Brown suggest here. It has been argued (Phillips and Pugh, 1987) that science departments often operate their postgraduate programmes as part of a specific long-term departmental project based on a grant, whereas humanities or social science postgraduate studies are more often individual projects, 'curiosity driven', and less demanding of equipment and resource funds. The consequences are that students must more often 'fit' into a project in science departments than they might do in a humanities department. We also have some empirical evidence that science students exhibit a preference for an assimilative learning style (Kolb, 1985), and more prescriptive curricula and conventional presentation and teaching practice (Isaacs, 1986). While Baxter's (1989) study of the same department considered in Isaacs' study did not attempt to align departmental style with its staff's reluctance to accept an unconventional teaching method, it portrayed a culture which found it difficult to accept alternative methodologies without extensive staff development activities.

Traditionally of course, the 'hard' disciplines of science, because of the nature and extent of the subject matter, have approached teaching through large-group lectures and laboratory sessions, while the humanities/social sciences have structured their teaching through large-group lectures and small-group seminars because 'knowledge' in these areas is considered open to interpretation and is therefore more 'negotiable'. Neither approach prepares the academic or the student for the intense one-to-one relationship which is postgraduate study — although the science postgraduate who is part of a project team is still largely working in a group situation, and may rarely see the supervisor outside the group.

But in consequence of these conventional approaches — which are only slowly changing — I would tentatively suggest that science departments might find a checklist more akin to a systems approach, a more comfortable and familiar strategy for assuring productive and satisfying postgraduate experiences for supervisor and student, while humanities and social science departments might prefer contracts In this regard, the recent work of Becher et al. (1994) on disciplinary differences in postgraduate education, might prove a useful focus for departments.

I would reiterate that the decision must be made at departmental level, both to secure as large a measure of commitment to the process as is possible in the university culture, and to ensure that there will be a procedure which is understood and accepted by every potential supervisor. And while there might well be a departmental proforma, there should also be the latitude for individual staff and students to add not only the specifics — six-weekly meetings or four-weekly; written or oral reports in the first six months or both; interim publication or not — as appropriate to the discipline, but also the idiosyncracies peculiar to the individual staff member or student, such as polishing a first draft immediately following a critique, or completing the thesis in first draft before polishing. As long as these items are made 'visible' and are **explicit** in the contract or checklist, there is room for individuality.

Staff development activities in Australian universities have almost invariably relied on individual staff identifying a personal/professional need in the area of teaching and learning and 'self-selecting' for attendance at professional workshops. Improving postgraduate supervision has similarly been the concern of individuals. Activities such as Zuber-Skerritt's Department of Employment Education and Training (DEET) sponsored Seminar on Postgraduate Supervision in 1993 were designed to have a ripple effect within an institution or department, but still depend on the enthusiasm of the individuals involved in peer training. However, utilizing more concerted approaches such as contracts and checklists necessitates departmental decision making and intense discussion on the purposes and meaning of postgraduate studies — for departments, supervisors and students. This goes to the heart of university culture, combining as it does the essence of research and scholarship, and the most intense teaching and learning relationship — one-to-one — possible in our education system.

Conclusion

I began by arguing that it was not only the sheer numbers of postgraduate students that stimulated interest in supervision processes, but also the nature of the students themselves. Academics have an increasingly demanding and experienced — perhaps even cynical — clientele, older and busier, less interested in the 'dreaming spires' and more interested in jumping hurdles. If the procedures and expectations of the 'postgrad process' were clarified through methods such as contracts and checklists, eliminating the misunderstandings and failures of performance which seem to dog students and supervisors, we might yet be able to make postgraduate study the 'adventure of the mind' that Medawar (quoted in Phillips and Pugh, 1987: 13) tells us it should be, and that we know it can be.

Appendix

Supervisor Checklist

- Have we set a timetable for regular meetings?
- Do I have a copy of the study plan jointly devized with the student?
- Is this weekly? Monthly? Six-weekly?
- Is this being met?
- Am I keeping notes of each meeting and providing a copy to the student?
- Have I established with the student whether I require oral or written reports of progress at each meeting? A journal?
- Does the student's initial proposal genuinely fit my own research interests and knowledge of the area?
- Does the library have the resources to cover the field adequately? If not, what funding can be arranged?
- Have I told the student where I perceive I may not be able to assist? Can I get someone else to help, or arrange resources to cover that gap?
- Is the proposed topic still manageable in size at this stage of the thesis?
- Will the findings be a genuine extension of knowledge in the field?
- Have I ensured that the student understands the ethics of this relationship as I perceive them in relation to co-authorship/publication?
- Do I feel comfortable in the relationship with the student?
- If not, what have I done about it?
- Do I feel comfortable with the methodological implications of the study?

- Has the student understood fully the expectations for a Masters/PhD study as explained in the department's checklist?

- Have I checked with the student recently to ensure that he/she feels the department is meeting its obligations in terms of space? Funding? Conference travel?

Student Contract

I undertake:

- to attend the library's advanced information retrieval course in March
- to maintain our negotiated schedule of monthly meetings, and bring to those meetings a written report of at least 500 words on the work I have undertaken during the month, including reading, the questions raised by that reading in relation to my proposed study, and my progress on the computer course, as well as my assessment of my progress on our agreed schedule; the reading list will be annotated to assist in the literature review expected at the end of this six-month period
- to bring any difficulty I may have in relation to methodology, time, resources, or personal matters to the supervisor's attention between these meetings if they seem to threaten my progress
- to attend the fortnightly meetings of postgraduate students in the department, and to discuss my work with the group
- to prepare a 10-minute explication of my proposal for April 20th, to be given to a departmental seminar
- to complete the ERIC search by June 30th
- to contact the Postgraduate Office regarding the possibility of travel grants for the field trip
- to resubmit my proposal to the Ethics Committee by April 10th for clearance, given that the methodology has changed since my original proposal.

References

Baxter, E.P. (1989). *Resource Based Education in Chemical Engineering: Responding to Staff Perceptions of a Teaching Innovation*. Brisbane: Tertiary Education Institute, The University of Queensland.

Becher, T., Henkel, M. and Kogan, M. (1994). *Graduate Education in Britain*. London: Jessica Kingsley.

Connell, R. (1985). 'How to supervise a PhD'. *Australian Universities Review* 28(2): 38-41.

Ferrier, F. (1992). 'Not more of the same stuff: Student dissatisfaction with postgraduate courses'. *Academia under Pressure: Research and Development in Higher Education*, Vol. 15. Sydney: HERDSA, pp. 381-387.

Isaacs, G. (1986). 'Learner-oriented subjects in a teacher-oriented course'. *Research and Development in Higher Education*, 9. Sydney: HERDSA, pp. 87-91.

Knowles, M. (1990). *The Adult Learner: A Neglected Species*, 4th edn. Houston: Gulf.

Kolb, D. (1985). *Learning Styles Inventory*. Boston: McBer and Co.

Moses, I. (1985). *Supervising Postgraduates*. HERDSA Green Guide No. 3. Sydney: HERDSA.

Parry, S. and Hayden, M. (1994). *Supervising Higher Degree Research Students*. Canberra: AGPS.

Perry, C. (1993). 'A structured approach to presenting PhD Theses'. Notes for candidates and their supervisors. Brisbane: Faculty of Business, QUT.

Phillips, E.M. and Pugh, D.S. (1987). *How to Get a PhD*. Buckingham: Open University Press.

Ryan, Y. (1979). 'Between the Idea and the Reality: A Study of 46 Mature Age Students at a Regional College'. Unpublished MEd Thesis: University of Melbourne.

Science and Engineering Research Council. (1983). *Research Student and Supervisor: An Approach to Good Supervisory Practice*. London: SERC.

Chapter 14

'Guidelines for Discussion': A Tool for Managing Postgraduate Supervision

Barbara Grant and Adele Graham
with an Afterword by John Jones

Introduction

As staff developers in the area of postgraduate supervision we have been interested to hear academics tell of their personal experiences of being supervised as postgraduate students — frequently they were dismal! And many students currently enrolled tell similar stories. In this chapter we describe 'Postgraduate Supervision: Guidelines for discussion' (Graham and Grant, 1993) which we have developed to assist supervisors and students in the process of clarifying mutual expectations of the supervision process. This description is set amidst a consideration of the current literature on postgraduate supervision, as well as stories from students' experiences of using the document with their supervisors. In addition we offer some discussion — from critical education and Foucauldian perspectives — of the power dynamics of the student-supervisor relationship in an effort to understand this sometimes troubled ground.

Our experience of postgraduate supervision has been that it is a difficult terrain. From the perspectives of both the student and the supervisor,[1] there are often major concerns which frequently neither party has the skills to resolve. However, in acknowledging that both parties do have concerns, we do not want to overlook the relative importance of successful completion to the student. Indeed the unequal underpinnings at the level of lived experience — insofar as it is likely to be the student's major work focus while it is one small aspect of the supervisor's current workload — is probably one of the main factors implicated in the miscommunication and frustration described to us by many students and supervisors. This is not to say that supervision is never successful and enjoyable: it is often successful in terms of academic outcomes in spite of the frustration experienced by one or both parties, and it is sometimes enjoyable.

As numbers of postgraduate students climb with no corresponding increase in numbers of supervising staff, the potential for supervision problems grows. Also, the changed demographic structure of the postgraduate student cohort (as described by Yoni Ryan) may have some implications for what students will accept as adequate supervision.

What are some of the many concerns described by students and supervisors? Frequently from the student's perspective there are concerns with supervisors not being available, not being supportive, or not giving adequate feedback. From the supervisor's perspective, common concerns include students who appear unmotivated, who avoid the supervisor, who do not produce written work, who have unrealistic goals, or who do not have a 'thesis'.

So-called 'wastage' figures in the postgraduate cohort are high enough to cause concern and have been the subject of some research (Moses, 1985; DEET referred to in Powles, 1988; Zuber-Skerritt, 1992). Dissatisfaction with supervision emerges as a significant factor in non-completion although there are some interesting twists in these findings. For example in a recent comprehensive review of the organization of graduate studies in Canada (Holdaway et al., 1994), while 'proper supervision' was listed as the number one factor thought to influence successful completion of graduate programmes, it was ranked mid-way among those factors thought to be most influential in preventing such completion. 'Motivation' — a variable which in our experience is often linked to the dynamics of the supervision relationship — was ranked more highly. This aligns with the picture provided by our institution's official supervision guidelines, in which after a detailed listing of the reciprocal responsibilities of supervisor and student, the student is told that she or he is ultimately responsible for the success or failure of the thesis. It would seem that while it is clearly to the supervisor's credit if a student does well, it is **not** clearly to their discredit if the student fails. Yet from the stories that students tell us we know the supervision relationship itself can be a great source of motivation or, equally, a cause for loss of motivation and, further, we know that the supervisor's advice is sometimes contradictory or misleading or at odds with the student's goals. For these reasons, it is not surprising that researchers such as Phillips and Pugh (1987) suggest the heart of a successful supervision process is the quality of the relationship between supervisor and student.

The student–supervisor relationship: a relation of power

There is indeed a variety of problems which can arise in the supervision relationship, some of sufficient significance from the student's point of view to cause withdrawal. These problems are frequently a function of poor communication between student and supervisor, as Estelle Phillips notes in Chapter 11. Indeed the notion that supervision is a 'relationship' has been contested within the academy, as Robert Brown points out in this collection. This is supported by our experience of working with university staff who, at times, vehemently contest the use of that word in connection with supervision, insisting that it is an academic matter only.

While it is important to recognize the centrality of good communication to the supervision relationship, the question which must be asked is why communication between student and supervisor is so difficult when self-evidently they share the same goal — the successful completion of the 'quality' degree? As we have remarked, one of the factors must surely be the diverse perspectives arising from the fundamentally different material positions each occupies with respect to the work's centrality to their lives. However another factor is the place or play of power in this relationship. In this chapter, we explore some different ways of understanding this deeper dimension of the supervision relationship, first by looking at the common sense way of talking about power in education, then by exploring the radical educational analysis of top-down (and from the student's perspective perhaps out-of-control) power, and finally adding a Foucauldian definition of power as relational and therefore partly controllable.

Power between supervisor and student can be understood in several ways. The common sense or liberal understanding avoids talk of power *per se* and talks instead about the 'authority' of the supervisor, an authority which is based on her or his structural position as 'the one who knows'. The relevant questions with respect to supervision (as to other teaching practices) become those which, assuming supervisory authority to be simply necessary, explore the legitimate and illegitimate uses of that authority (Marshall, 1993). Thus discussion tends to centre around consideration of the ways in which the supervisor 'knows what is best' for the student (and hence can justify the use of her or his authority), a discussion which often takes a paternalistic turn because of the conflation — in either the student's or the supervisor's mind — of legitimate academic authority and other less legitimate forms of authority. For instance the authority of the supervisor to pronounce on the clarity of the student's argument in the text becomes an authority to also pronounce on the worth of the student. Thus not only is the student's academic behaviour controlled, more or less productively, but so are other aspects of her or his behaviour, some of which will be relevant to the supervision relationship. One striking thing about this authority — particularly within supervision — is that its illegitimate effects are in a zone of silence and thus it is a fertile ground for misunderstanding.

Radical educators, on the other hand, tend to call power by name and talk explicitly of relations of domination and subordination (Apple, 1986). In this way they draw our attention to the structured top-down aspect of power where some individuals are seen, because of their material location, to have more than others. In this view, supervisors by virtue of their institutional position have power over students insofar as they are seen to know more (about the research process and, at Masters level, the disciplinary field) and — crucially — they frequently have an active role in assessing the student's work. This analysis brings various problems into view which are not so visible from the common sense perspective, particularly those that arise from the student's sense of her or himself as powerless. This perception can engender a fear of behaving in certain sorts of ways — for instance, assertively — in case the supervisor punishes with their greater power, for example through the assessment process or by obstructing future career options. Other factors which radical educators bring into focus are those axes of power in the wider society — the axes of gender, ethnicity, class, age, sexual orientation and so on. These too will bear on the relationship between student and supervisor, influencing each one in distinctive ways.

In contrast to the entrenched authority of the liberal perspective or the sovereign power implied in the radical view, a Foucauldian view of the place and play of power between student and supervisor suggests that it is relational. In Foucault's view, power is not something which some people have and others do not, but is a relation which exists between two individuals who are both capable of acting: 'it is ... always a way of acting upon an acting subject or acting subjects by virtue of their acting or being capable of action' (Foucault, 1986: 427). In this view the supervision relationship is, like any other relationship between two acting subjects, always/ already a power relation; it 'is exercised on and by individuals over others as well as themselves' (Sawicki, 1991: 25). Forged within the hegemonic (or common sense) beliefs, values, language and practices — the discourse — of the liberal university, it is likely to be lived out in some various but, importantly, constrained ways. While this discourse of the liberal university makes some responses on the part of both supervisor and student to the supervision relationship more likely, because power is productive — rather than merely repressive — there is always a possibility for struggle and resistance. This possibility for 'freedom, construed as the potential for autonomous recalcitrance' (Howley and Hartnett, 1992: 272) against the constraints imposed without and within the relationship exists because of the subject's capacity for action. Therefore things do not **have** to continue as sometimes, from a common sense point of view, it seems they must: with insight, and some tools, either student or supervisor can interrupt the present relation of power in the supervision.

Understanding power to be both structural (as the radical viewpoint makes plain) and relational seems to be important for understanding the issues of concern in supervision, especially those of poor communication: there is the material reality of the supervisor's more powerful structural position and the ways in which this position can be used to block access to privilege and reward. We have heard too many stories of abuse of this power — from students, from staff of their own experience as postgraduate students, and from our institution's mediator — to be able to discount its operation and effectiveness. It must be accounted for by students in their dealings with their supervisors. Yet at the same time we can decentre sovereign power because Foucault allows us to understand that this rule of supervisory power is neither complete, nor is it unmediated by the students: both the student and the supervisor are acting subjects who may act on the actions of the other. Offering students tools such as the 'Guidelines' discussed below (as well, for instance, as other ways of speaking about supervision and speaking to supervisors) may also offer them other ways of acting within the supervision relationship than the obvious ones. This is in spite of the fact that a plethora of institutional practices (what Foucault calls the microphysics of power) including the regulations of the institution, the often inscrutable behaviour of their supervisors, and their experience as undergraduates (Grant, 1993) have prepared them to act in particular ways.

Let us leave this discussion of power for now and look more closely at the document (which we hope will interrupt the dominant practices of the supervisory power relation) and the experience of students who have used it.

The 'Guidelines for Discussion': a tool for managing supervision

In her chapter, Yoni Ryan outlines the usefulness of either a contract or a checklist as two procedures for alleviating 'the problems inherent in the current "postgrad process"'. In this section we describe a document which has elements of both and which is being increasingly used in our institution (although neither extensively yet nor as a matter of institutional policy).

The argument of this chapter is that if many supervision problems are to be avoided, good communication — based on mutual respect and leading to mutual trust — is essential. The mediator at our university has pointed out that frequently the underlying issue in breakdown of supervision was an initial lack of clarification of mutual expectations and responsibilities. While the University of Auckland does publish sets of guidelines for the conduct of Masters and PhD supervision, they are sketchy and leave a great deal to be negotiated by the student-supervisor pair. Unfortunately, as a survey we recently carried out in a department indicates, this initial process of negotiation often does not take place: perhaps supervisors are too busy to think of it, or, often being people of good will, think it is unnecessary, and we know students are frequently too timid to initiate it.

With this in mind, we have developed 'Postgraduate Supervision: Guidelines for Discussion' (Graham and Grant, 1993). This ten-page document, set out like a workbook, is designed to be used as the basis for open discussion between student and supervisor early in the supervision. When talking to students or supervisors about the document we suggest that, during the discussion, the answers to each of the questions are noted on the document which is later photocopied so that both parties have a record of what they agreed. The questions are grouped into three categories: supervisor/ student understandings; departmental expectations and resources; and university requirements. The questions are very explicit, covering issues such as:

- What does 'thesis' mean?
- What is meant by originality?
- Frequency and duration of meetings?
- Expectations of feedback: how much, how often, in what form, with how much notice?
- In the case of joint supervision: what roles will be taken by each supervisor?
- What access does the student have to a study place, pigeon-hole, tea/coffee (and so on)?

While some of the answers to the questions are not up for negotiation, especially in the second and third sections, the questions still need to be addressed as we have found that many students do not know (and often neither do their supervisors) their department's expectations, nor their rights and privileges. On the other hand, the answers to the questions in the first section, which addresses the student/supervisor working relationship, will vary because there is, for instance, no one right answer to the question about meeting frequency and duration. Further, the answers to those kinds of questions may change over time within a given supervision relationship and so will need to be understood as open to renegotiation.

When we introduce this document to students in thesis management workshops we face a range of reactions. One of the most common is an unwillingness to go to a supervisor and put the document on the table for negotiation — many students feel this to be an inappropriate behaviour, one which risks the supervisor's disfavour and thus prejudices the success of the supervision of their thesis. We have found that simply giving out the document without skilling students in ways to introduce it to the supervisor is not effective and so we spend some time with students using role play and discussion of opening lines to prepare them for handling the interaction. We have also developed a policy of sending a copy of the document to the students' supervisors, within a day or so of the workshop, with a covering letter explaining to them why we think that working through it is a good idea. In this way we pick up the responsibility (in our roles as staff/student developers) of advocating the document's use and any supervisor's wrath may then be directed at us. Not surprisingly we have not had too much wrath and many students report back to us that their supervisor subsequently initiated discussion of the document.

There is a range of ways in which the document might be used. The ideal is that either the student or the supervisor initiates the discussion and they work through at least the first section together: in this case, both the process of doing this and the outcomes in terms of shared understandings will be productive for the relationship. The agreements reached should be recorded and a copy held by each person. The second and third sections can be treated in the same manner but may just as well be covered in a group induction with all the postgraduate students (and their supervisors) within a department together. (Some departments at the University of Auckland now produce a booklet for their postgraduates which outlines all the issues covered in these sections. In this event only the first section needs to be provided — the layout of the document makes it easy to adapt.) The document may also be used in a more 'covert' manner, that is the student can take several questions at a time and introduce them into a supervision meeting agenda, and thus work through the sections over a series of meetings. We advise students to record any agreements made at supervision meetings and send a copy to their supervisor — apart from anything else, it is convenient for a busy supervisor to be able to easily check back to a record of the last meeting in preparation for the upcoming one. This way of using the document, while not ideal, works for students who do not feel confident enough to ask their supervisors to work through the document with them.

The experience of students who have been introduced to the 'Guidelines'

Late last year we held a 'Getting started on your thesis' mini-conference for 50 Masters research students from a variety of departments. As part of the programme we gave a workshop on the Guidelines in which, as well as discussing the rationale for the document, we explored the students' responses to the idea of presenting it to their supervisors. There was resistance, as there has been on other such occasions, and so we spent some time talking about how they might introduce it to their supervisor, with the students trying out opening lines on each other, and role-playing such interactions. With their consent, we also sent copies of the Guidelines to all their supervisors (if they knew who they were) with a covering letter explaining that we had recommended them to their students who might, in the near future, suggest their use. Six months later, Adele Graham carried out follow-up interviews with 20 of these students to gauge the effects of the mini-conference on their progress and supervision.[2] Among other questions, she specifically asked about their use of the Guidelines — she found many different stories, some fragments of which are presented here.

Despite the preparation we gave them during the mini-conference, some students remained either ambivalent or anxious about presenting the Guidelines to their supervisor, perhaps because this action would break the code of being the supervised (passive and obedient) student:

I wanted to use them — I thought the Guidelines were really good. They covered everything ... a lot of things I wouldn't have thought of myself. I showed them to both my supervisors and one basically ignored it and the other said, 'that's a good idea' but did nothing about it. And when I actually tried to push it on them, whenever I brought it up, they just ignored it. So I never did use them and there were a lot of things I would have liked to discuss because there were a lot of things that I didn't think were fair which could have been sorted out at the beginning of the year which might have made a difference ....

However, some of the students were surprised and relieved when their supervisor initiated discussion of the Guidelines:

I originally started drip-feeding [my supervisor] these questions without letting on where they came from. And then when [he] got the document in the internal mail, he actually asked me about it so that I knew it was okay ....
We had a group meeting planned and [my supervisor] put on the memo that we would be discussing the Guidelines at the group meeting and that we should have read through them [to] ... see if there were any issues that we specifically wanted to bring up. ... It was good that we didn't have to show it to her, she brought it to us ....

Others made the decision to raise it with their supervisor and, in different stories, there were both positive and negative responses reported:

He thought it was a really good idea and was completely open. We didn't work through it as such but basically covered all the main points in it and devised some extra points.
I raised it with him — I went to see him soon afterwards and took a copy for him and for me. ... We had it there but didn't fill it out. [My supervisor] flicked it off in a way — but not in a malicious way. Like the attitude was 'I know all this'. ... He doesn't see it as an essential tool for the supervision of a postgraduate student — which, I sort of felt disappointed about really, because I think it is a valuable tool, it sets the groundrules.

Some students hadn't used the Guidelines at all because they felt it would be unwise:

[Before establishing supervision] with my actual supervisor, I was talking with [another member of the Department] and he said 'Oh those HERO people, are they still pushing that contract thing?' And it sort of threw me off guard. There was another lecturer there at the time and I got the feeling that the whole Department didn't approve.

This student decided not to introduce the Guidelines because she didn't want to jeopardize her chances of getting the person she wanted to supervise her. Another student told a similar story:

No way did I mention the Guidelines for Discussion to him. I'm too scared to do that.

By contrast, one student used the Guidelines to help him check out potential supervisors:

I used it in evaluating who I was going with ... I had it with me when I went to talk with them [the two possible supervisors]. It was excellent. I'm a great liker of criteria ... I didn't go through it question by question, but I used it as a guide and said 'have you seen this?', and they both said 'yes'. And I said, 'are you happy with it?' and they both said 'yes'. So that was good ....

In this student's story, if one 'candidate' had been unwilling to work with such a tool, he would not have chosen her or him as a supervisor in the belief that open communication about the issues within would be essential to a successful supervision. It was a very powerful use of the Guidelines.

Some students found that the Guidelines were useful for clarifying different expectations on the part of joint supervisors:

Some of it was interesting because it made them think about what a thesis was too and their actual definitions were quite different at times ....

We have heard many stories from students caught between joint supervisors with different expectations. For this reason we recommended that the Guidelines be used in an initial meeting with all parties present so that the various roles and expectations could be clarified. (We also suggested that such meetings be held every so often so that the student does not get caught between different — or, as sometimes happens, opposing — perspectives and feedback further down the line.)

In a small number of stories, the Guidelines were used in the ideal way (as described above); mostly however they were used, either overtly or covertly, as a guide to discussion, with the student only keeping notes of what was discussed and agreed. Nearly all the students felt that they were useful especially in raising their awareness of what might be important. In some cases this awareness was passed on to other students:

I know several people who didn't come to the conference [who] we talked to about the Guidelines and they actually went and spoke to their supervisors about them. And I've got an office mate and we spoke to her specifically about the issue of papers coming out at the end and warning her about what her supervisor's point of view might be. And she came back afterwards and said [that when] they went through the document, her supervisor had spent a lot of time discussing with her about that point.

Overall, from the students' feedback, some themes stand out. Perhaps the most significant in terms of understanding how the structured power inequality impacts on the supervision relationship is that it is evident that, in many cases, it is up to the supervisor to decide on use of the Guidelines. One student who had not been successful in getting them used with her supervisor said:

> There was nothing else more you could have done to prepare us to present them. Like I'm not normally a very tactful person and you showed me how to do it in a tactful way and it didn't make any difference. The fact they received them beforehand [in our mailout] and didn't give any indication [that] they had ... I think it was just the people themselves rather than the way I approached them or [how] you prepared us....

Yet, on the other hand, from the evidence we find in the students' stories, some students operated more powerfully than others in terms of getting what they wanted within the supervision relationship — like the student who used the potential supervisors' attitudes towards the Guidelines to help him select a supervisor. In this way we can see that the issue of power is not a simple one of the supervisor having it all and the student having none — there is indeed a relation of power which is more or less susceptible to change. What factors might make change more or less likely bears further exploration.

At the same time, there is little doubt that the power relations in supervision tend to be seen by many students as uneven and relatively fixed. For example, they worry about their supervisors' perceptions of them and how this might affect the supervision:

> I asked [my joint supervisors] if they would be prepared to fill in something like this. We didn't fill it in formally, but I just went through it as a guideline to discussion and afterwards just wrote up what they said to clarify it in my own mind. I should have formalized it by giving it back to them or giving them a copy to check but I decided it took it too far — but they thought I was too organized as it was.

It is not often that we hear supervisors complain of students who are too organized but from the student's point of view there is an ongoing concern about how to strike the right balance of behaviour or demeanour in the relationship. This is a difficult balance to find and maintain, causing frustration and motivational failure in many students.

Conclusion

In expecting the essential communication processes needed for a successful supervision relationship to arise spontaneously from such a complex terrain, the institution is unrealistic. As student and staff developers we have come to realize that we must not only provide the concrete tools to structure and thereby support these processes but also the skills needed to use these tools effectively in the first place. Time spent in the mini-conference working with students on the skills required to present the Guidelines to their supervisors in a positive non-threatening way meant that many more students than we expected had initiated their use. However overall this was still only a third of the group. It is clear to us that in many cases interruptions such as the mini-conference and the Guidelines themselves are not enough to restructure the power relations inherent in the supervision process which have their roots in the past experiences of both supervisor and student and indeed in the traditions of the institution itself.

Afterword: The 'Guidelines' and staff development

Adele, Barbara and I work together in a unit which is responsible for academic staff development at the University of Auckland. In this Afterword I would like to use the specifics of the Guidelines to reflect more broadly upon the whole business of postgraduate supervision, and the potential that it has for interrupting and transforming the discourses associated with 'staff development' —and promoting critical reflection upon conceptions of teaching.

The question, 'How do staff arrive at their conceptions of teaching?' has been largely ignored in the literature, and that presents problems for staff developers or those who wish to operate within a critically reflective paradigm at least. Webb (1992) has outlined three 'pretexts' which, associated with the positivist, interpretive and critical paradigms respectively, may be used to inform the activities of higher education staff developers. In summary, the rationales for the various types of activity are as follows.

The **positivist** rationale is concerned with empirical, experimental research which demonstrates that students of different types learn best under particular conditions. So the advice given to academic staff from this perspective might be: 'teach and construct courses according to the following principles (x, y and z) and your students will learn better. As a staff developer I can supply you with appropriate information, and help you to convert generality into specific practice'.

On the other hand the **interpretive** rationale generates largely qualitative research which suggests that students perceive and interpret the 'reality' of courses in different ways. Context is crucial. 'As a staff developer I can expose you to these ideas and help you to ascertain students' perspectives of the factors that inhibit their "deep" learning, in order that they may be removed and students achieve better quality learning'.

Then there is the **critical** rationale in which the educational is also the political. Classrooms (and curricula which underpin what takes place there) are sites in which the dynamics of the power relationship have become enshrined in conventional practices. As staff developers we need to interrupt that hegemony (or taken-for-granted status quo) in order to help staff and students to work together, reflect upon their practices and the contexts in which they occur, and eliminate distortions in order to create more just educational practices and contexts.

Almost all staff development work is informed by the positivist and interpretive paradigms. That is not surprising, as they are consistent with the dominant ethos of universities. Practices consistent with those perspectives are what staff want, expect and are prepared to engage in. However, as radical educators, we are also committed to the critical paradigm, and the utilization of opportunities for drawing those with whom we work into a more critical approach to their practice. The Guidelines present one such opportunity.

Power is a concept that is central to a critical approach to education. It is manifest in all relationships between students and staff, and in the interactions of staff developers and academics. Webb (1992) writes as follows:

> In the end we are brought back to the power relationships pertaining between us as educational developers and our 'clients'. Indeed the very language here is indicative of the relationship we might wish to pursue. The term 'client' may bring with it some useful overtones concerning 'professionalism' and ethical behaviour, but it also conveys a power relationship which may act against movement in the direction of emancipation and participation: such movement makes problematic the notion of 'professionalism'.

Any serious move to change education radically has to address the power dynamic head on — and interrupt it, so that it can be reflected upon and potentially reconstructed in a way which more rationally serves the best interests of those involved: students and staff. Conventionally, academic research has been an arcane activity carried out by 'insiders' who have been socialized into an elite. Supervisors are potentially in the position of luminaries who point out a path (more or less clearly) via which students may enter this elite — and of judging whether those students are worthy of entry. It is a position of great power especially when the gate-keeping function is associated with a broader sweep of social privilege that is bound up in the attainment of a higher degree. The Guidelines represent one (possibly small) step in freeing up students from a structural mysticism that often surrounds the production of a thesis. Used to its full extent it clarifies many aspects of doing a thesis that were previously tacit in academic culture — or in some cases leads to an articulation of the fact that the whole process is fuzzy.

The culture implied by common university teaching practices involves the teacher as expert and authority, with the student as apprentice, disciple, acolyte. The practices are steeped in a power dynamic which hold them in place as new staff enter the academy. To radically shift the culture of university teaching — 'improve teaching', if you will — it is necessary to interrupt that power dynamic. So far it has been remarkably resistant to change, with innovations in teaching consisting of cosmetic pedagogical moves which hardly impact at all on the fundamental meta-practices of institutions (Jones, 1990). Perhaps the Guidelines and similar documents provide something of a potential for such an interruption in the following ways.

For one thing, many current postgraduate students are themselves teachers through their work as part-time tutors in the departments in which they are enrolled. A qualitatively different power dynamic in their own relationships with their supervisor might flow into their practices and relationships with the students for whom they are tutors (see Elton in this collection). More importantly, though, it is from current students that future cohorts of academic staff will be drawn. A fundamental interruption of power dynamics in supervisor-student relationships offers at least the potential for providing an experience, a situational modelling, which the student-turned-staff member can draw on in future. It offers the possibility of a 'site for resistance' (Giroux, 1983) to the historically reproduced power relationships that are dominant in conventional university education.

However, the Guidelines on their own are not enough. Students have to be enabled to move past the threat that is implied in the dominant system of power relationships. Any student prepared to stand up to and challenge the system on their own is very brave, stupid, or brilliant — most are not. At the heart of critical educational theory is the notion of collective action: students can be empowered to act by the knowledge that they belong to a collectivity. In this respect the workshops and mini-conference that contextualize the Guidelines are crucial. They do two things: first, they 'skill' students (in matters of negotiation, etc.), so that at a level of embodied self-efficacy (Bandura, 1977) students become more able and empowered to take the action that they know is in their best interests. Second, they bring together a group with common goals to constitute the critical mass of a support group.

At one level then, the development and introduction of the Guidelines can be seen as a simple technical device — a workbook — that helps students and supervisors to clarify expectations and assists in the efficient and effective production of a thesis. From a different perspective though, a critical one, it provides a small opportunity to interrupt the dominant discourse of education, and the power relationships to which it gives rise, and perhaps bring about a 'perspective transformation' at the level of the individuals concerned, or of the community that they constitute.

Notes

Note: Copies of the Guidelines are available from the authors on request at HERO, University of Auckland, Private Bag 92019, Auckland, New Zealand.

1   While throughout this chapter we refer to the supervisor, we understand that it is increasingly common for there to be more than one supervisor in any supervision. Some of the concerns described in the opening section are thus made more difficult to resolve and, as Phillips argues in her chapter here, we suggest that steps be taken to pre-empt them.

2   For those readers who like numbers: of the 20 students interviewed, in eight cases the supervisor initiated discussion of the Guidelines, in seven the student did, and in five neither did.

References

Apple, M. (1986). *Teachers and Texts: A Political Economy of Class and Gender Relations in Education*. New York: Routledge and Kegan Paul.
Bandura, A. (1977). *Social Learning Theory*. Englewood Cliffs, NJ: Prentice-Hall.
Foucault, M. (1986). 'The subject and power', in B. Wallis (ed.), *Art After Modernism: Rethinking Representation*. New York: New Museum of Contemporary Art.

Giroux, H. (1983). 'Theories of reproduction and resistance in the new sociology of education: A critical analysis'. *Harvard Educational Review* 53(3): 257-294.

Graham, A. and Grant, B. (1993). 'Guidelines for Discussion'. Auckland: HERO, University of Auckland.

Grant, B. (1993). 'Making University Students: The Construction of Student Subjectivities'. Unpublished MA thesis: The University of Auckland.

Holdaway, E., Deblois, C. and Winchester, I. (1994). 'Practices and opinions reported by coordinators of graduate programs'. *Interchange* 25(1): 65-86.

Howley, A. and Hartnett, R. (1992). 'Pastoral power and the contemporary university: A Foucauldian analysis'. *Educational Theory* 42(3): 271-283.

Jones, J. (1990). 'Reflections upon the undergraduate curriculum', in I. Moses (ed.), *Higher Education in the Late Twentieth Century*. Sydney: HERDSA.

Marshall, J. (1993). 'Authority and power in education'. Unpublished paper, The University of Auckland.

Moses, I. (1985). *Supervising Postgraduates*. HERDSA Green Guide No. 3. Sydney: HERDSA.

Phillips, E. and Pugh, D. (1987). *How to get a PhD*. Buckingham: Open University Press.

Powles, M. (1988). *Know your PhD Students and How to Help Them*. Melbourne: CSHE.

Sawicki, J. (1991). *Disciplining Foucault: Feminism, Power and the Body*. New York: Routledge.

Webb, G. (1992). 'On pretexts for higher education development activities'. *Higher Education* 24(3): 351-362.

Zuber-Skerritt, O. (ed.) (1992). *Starting Research: Supervision and Training*. Brisbane: Tertiary Education Institute, The University of Queensland.